IMAGES
of America

FARMINGTON

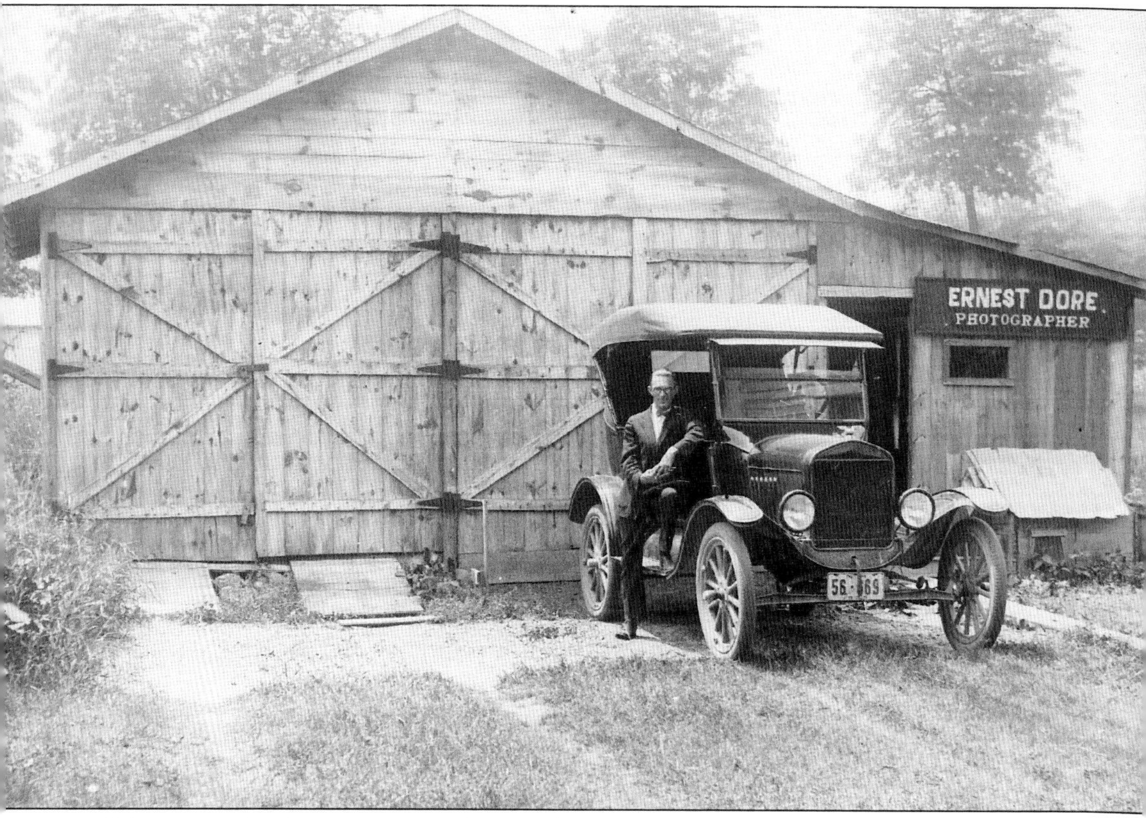

We are indebted to the many photographers of years past who recorded life as it was in Farmington. Their work has made this book possible.

IMAGES
of America

FARMINGTON

Farmington Historical Society

ARCADIA
PUBLISHING

ISBN 978-0-7385-9036-3

Published by Arcadia Publishing
Charleston, South Carolina

Printed in the United States of America

For all general information contact Arcadia Publishing at:
Telephone 843-853-2070
Fax 843-853-0044
E-mail sales@arcadiapublishing.com
For customer service and orders:
Toll-Free 1-888-313-2665

Visit us on the Internet at www.arcadiapublishing.com

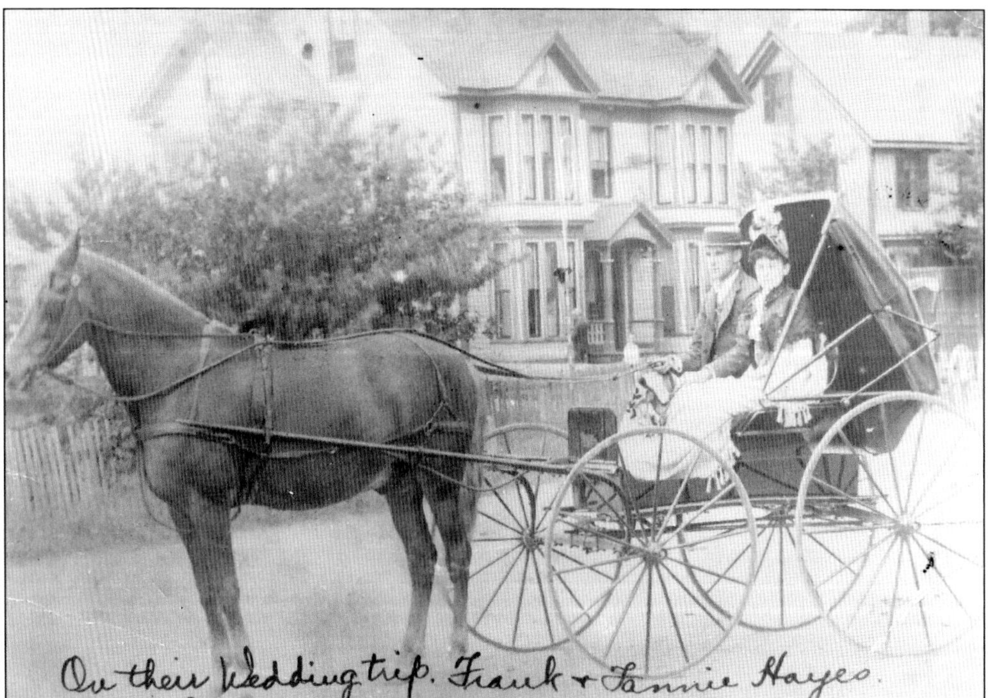

The wedding limousine of yesterday! Frank and Fannie Hayes leave Grove Street on their wedding trip, June 27, 1888.

Contents

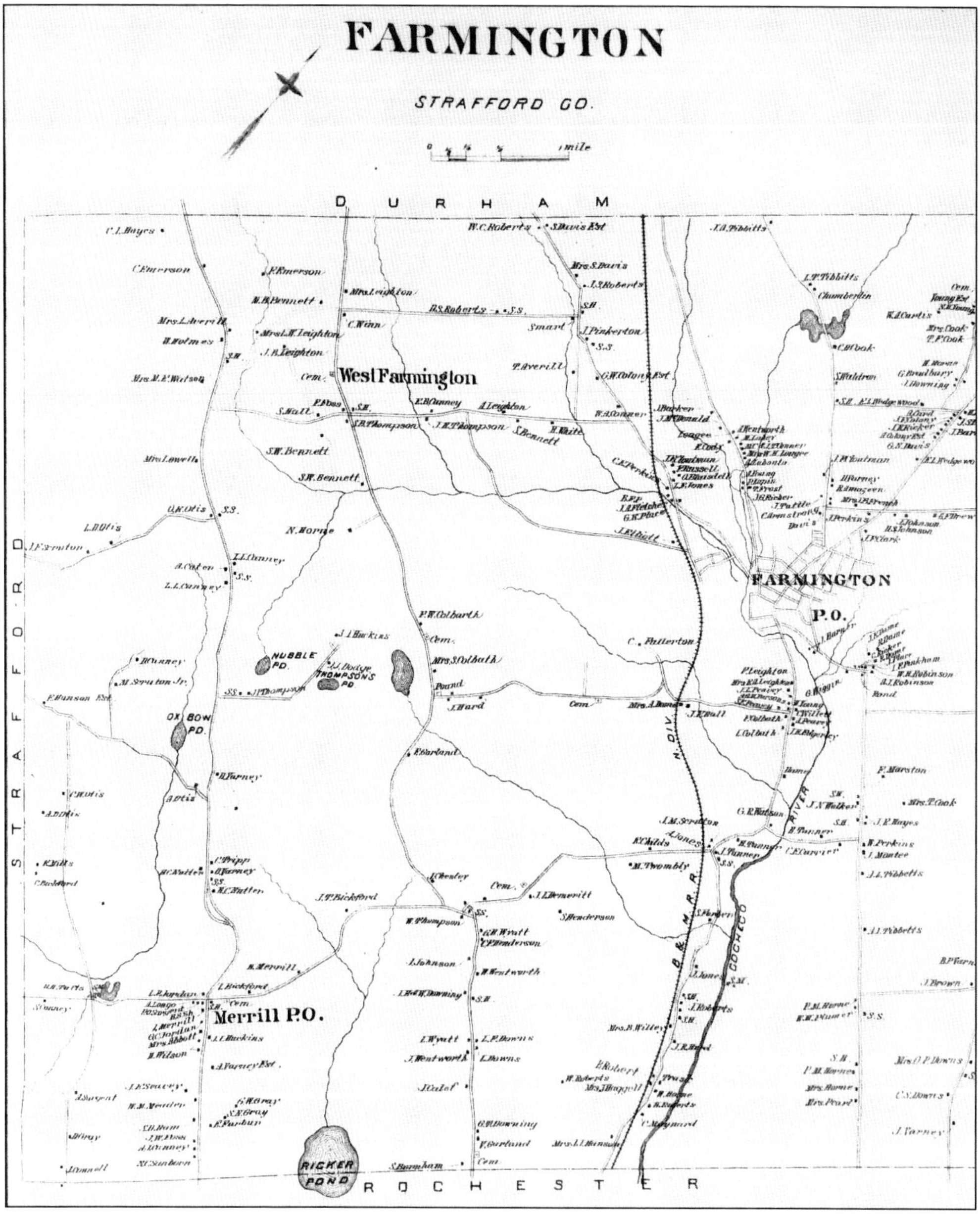

An 1892 map of Farmington, New Hampshire.

Introduction

Small towns abound in New England and the story of their growth and development is an integral part of the history of America. Farmington, located in the southeastern part of New Hampshire, exemplifies this.

The native Indians called the area "Chemung," meaning "canoe place." When settlers arrived in the 1770s, it was known as the Northwest Parish of Rochester. Distance and rough roads made it difficult for these first families to travel to the established church in Rochester, although they were taxed heavily to support it. This age old problem of taxation was the catalyst which caused the citizens to petition for a charter to incorporate a separate township of Farmington, and this was granted on December 1, 1798. The first town meeting was held on March 11, 1799, at the home of Simon Dame. The 141 voters present elected three selectmen: Ichabod Hayes, Lieutenant Ephraim Kimball, and David Roberts. This form of government has been maintained, with the addition of a town administrator, to this day.

Originally an agricultural settlement, the early homes were farms in the Merrill's Corner section, hence the town name. In the 1800s, the establishment of water-powered industries along the Cocheco, Ela, and Mad Rivers caused a population shift, with the present downtown area evolving near these rivers. The subsequent construction, in 1849, of a railroad through the mill area brought further prosperity and cemented the location of the town commercial center. In early days this business area was referred to as "The Dock" or "Puddledock," a name which endures today on the masthead of the local paper, *The Puddledock Press*.

Although Farmington began as an agricultural community, the principal industry to develop was shoe manufacturing. From its beginnings in 1836 when E.H. Badger built the first shoe shop on Spring Street, to its ending in 1991 when the last factory (the Alton Shoe Company) closed its doors, the shoe industry made the town's reputation and employed upwards of 2,000 people. It was as a cobbler that the most renowned native, Vice President Henry Wilson, got his start, journeying to the shoe capitol of Natick, Massachusetts, in 1833 to learn his trade.

Though difficult to envision today, the downtown area once contained several hotels, grocery stores, and even a movie theater and bowling alley. Farmington has had its ups and downs like any other community, with prosperity checked by disasters and economic depressions. Through good and bad times its generations of loyal residents have remained strong and supportive of one another, with deep pride in past accomplishments and optimism for the future.

It is hoped that the photographs presented here of a town and its people, how and where they worked and played, will bring enjoyment to the reader and, also, an understanding of the valuable heritage to be found in a small New Hampshire town.

Book Committee:
Dorothy Bean
Dorinda Howard
Norma Park
December, 1996

Acknowledgments

Publication of a book such as this depends upon many individuals for the contribution of both photographs and information. The Book Committee sincerely appreciates the assistance of the following: Roger Belanger, Pearl Bowden, Robert Cameron, Everett Carlsen, Martin Chagnon, Roscoe Chamberlin, Rosanna Chute, Evelyn Derby, Lois and Prisco DiPrizio, JoAnn and Charles Doke, Ardys Elliott, Jane and Norman Fall, Eileen Ferland, Farmington Fire and Police Departments, Steven Gardner, Uel Gardner, Lena George, Marshall Gibbs, Polly Gilman, Derald Goodwin, Eugene Goodwin, Jewell Gray, Norma Gray, Elsie Hart, Thom Hindle, Helen Houston, Richard Hunneman, Edith Jenness, Paula Kenyon, Esther Krisiak, Gladys Lepene, Jean Merrill, Lorraine Meyer, Eugene Nute, Roger Nutter, Norma Park, Paul Place, Joanne Pulsifer, Nancy Rabb-Cassinari, Louise Rollins, Rufus Rundlett, Barbara Russell, Pamela and George Sansoucy, Robert Schulte, Pauline and Frank Scruton, Nicholas Servetas, Mortimer Sullivan, Beulah and James Thayer, Frances Thayer, Norma and Robert Tilton, Ruby Towle, Charles and Sandra Wibel, and the Trustees and Librarians of the Goodwin Library.

One

Downtown

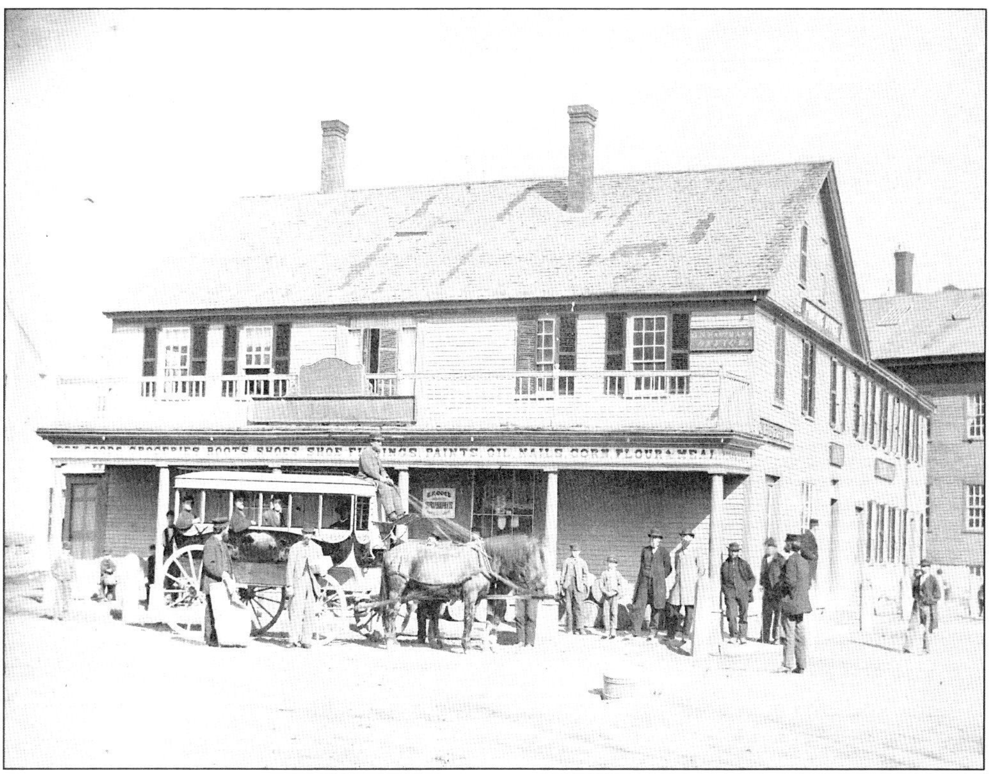

The former Steamboat Hotel, built in 1830 by Gilbert Horney on the corner of Main and Central Streets, appears here with the Perkins Jitney which served as transportation between the center of town and the railroad station. Reported to be the oldest commercial building still in existence, it currently houses a laundromat.

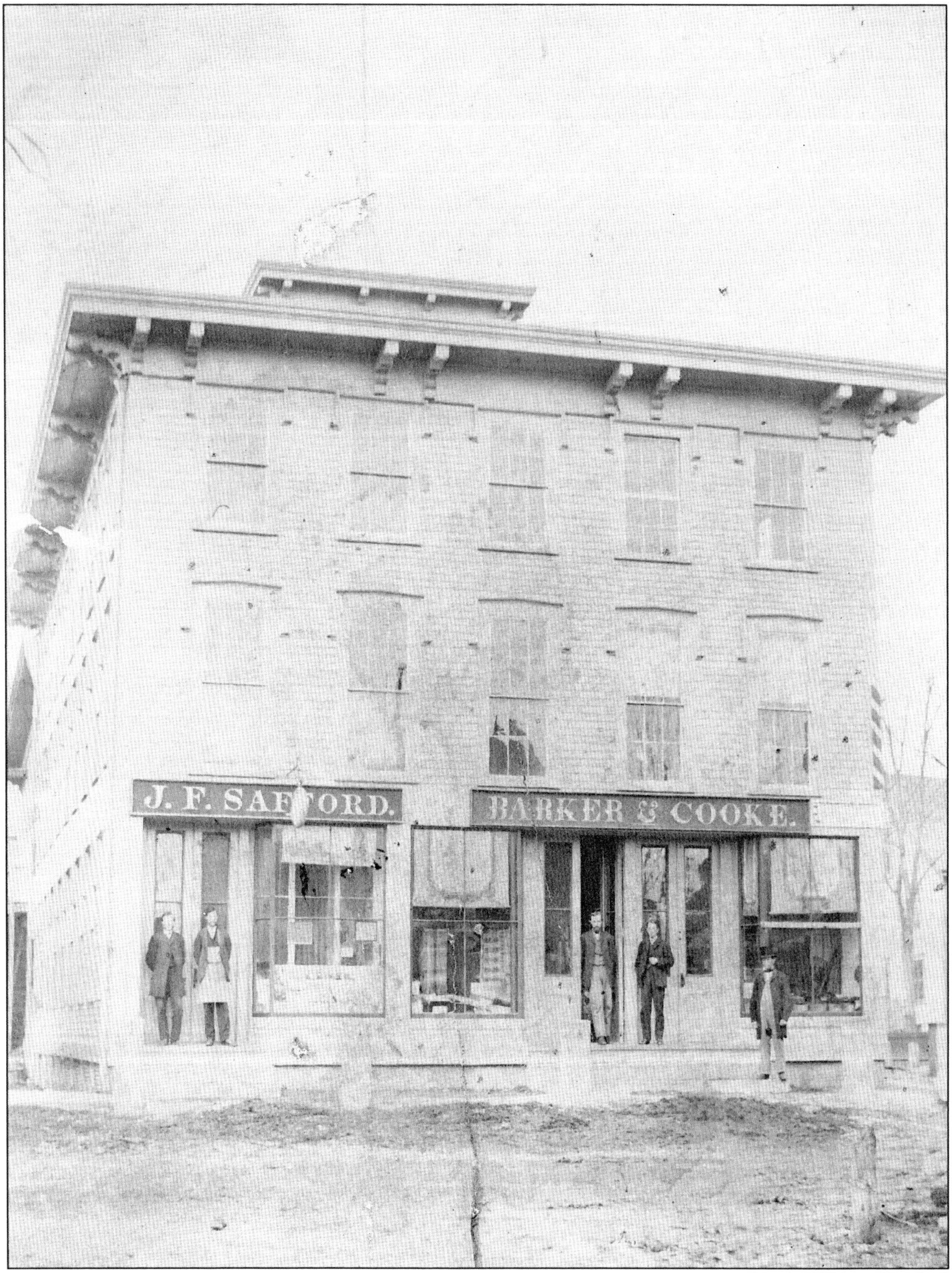

An 1869 photograph of the Barker Block on the corner of South Main and Central Streets. Jeweler and optician James Safford and a friend stand on the steps, along with store owner Thomas Cooke and clerk John Lougee. The top-hatted gentleman is Josiah B. Edgerly, Judge of the Police Court.

The Farmington Savings Bank was organized in 1868 and the Farmington National Bank in 1872, both banks operating in this brick building. A stairway on the left led to the Masonic Hall on the second floor.

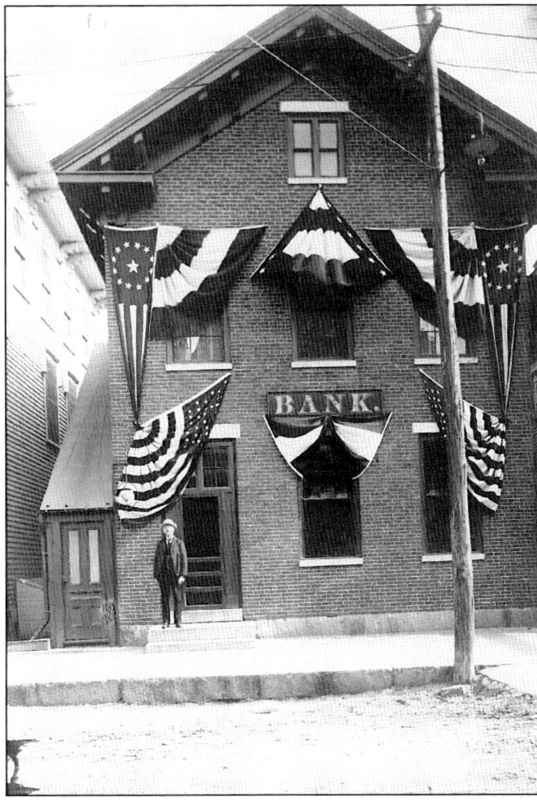

A festively decorated Boston Clothing Company was a later occupant of the Barker Block. Union Hall occupied the top floor. Today the Farmington Bank stands on this site.

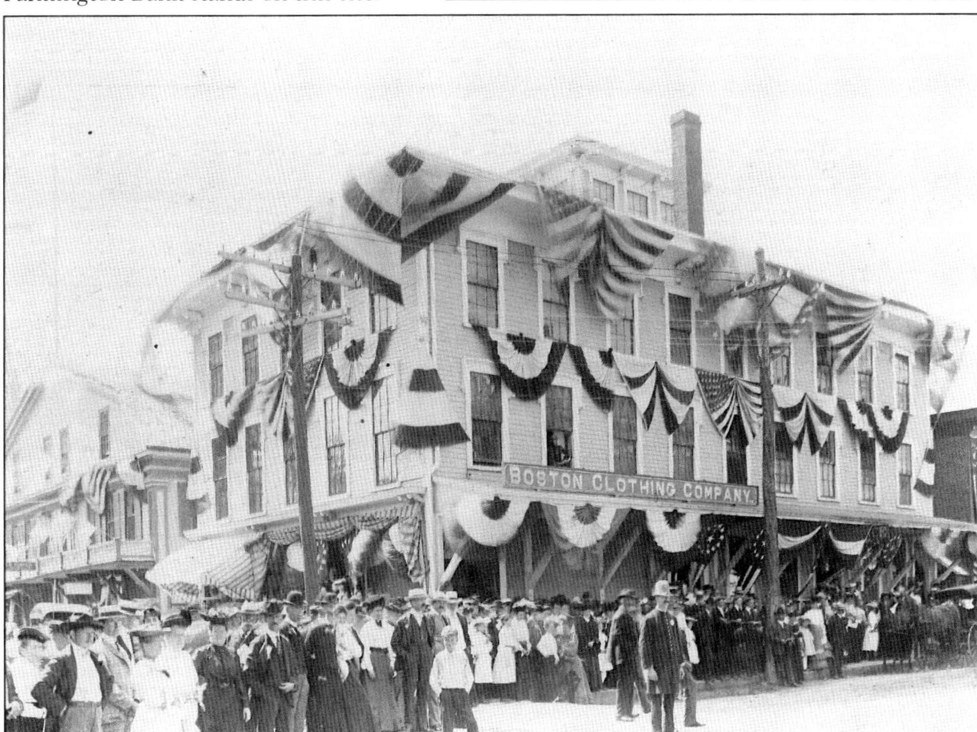

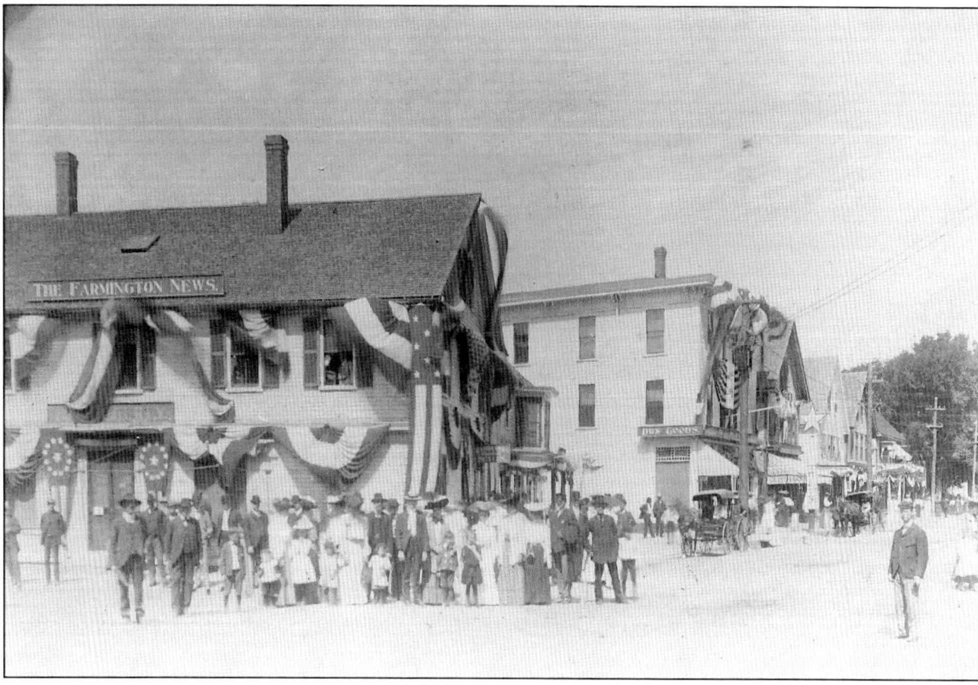

With offices on the second floor of the Steamboat Hotel building, *The Farmington News* was a weekly newspaper originated by James E. Fernald and his son. First issued on March 14, 1879, it was published in this building until 1955.

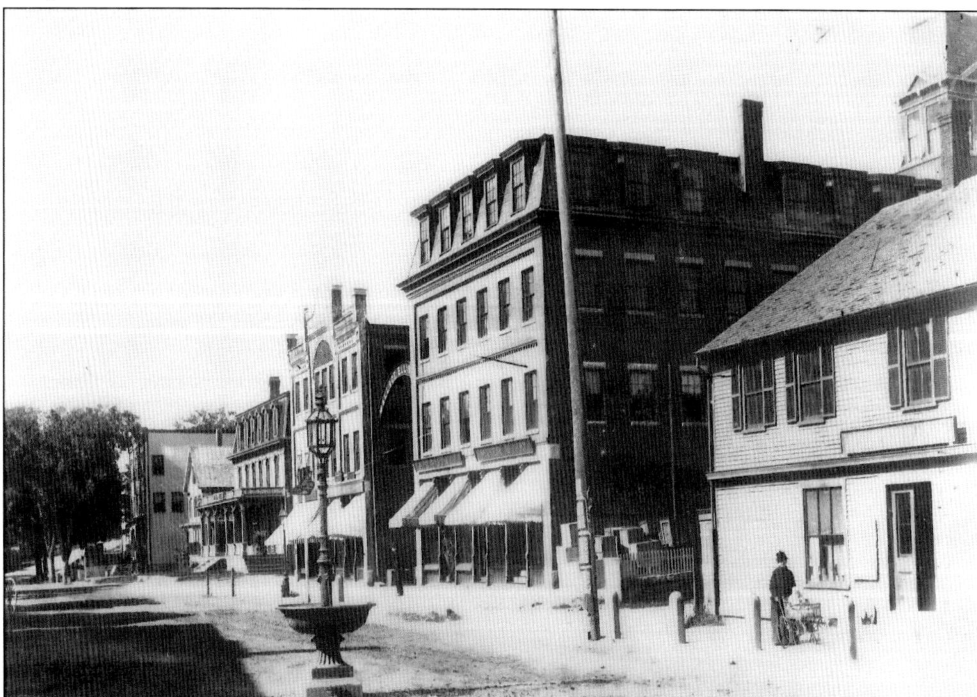

A Central Street view featuring the town watering trough, installed in 1887. It had dippers for people, a high basin for horses and cattle, and a low place for dogs!

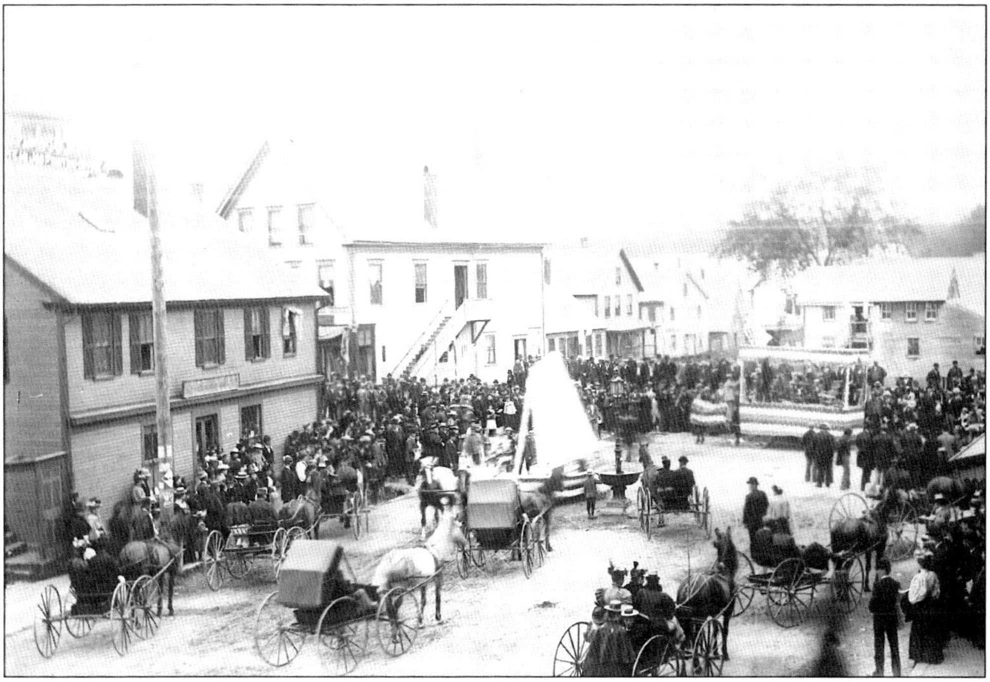

The Square has always been a site for public gatherings. This picture, taken prior to the construction of the Odd Fellows Block, shows the houses on Mechanic Street.

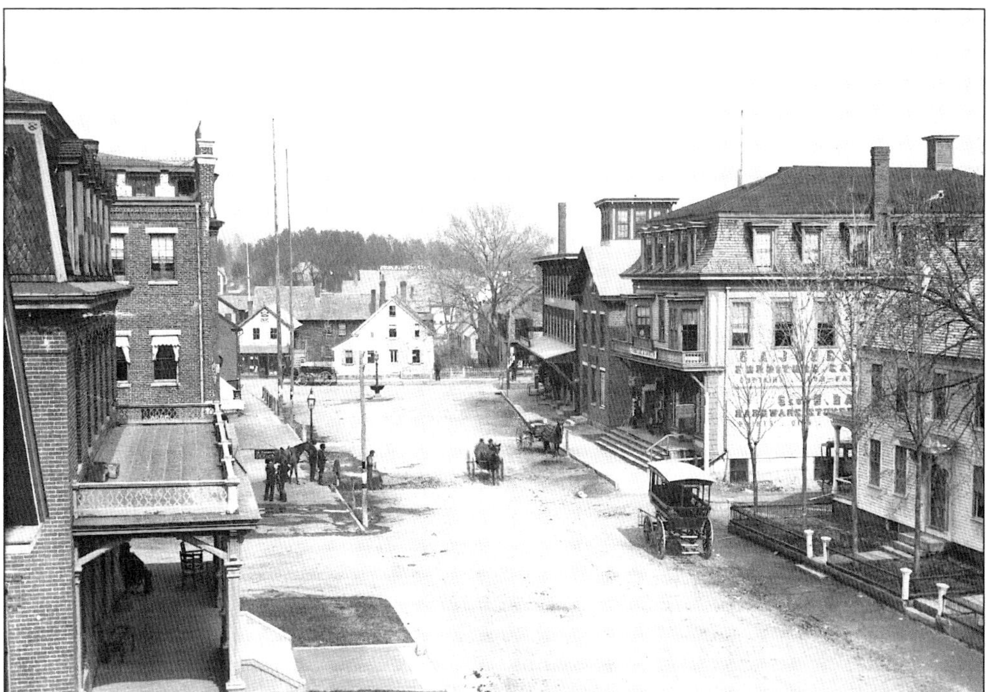

This 1895 photograph by Ralph White records the south side of Central Street when there were still residential dwellings at the Square. The Horn/Schulte House on the right was sacrificed for the bank parking lot in the 1970s.

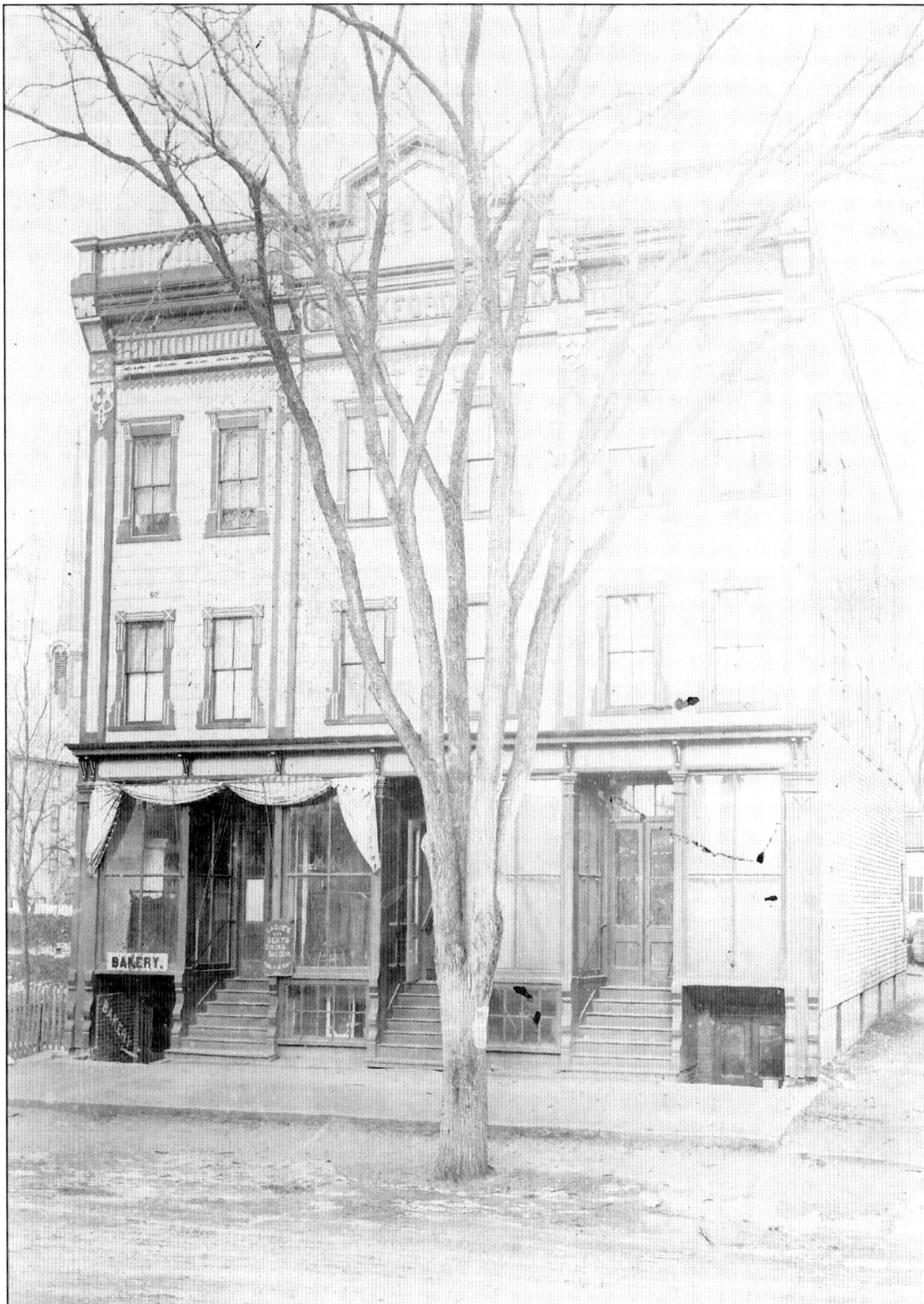

Farmington's most notable portrait photographer was Amasa W. Shackford, who had his studio in this building on Central Street. The U.S. Post Office was located on this site prior to May of 1995.

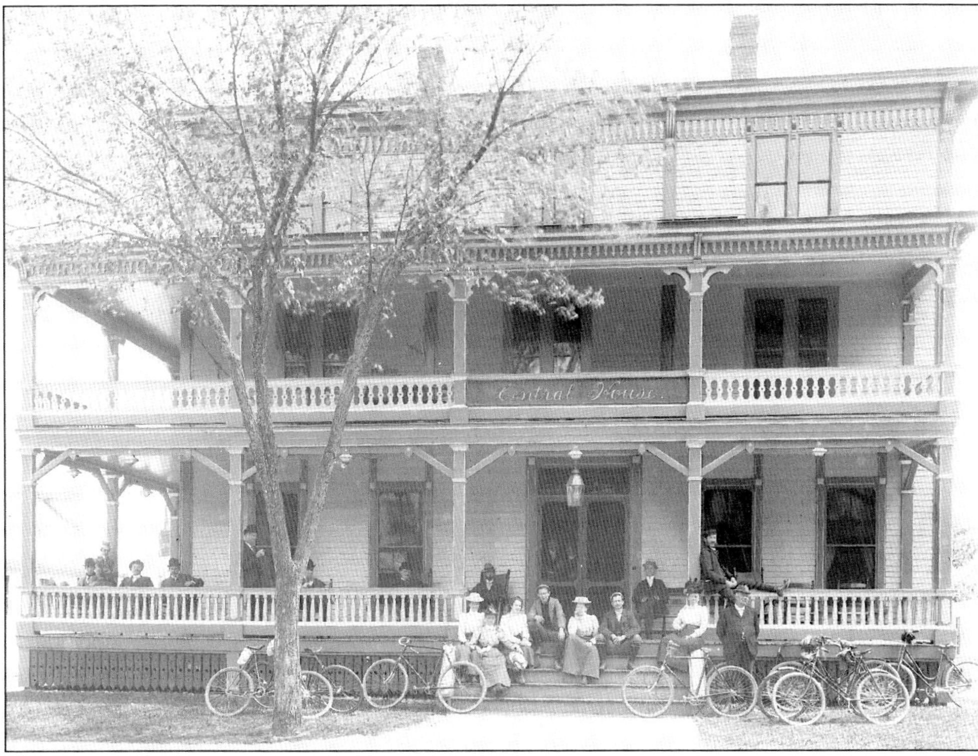

A prominent building on Central Street was the Central House Hotel, shown here with a group of "wheelers" in 1899. It was demolished in 1976.

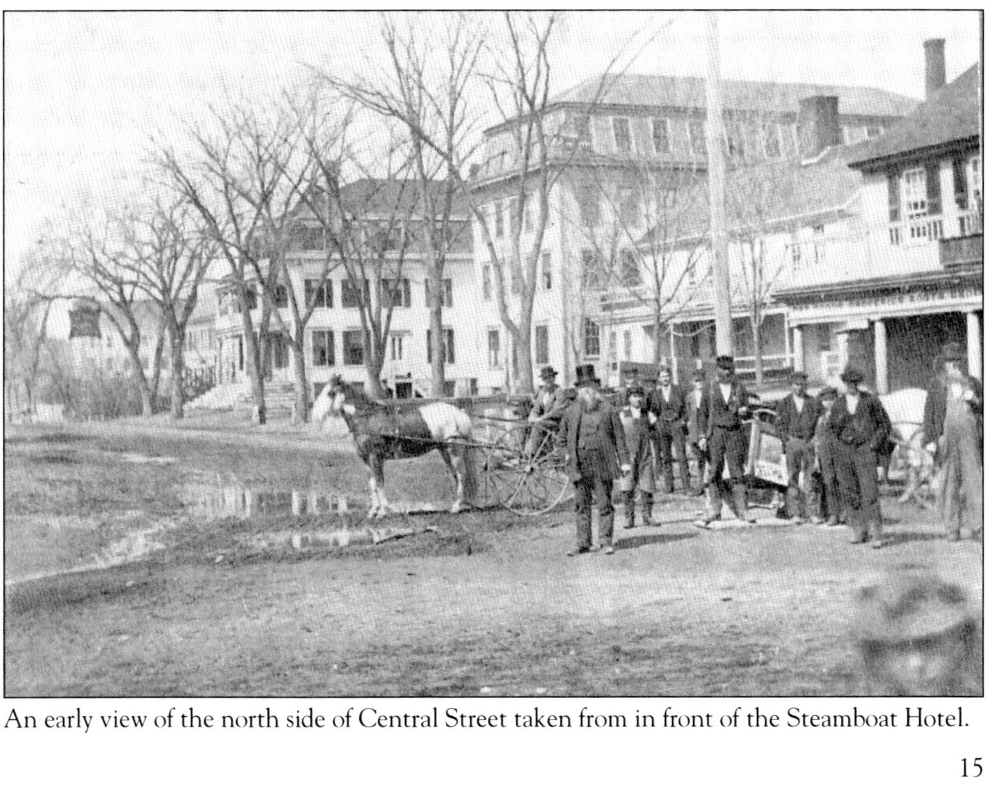

An early view of the north side of Central Street taken from in front of the Steamboat Hotel.

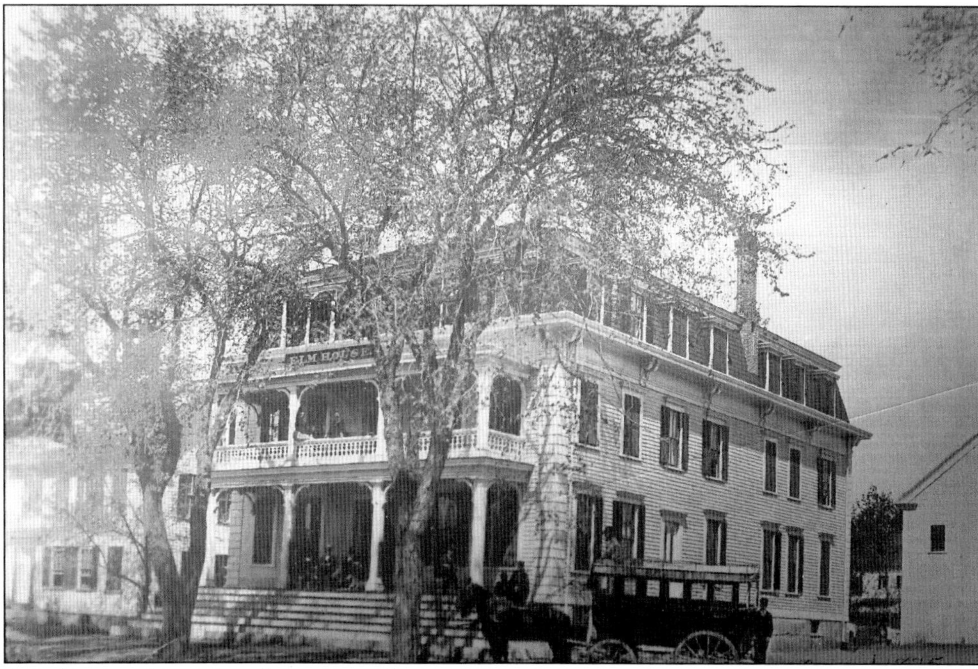

Another handsome hotel on Central Street was Elm House, which fell victim to fire in 1875 but was quickly rebuilt. It later became the Roosevelt House and then the Wilson House.

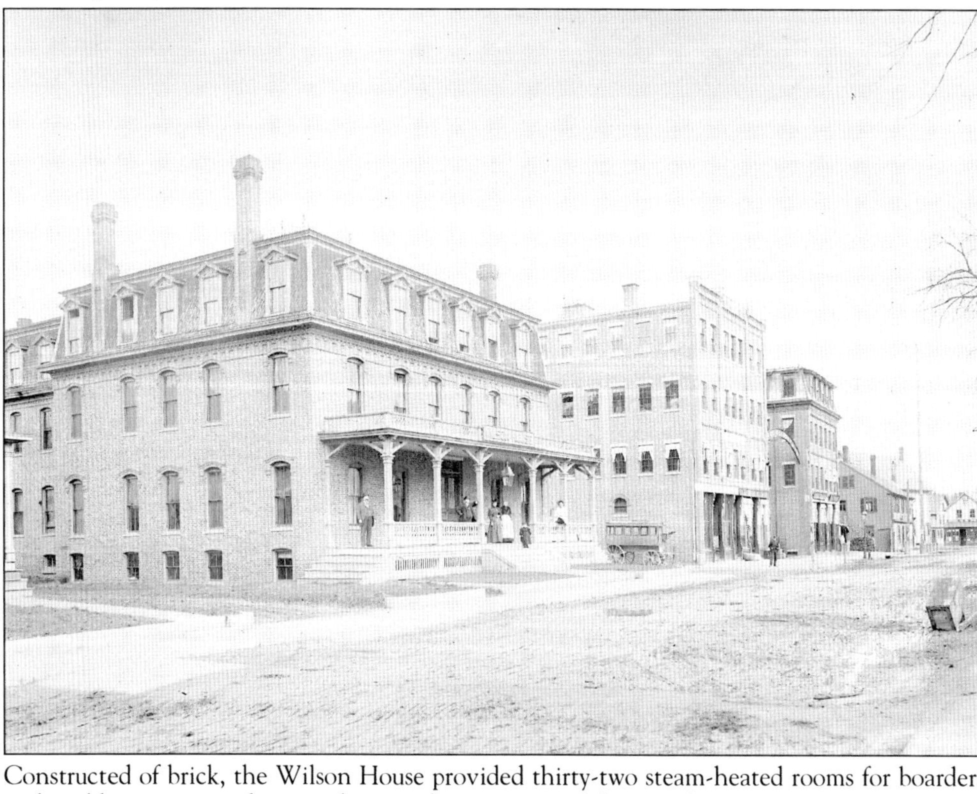

Constructed of brick, the Wilson House provided thirty-two steam-heated rooms for boarders and could seat seventy-five people in its dining room. Today it is the Fisher Apartments.

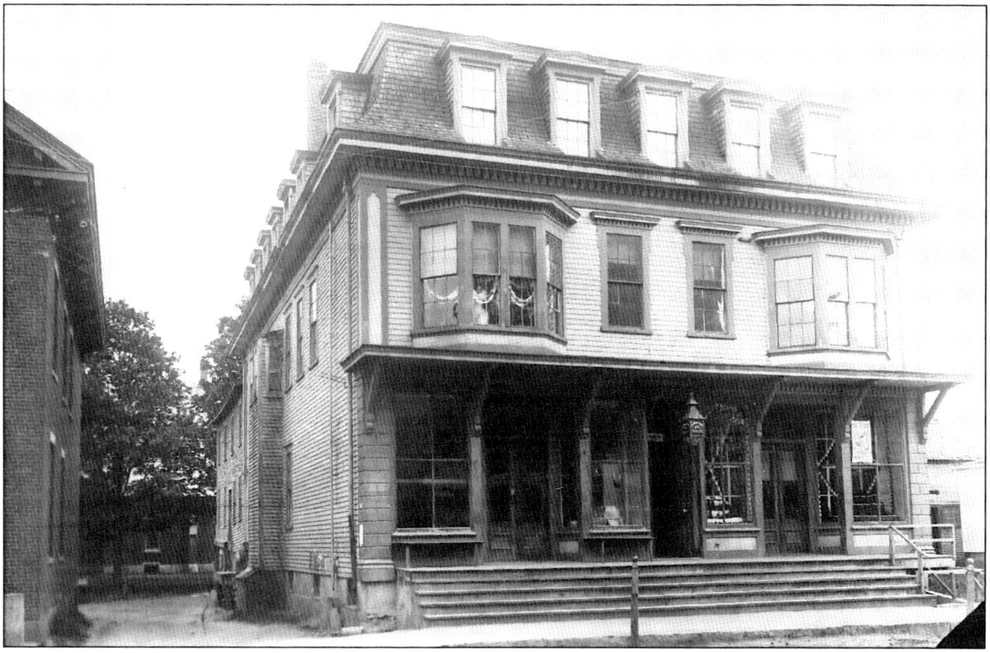

A popular shopping place for the ladies was Lucy Small's Millinery Shop on the second floor, for her ribbons, laces, feathers, and bonnets were much in demand. Stacks of codfish in the basement supplied Marcus Small's first-floor grocery.

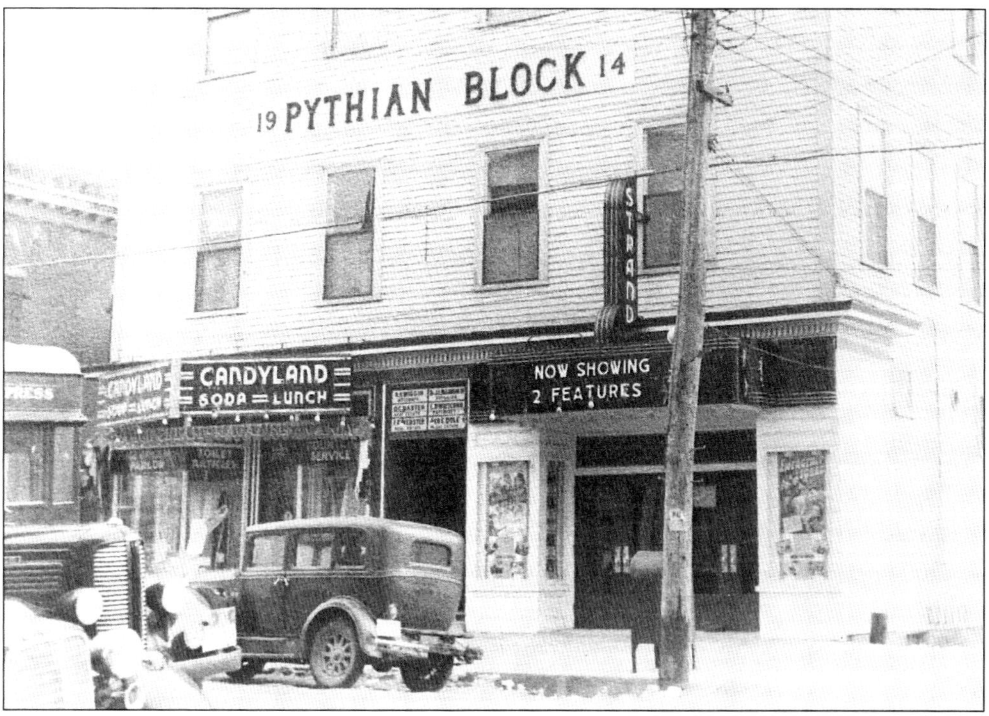

After a fire destroyed the Small Block, the Pythian Block was erected in 1914 as headquarters for the Knights of Pythias. The movie theater and Candyland served as an entertainment focal point until the 1960s.

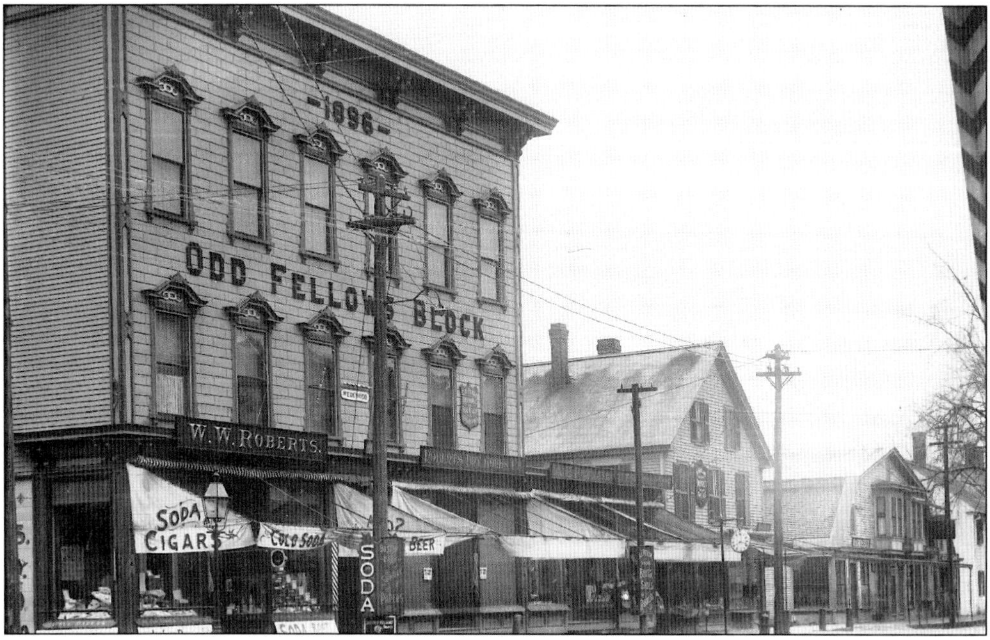

The formal opening of Odd Fellows Hall in October 1896 saw over five hundred people in attendance. For over fifty years the street floor was the location of Roberts Drug Store, which was sold in 1953 to Wilfred "Twink" Osgood, thus becoming Osgood's Pharmacy.

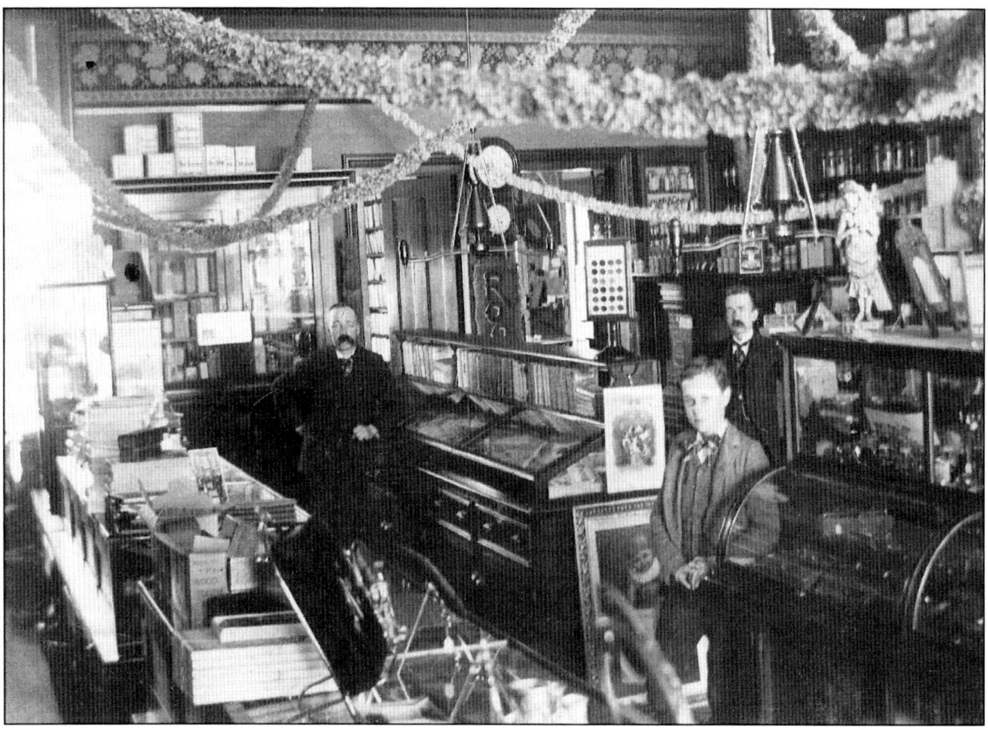
W.W. Roberts (on the left) and Will Peavey (behind the counter), both Farmington natives, formed a partnership in 1889 and opened their drug and stationery store at 21 North Main Street. A young Herbert Browne is in the foreground.

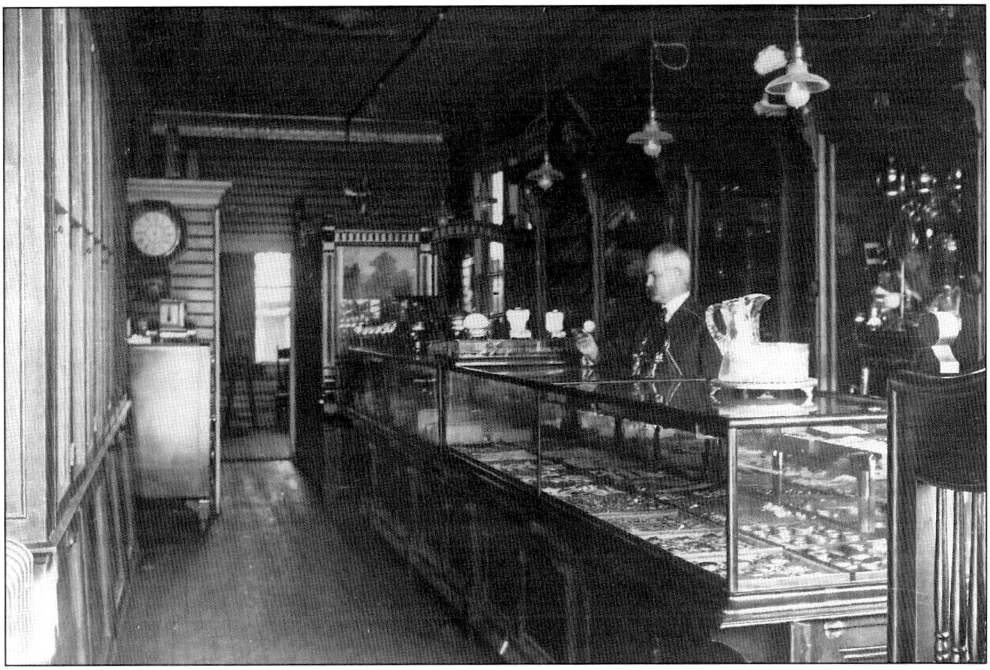

Edwin Legro was proprietor of a jewelry store next to the Odd Fellows Block for a number of years. His store later became the barbershop of Rufus Rundlett.

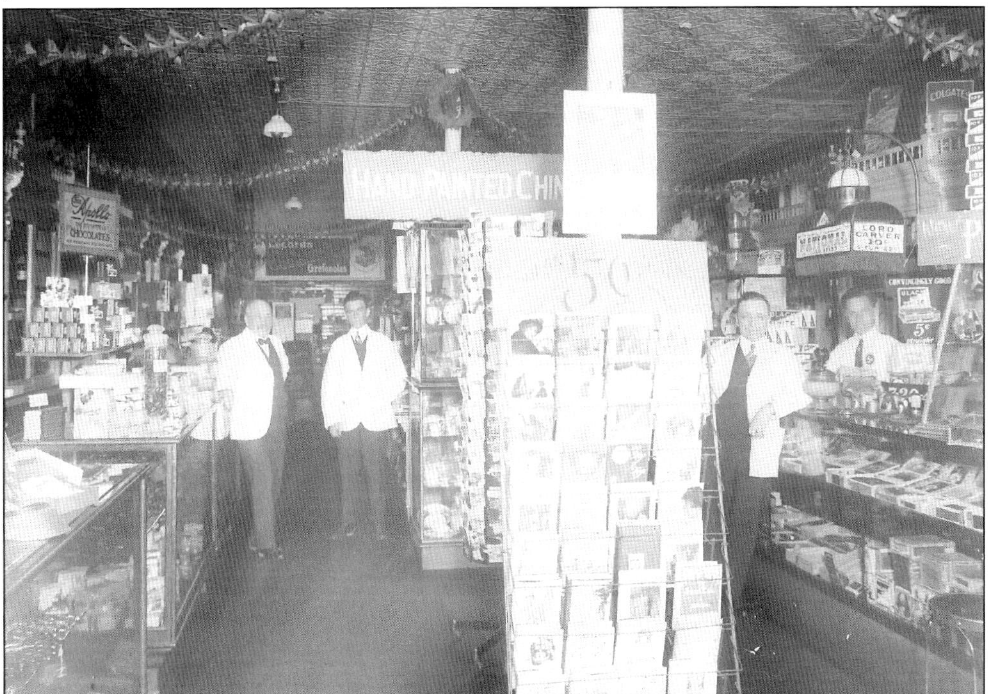

William Roberts purchased complete ownership of the drug store in 1894 when it was moved into the Odd Fellows Block. He is shown here with Clarence Blaisdell, his son George Roberts, and a grown-up Herbert Browne.

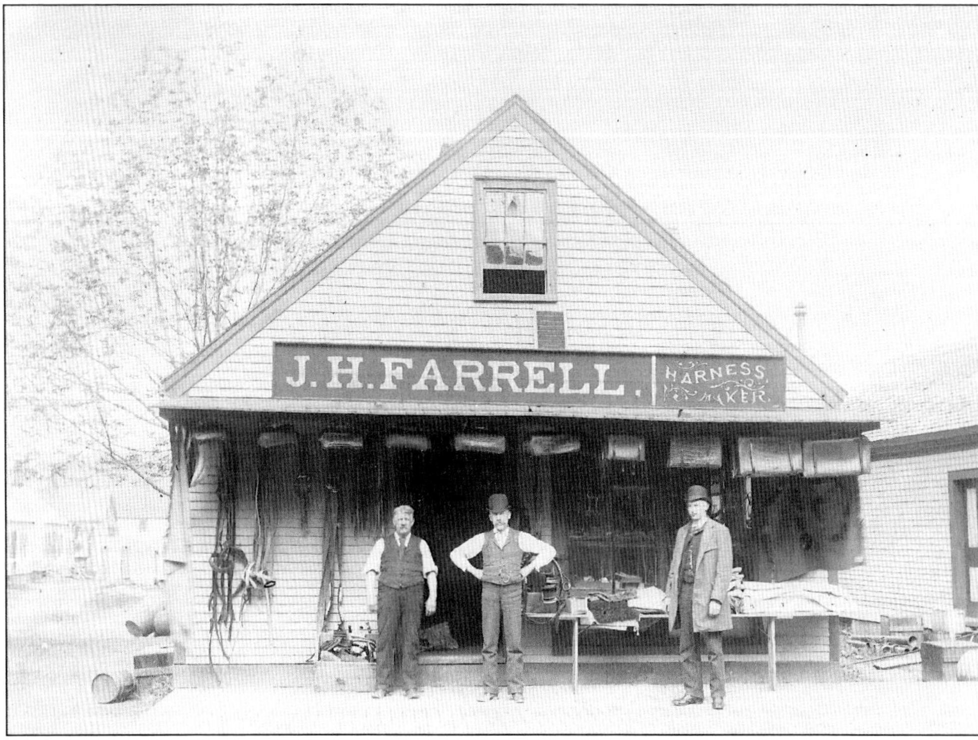

Before the advent of automobiles, harness making was a profitable business as can be seen by this establishment on Main Street.

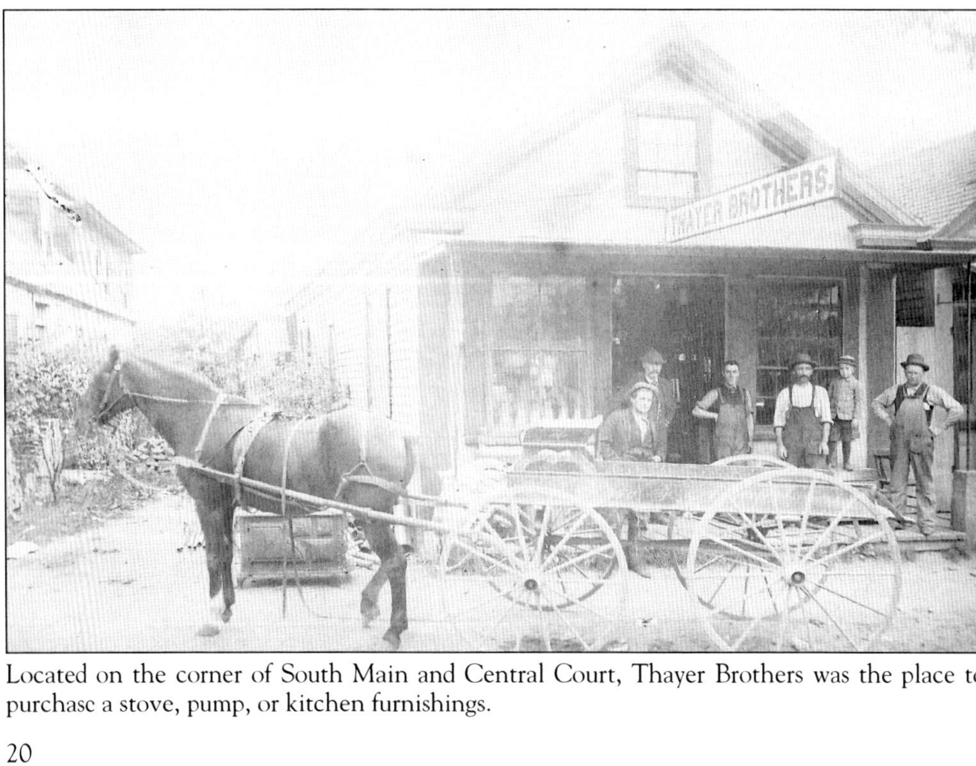

Located on the corner of South Main and Central Court, Thayer Brothers was the place to purchase a stove, pump, or kitchen furnishings.

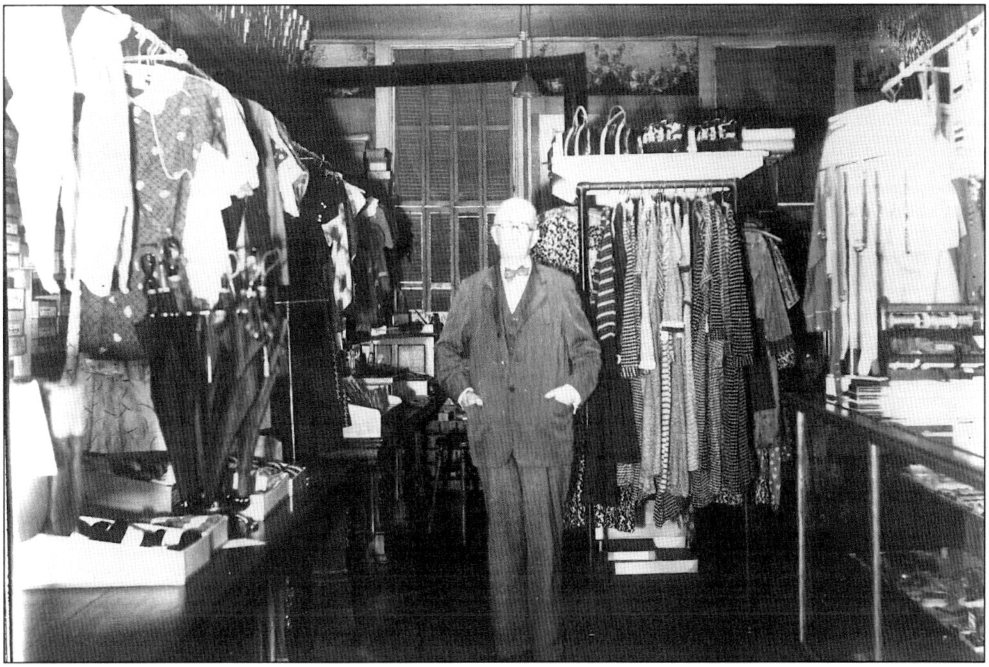

Proprietor of a dry goods store on Main Street until 1936, Ned L. Parker was one of the town's most civic-minded citizens. In addition to several terms in the state general court, he also served as town moderator, library trustee, and school board trustee. He was a frequent contributor to *The Farmington News* of well-researched articles on local history.

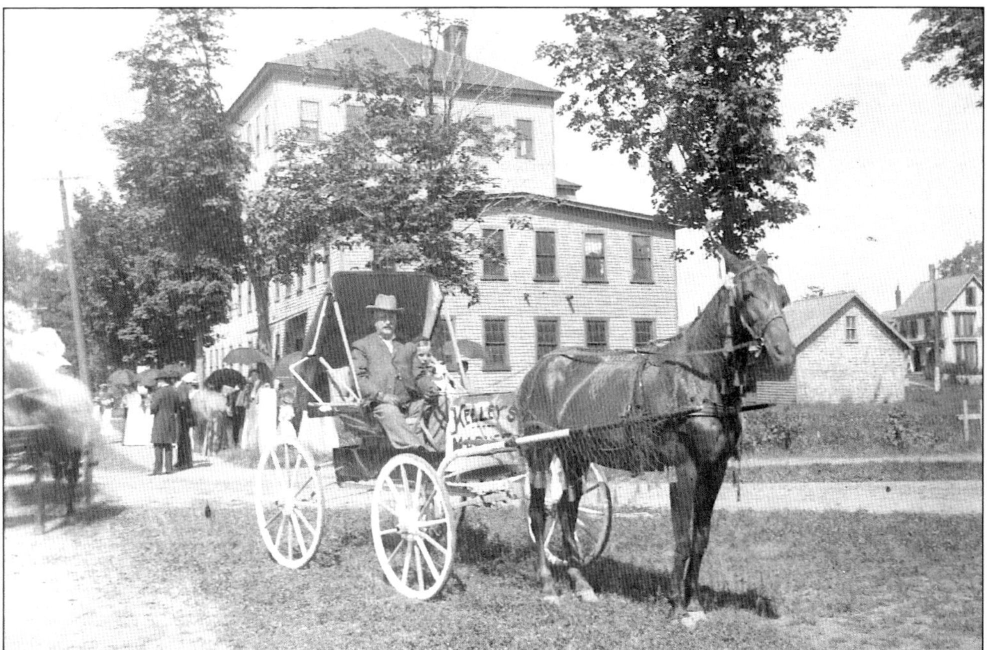

With the Cloutman shoe factory in the background, James Kelley, with son Ernest, advertises his market, which was located first in the Boston Clothing Company building and then in the Steamboat Hotel building. Note the fly net on the horse!

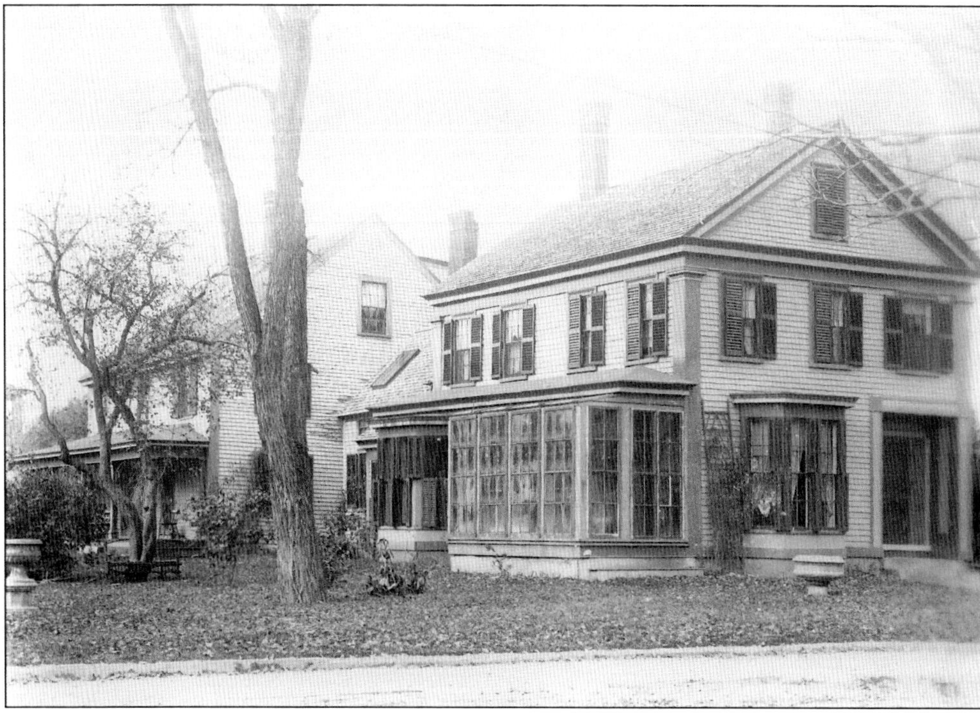

Across Main Street from his shoe factory, the residence of Alonzo Nute on the corner of Grove Street looks much the same today as when it was built in the mid-1800s.

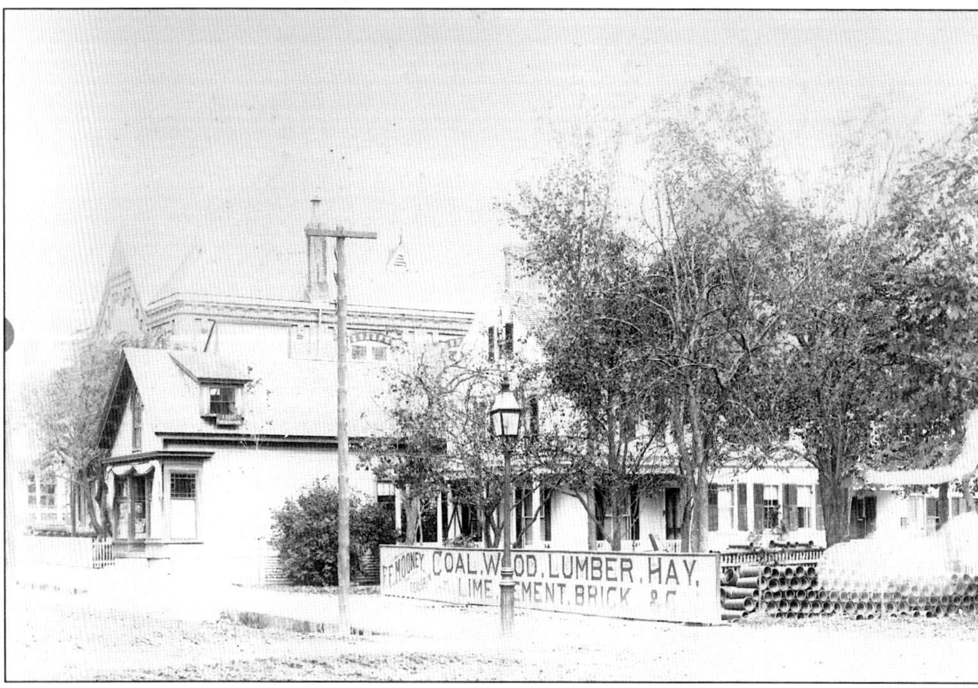

Originally built by Dr. David Parker in 1837, this house and barn next to the Old Court House became Frank Mooney's fuel and hardware business in the 1890s. Today the buildings serve as apartments and a law office.

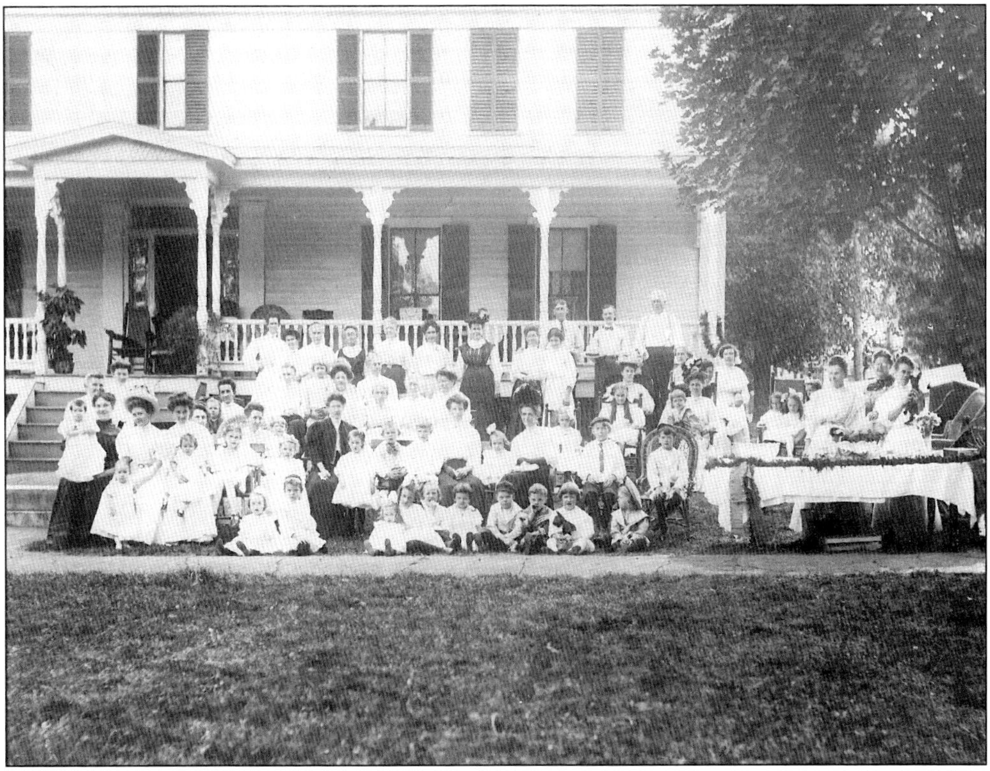

This festive occasion took place in front of the Currier Rooming House. The building later housed the Main Street Restaurant, a most modern establishment as it was lighted by electricity!

TABLE BOARD
AND FURNISHED ROOMS.

CENTRALLY LOCATED.
LARGE AND AIRY ROOMS.

Main Street Restaurant

46 AND 48 NORTH MAIN STREET.

MRS. HESTER E. PINKHAM,
PROPRIETOR.

TRANSIENT CUSTOM SOLICITED.
LIGHTED BY ELECTRICITY.
(OVER)

FARMINGTON,
NEW HAMPSHIRE.

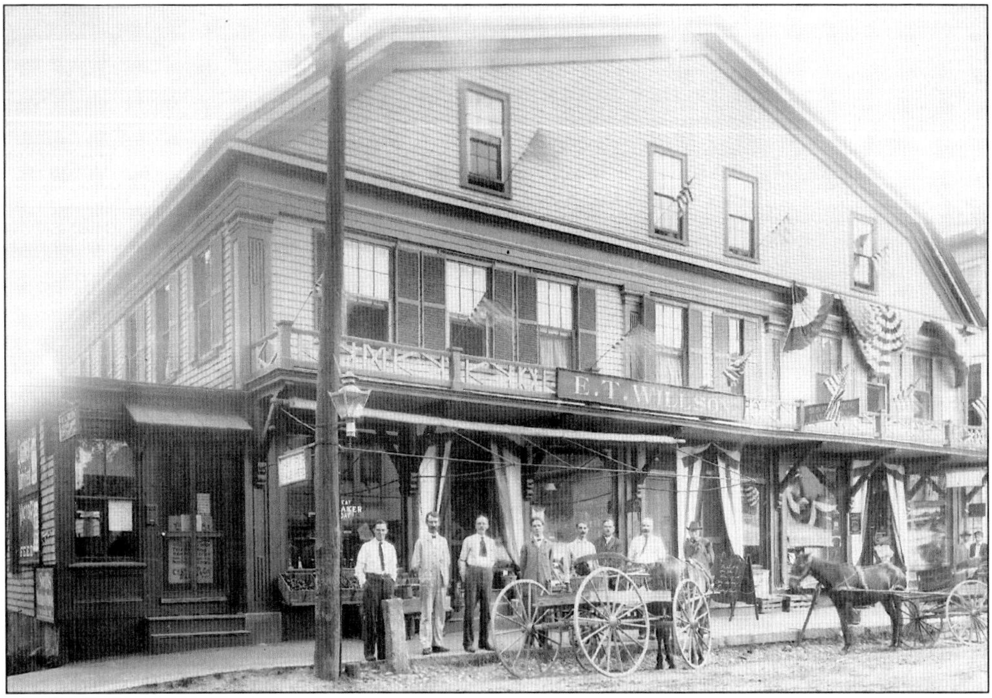

Now the site of the Goodwin Public Library, in 1871 Charles Talpey established a general store in this building. From 1882 until the fire of 1910, this was the Edward T. Willson Store, selling everything but clothing and dry goods.

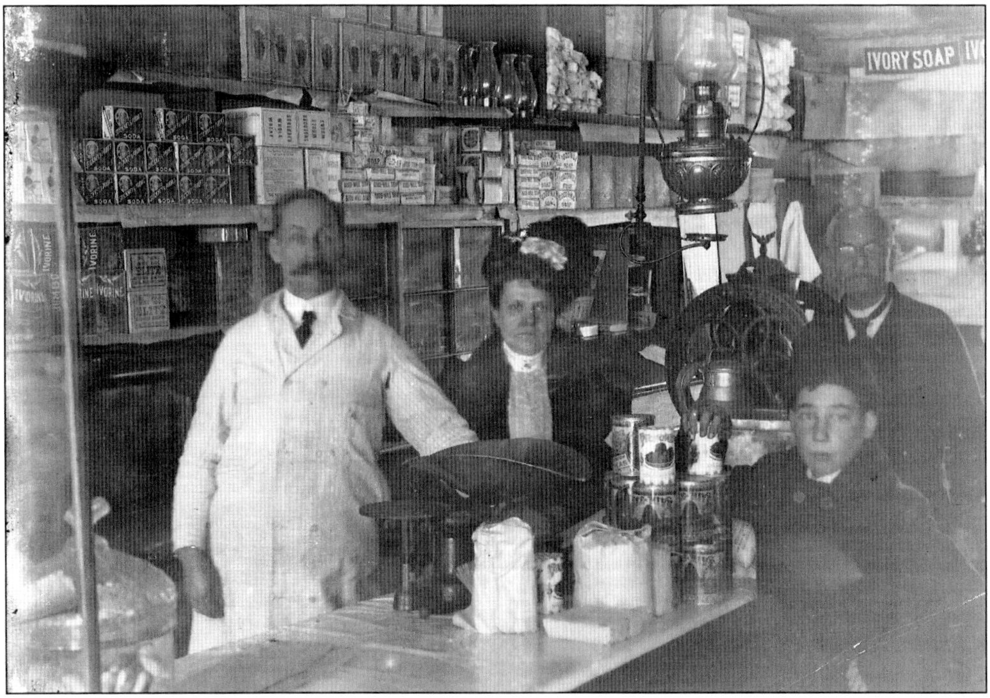

The interior of E.T. Willson's in the era when groceries were wrapped instead of bagged and there was no such thing as self-service.

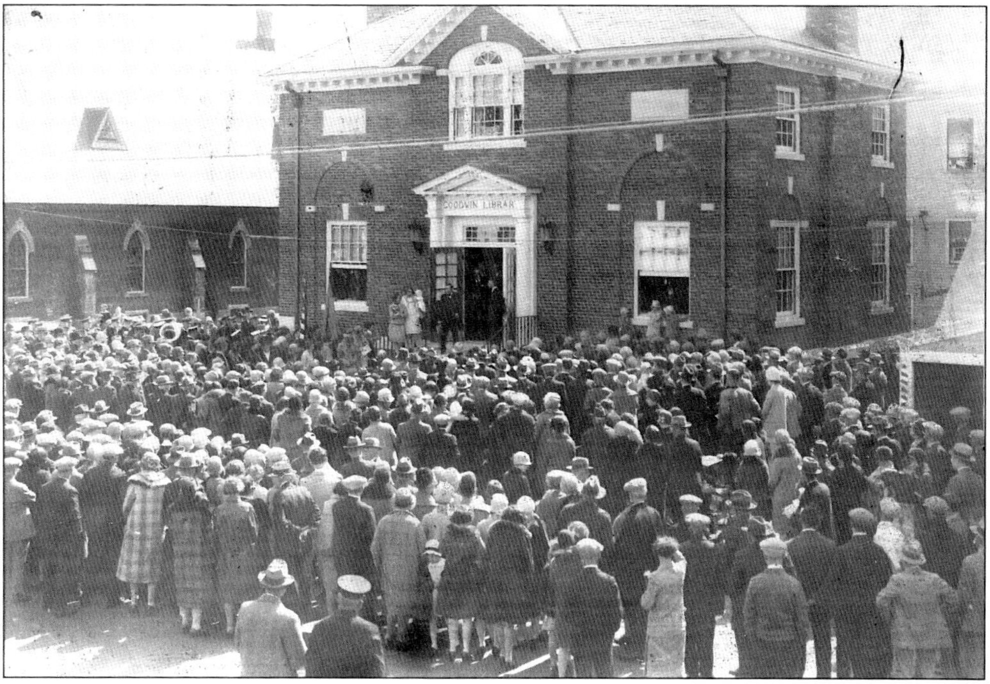

The dedication of the Goodwin Public Library took place on May 10, 1929. The previous library in the Opera House was destroyed by fire in 1928. This was the impetus for a separate library building, and George Goodwin of West Milton agreed to provide funds for its construction.

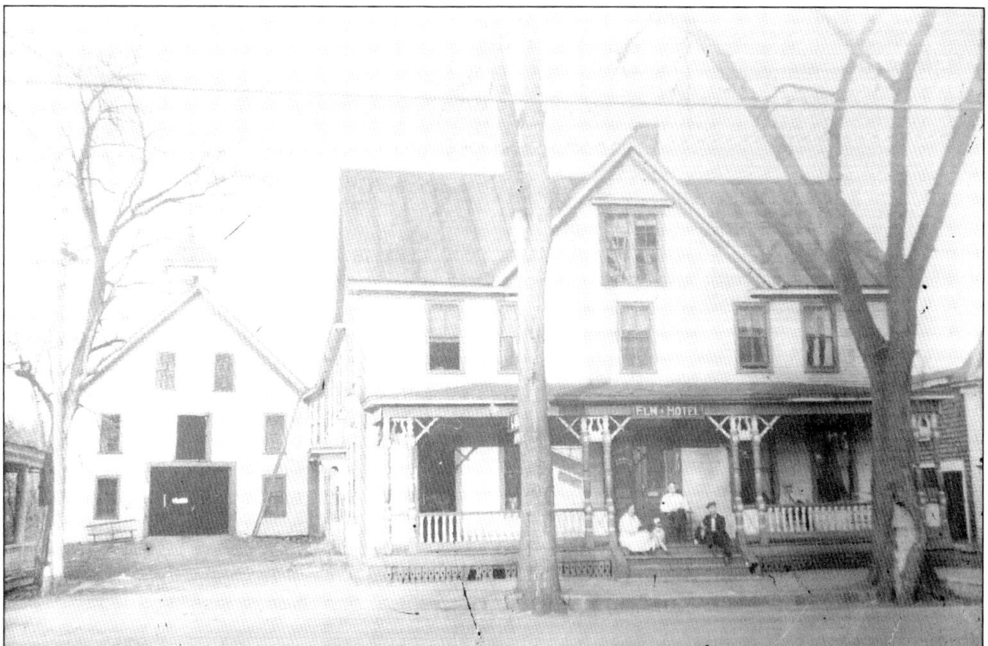

Both its namesake trees and the Elm Hotel are gone now, but this popular stopping place for transients once stood on South Main across from the Congregational church.

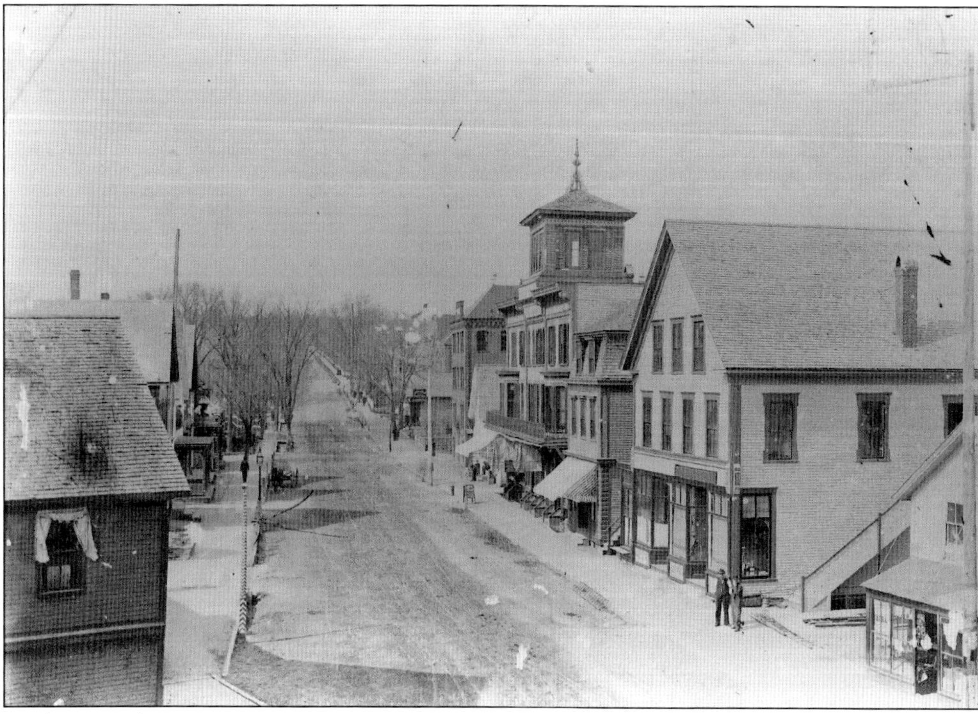

Looking north on Main Street *c.* 1890 prior to construction of the Odd Fellows Block. Note the barber pole and street light on the lower left.

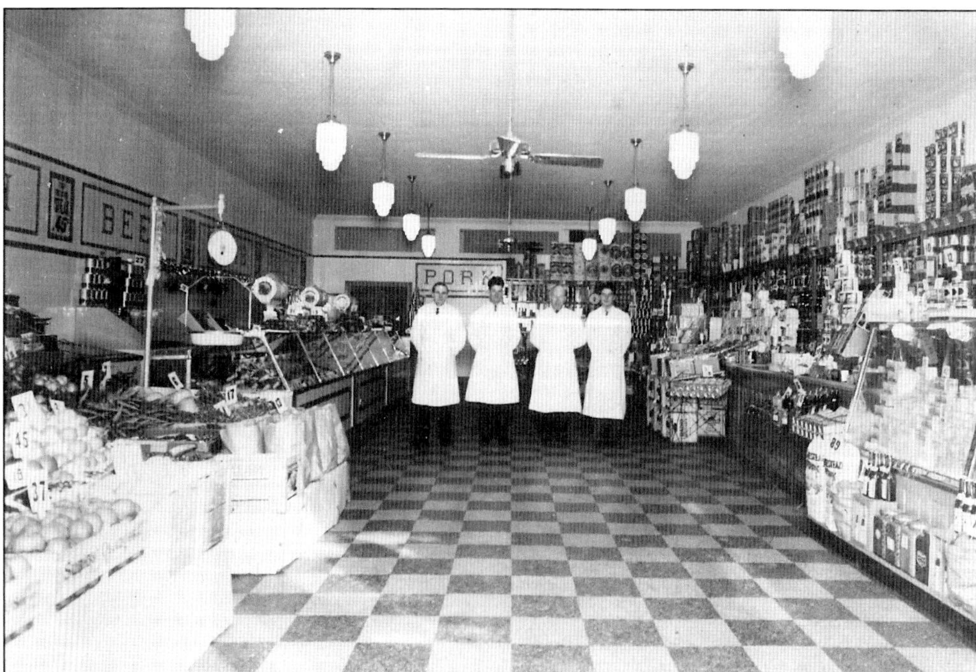

A 1934 photograph of the First National Store with employees Herb Weston, Ray Moreshead, James Hoage, and "Twink" Osgood. Currently a video store and beauty parlor are resident here.

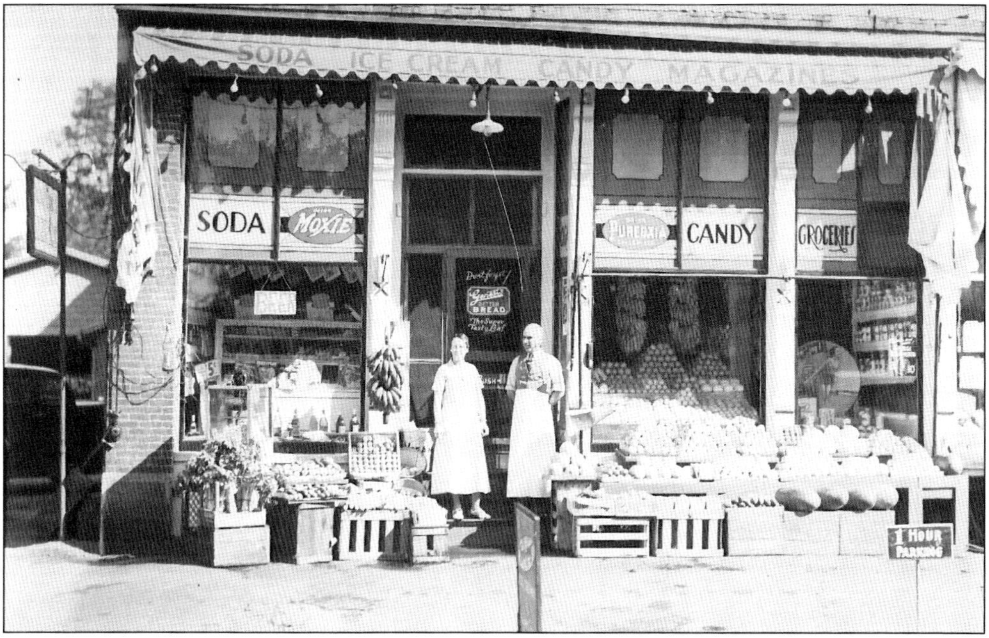

John Brooks and Margarite Furber pose in front of his store on Central Street where the Union Telephone Company is now located.

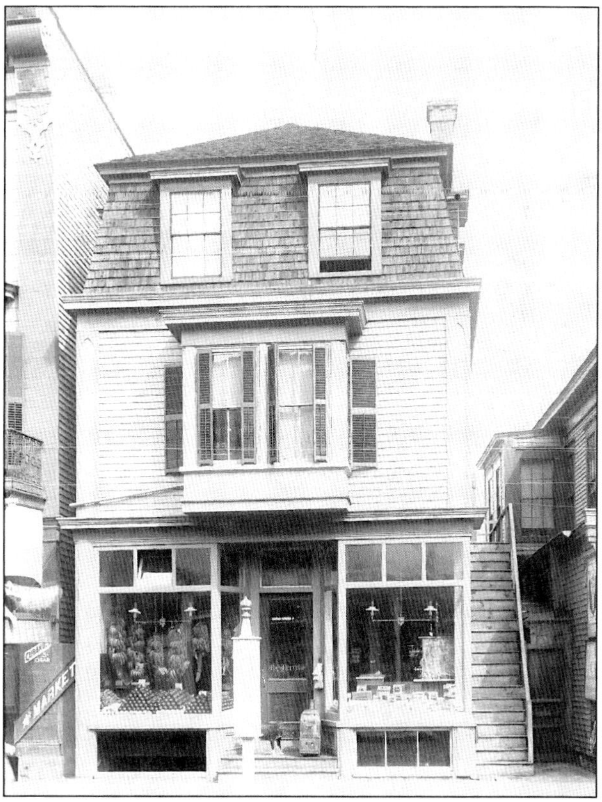

In 1896 Ralph Ferretti opened his fruit and ice cream parlor, advertising "three flavors constantly on hand." You could satisfy your chocolate craving there, at $1.00 per 5-pound box! Gelinas' Market later occupied this site.

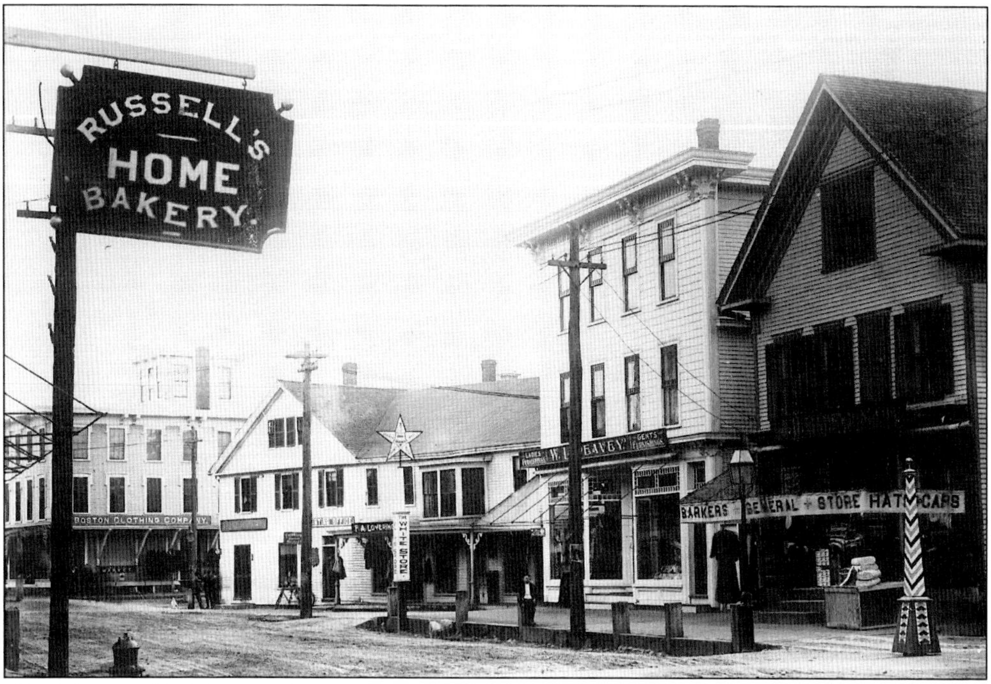

The Masonic Building, with its meeting hall upstairs, had on its first floor The White Store. The 1860 Reed Block next door, which housed John Barker's general merchandise store, burned in 1969.

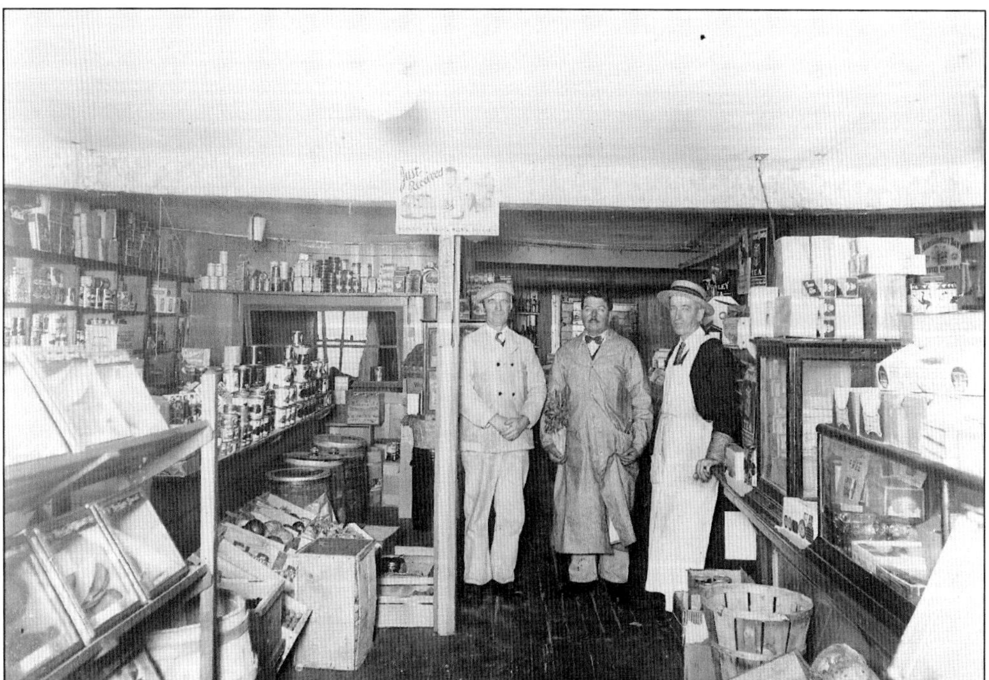

Another grocery on the Square was Nutter's Market, seen here with Harry Pulsifer, Harry Nutter, and Walt Pulsifer.

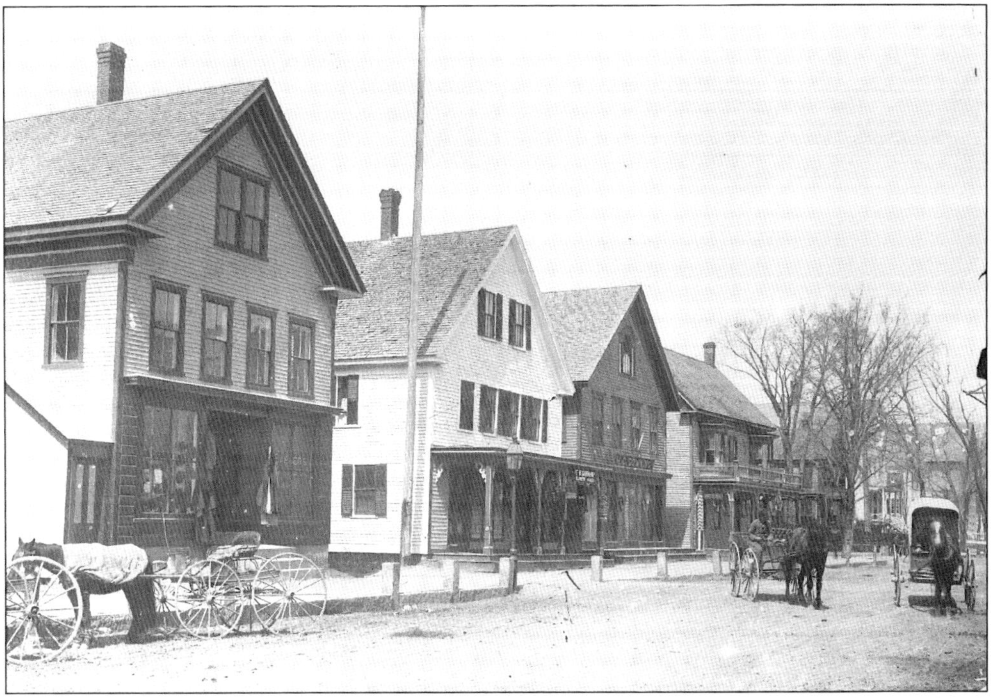

Looking up Main Street before traffic became a problem. These buildings, although remodeled, are still in existence.

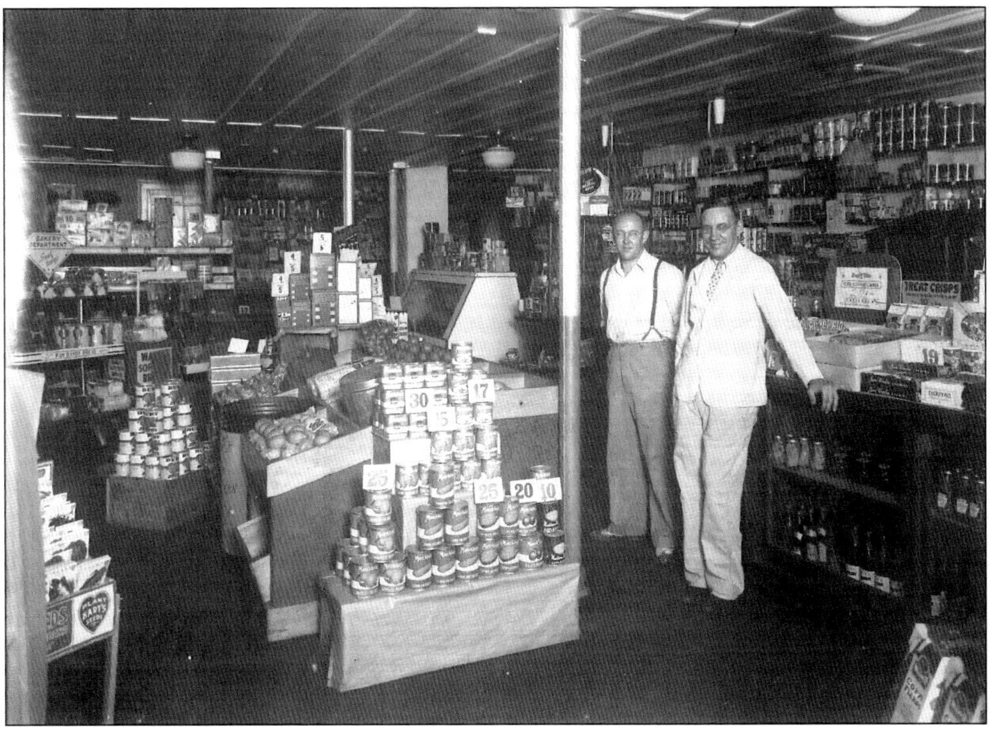

Ernest Kelley, shown here with George Butler, followed in his father's footsteps, establishing his own "Kelley's Grocery" in 1920.

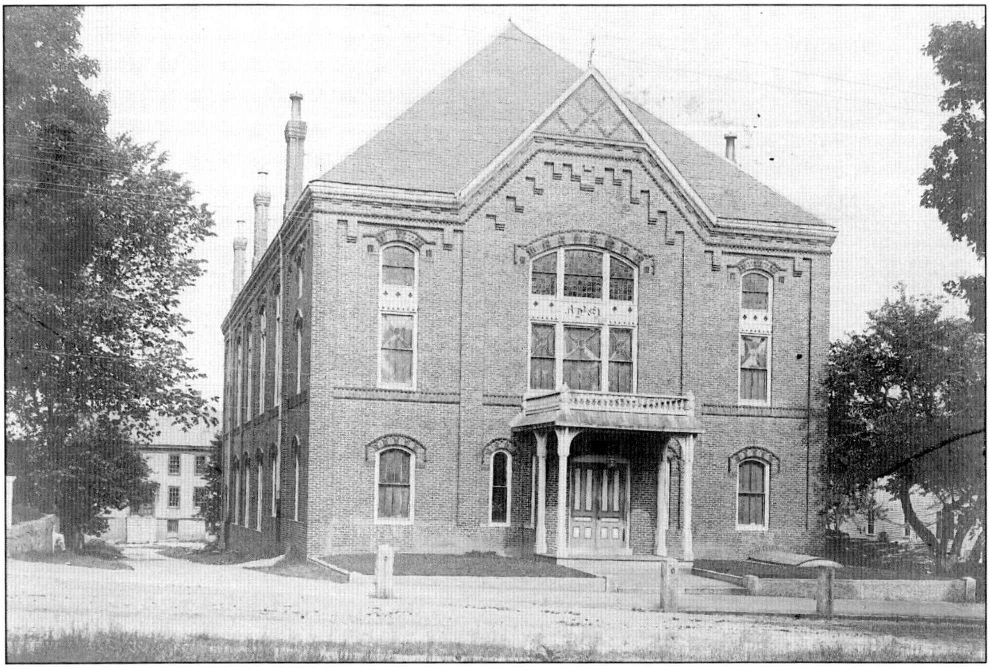

Built in 1881 at a cost of $21,355.76, the Opera House was Farmington's cultural center, hosting plays, dances, and concerts. Since the town offices were located here, its destruction by fire in 1928 caused the irretrievable loss of many town records.

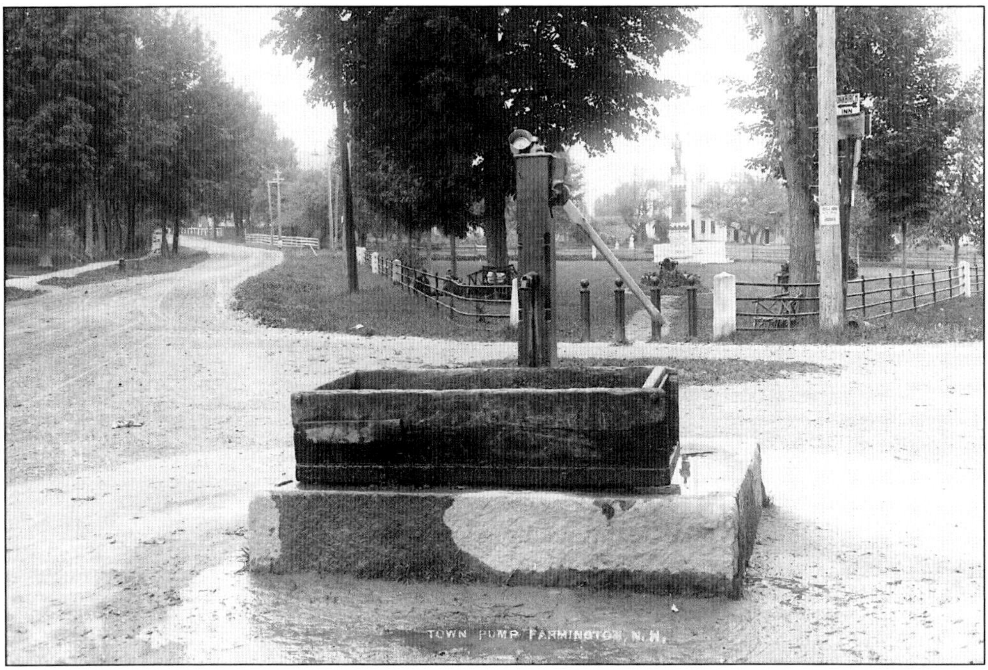

The old town pump with its tin dipper and watering trough stood for sixty years at the intersection of Charles and North Main Streets. After its well was condemned, it was replaced by an artificial pump. Edgerly Park in the background was a gift to the town from James Edgerly in memory of his Civil War comrades.

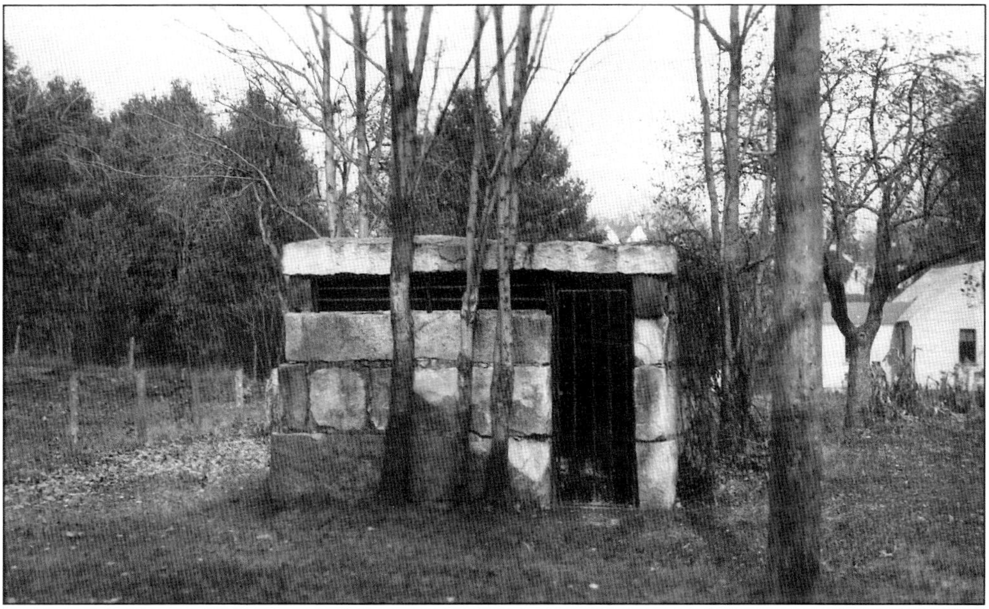

The Stone Lobby, later referred to as "The Lock-Up," was built in 1859 on the corner of Church and Union Streets by William Sampson to confine the lawless element until some legal tribunal pronounced judgment. It was 10 feet long, 10 feet wide, and stood 6.5 feet tall.

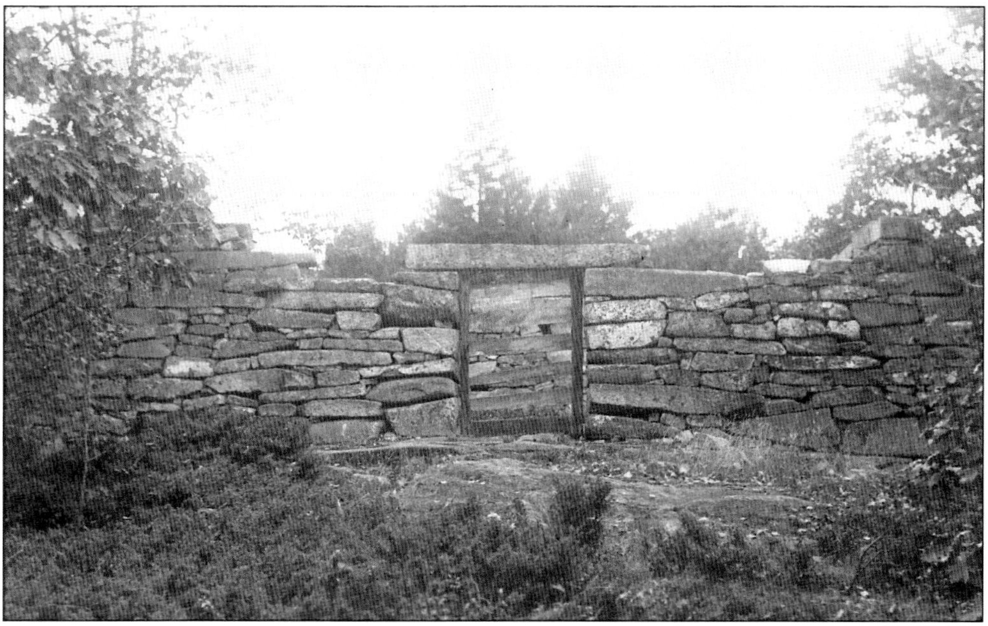

In the early nineteenth century each town was required to maintain an animal pound to restrain strays. Farmington's Town Pound, located on the Pound Road near the geographic center of town, is still an impressive edifice. Constructed in 1823 by Nicholas Colbath, it measures 40 feet square with walls 8 feet high. Due largely to the efforts of Edmund Demers, it was placed on the U.S. Department of the Interior's National Register of Historic Places in 1993.

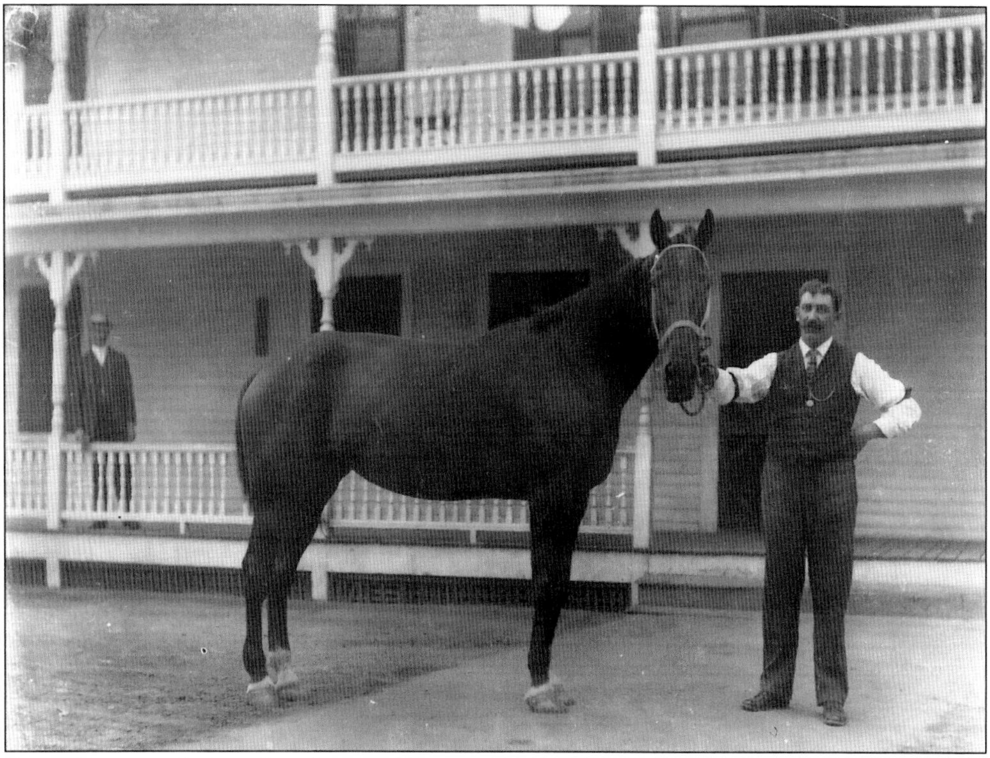

A vital business before the advent of the auto was Locke's Livery on Crowley and Mechanic Streets. Begun in 1889 by J. Wesley Locke, it was here that one could hire or buy horses and carriages.

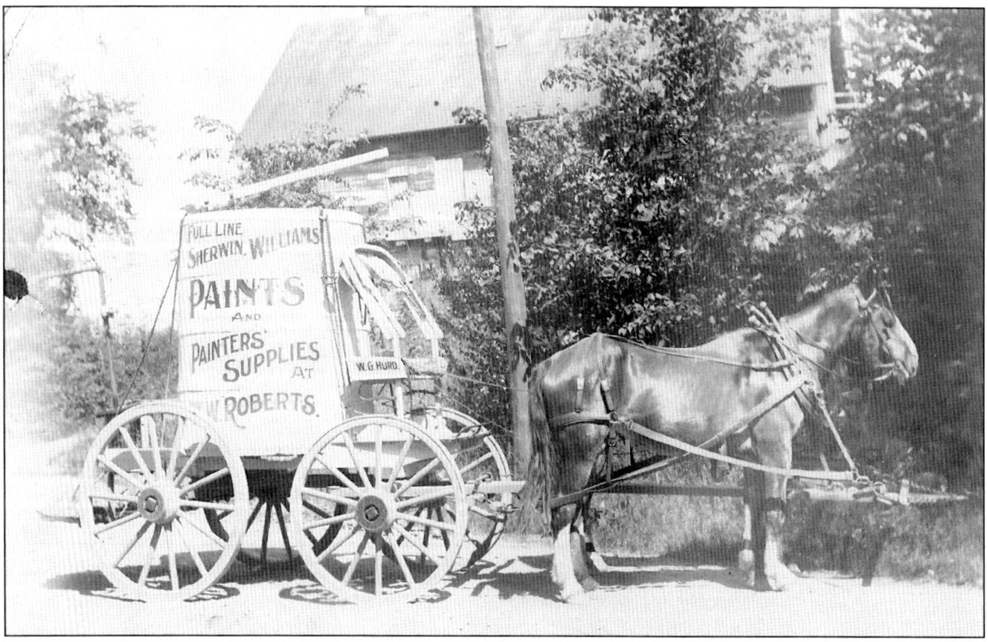

Dust from dirt roads would have been intolerable were it not for the efforts of Will Hurd, who was paid $15.00 weekly by merchants to operate the town sprinkler.

Two

Work: Industry and Agriculture

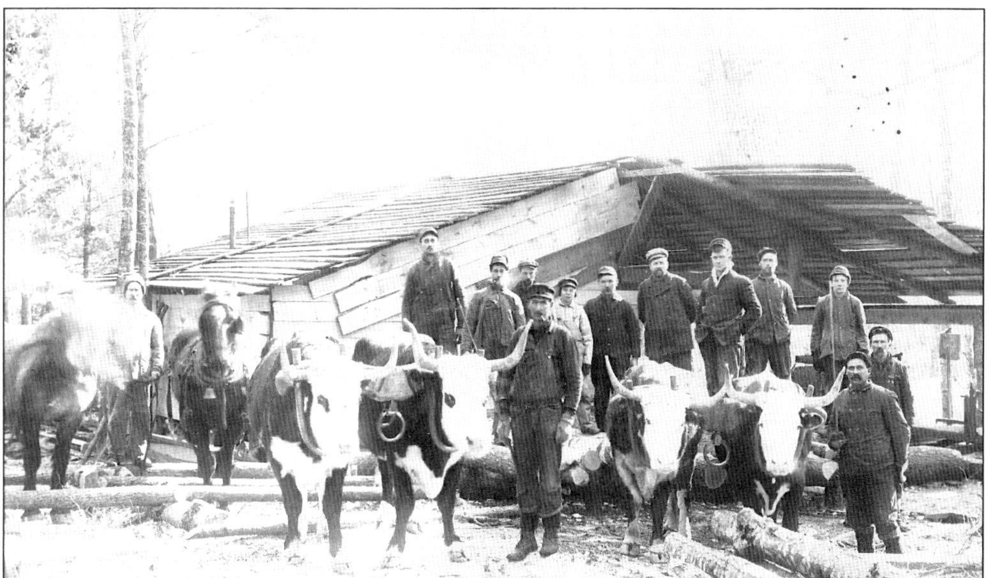

George Wyatt's sawmill *c.* 1913 on Ivory Bean's Meeting House Hill Road wood lot. Oxen teams were the "skidders" in those days.

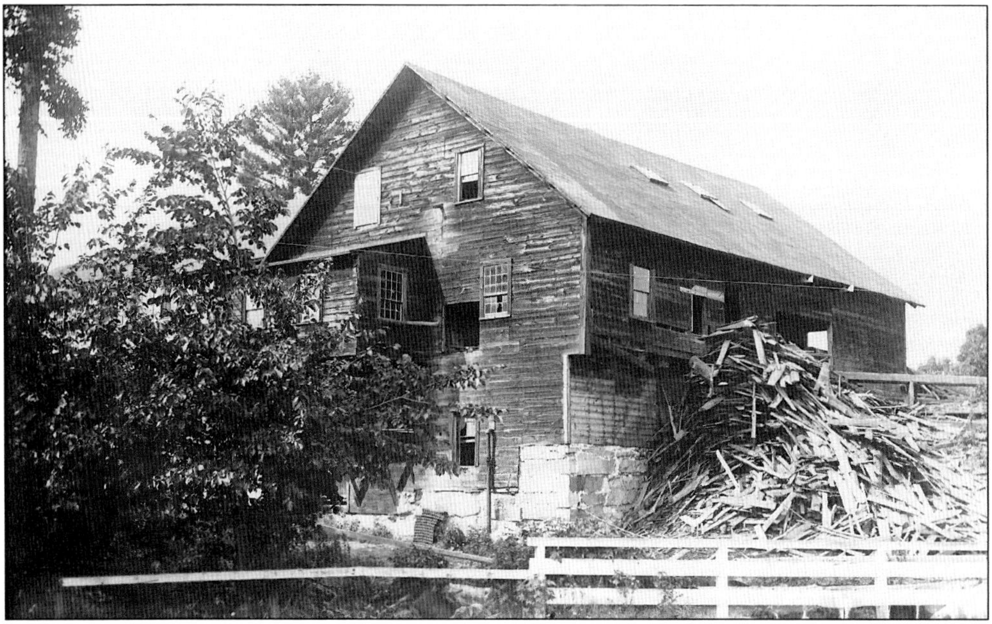

Originally built in the early 1700s on Central Street, the Waldron Mill obtained its power from the Ela River. In later years the mill was replaced by the Electric Light Station, bringing electric street lights to town in 1910.

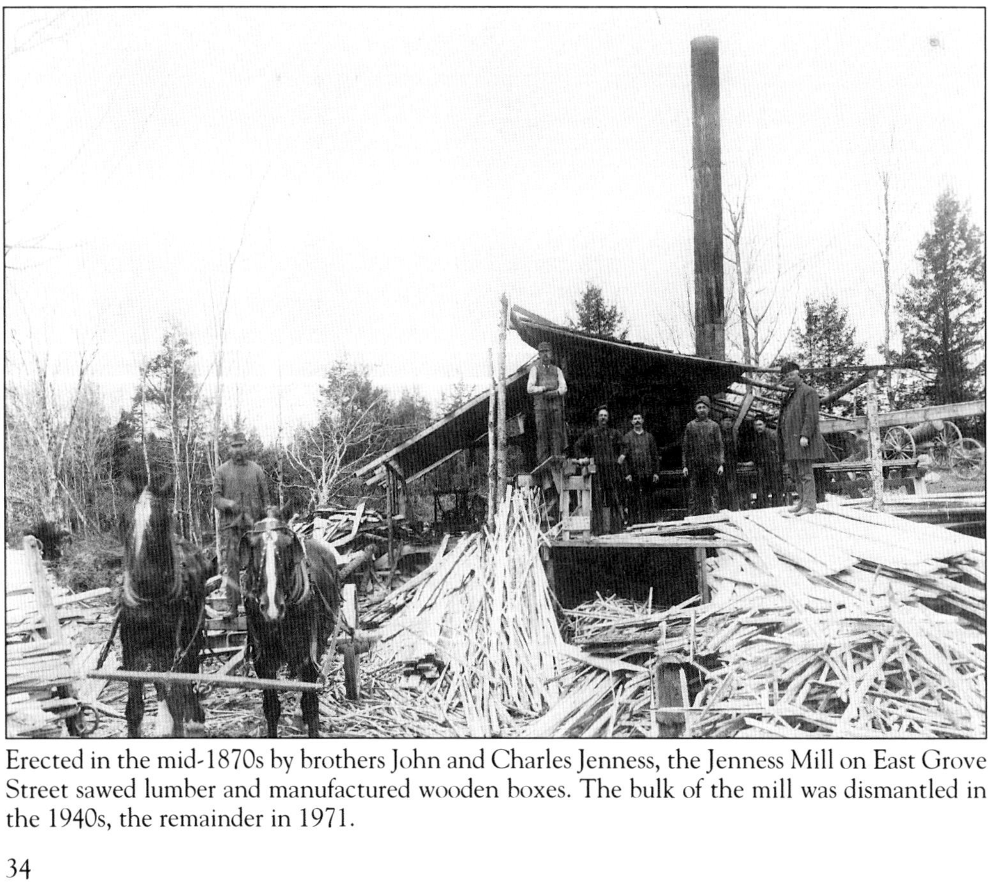

Erected in the mid-1870s by brothers John and Charles Jenness, the Jenness Mill on East Grove Street sawed lumber and manufactured wooden boxes. The bulk of the mill was dismantled in the 1940s, the remainder in 1971.

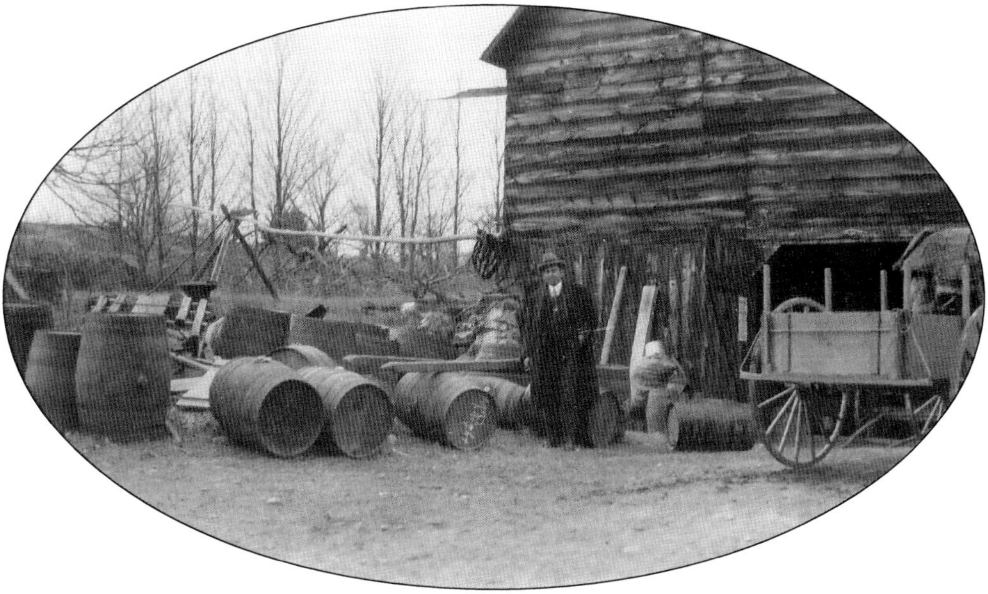

This barrel factory on East Grove Street kept a number of coopers employed, for the wooden barrel was the major container for the storage and sale of items such as flour, sugar, apples, and cider.

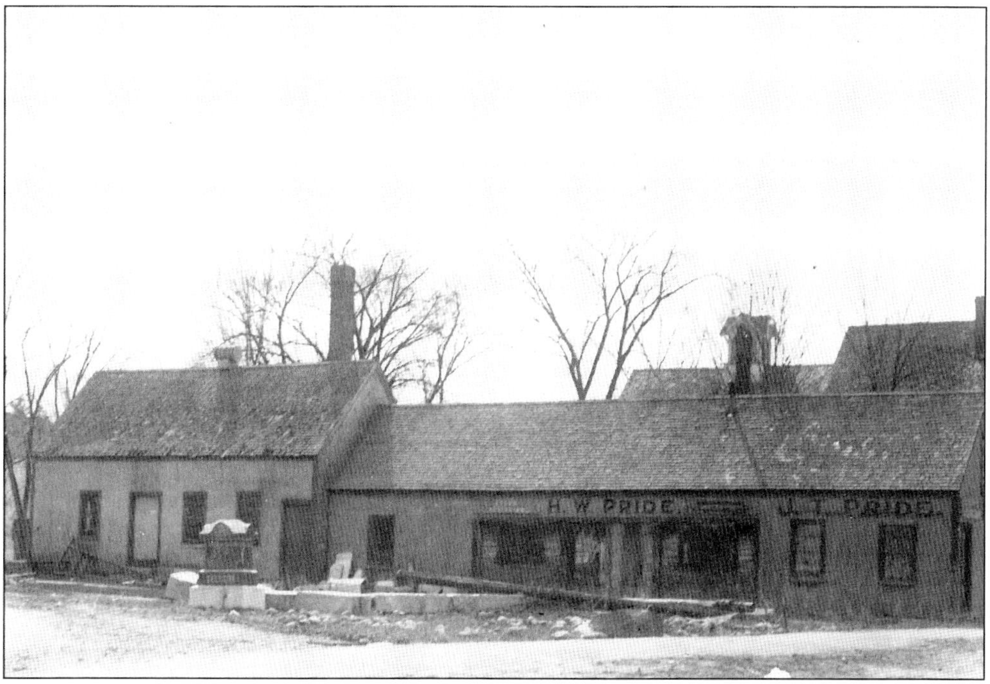

The Pride family operated a stone monument works in the 1880s at the junction of Central and Tappan Streets near where the Catholic church now stands. Many a granite tombstone in Pine Grove Cemetery was manufactured here.

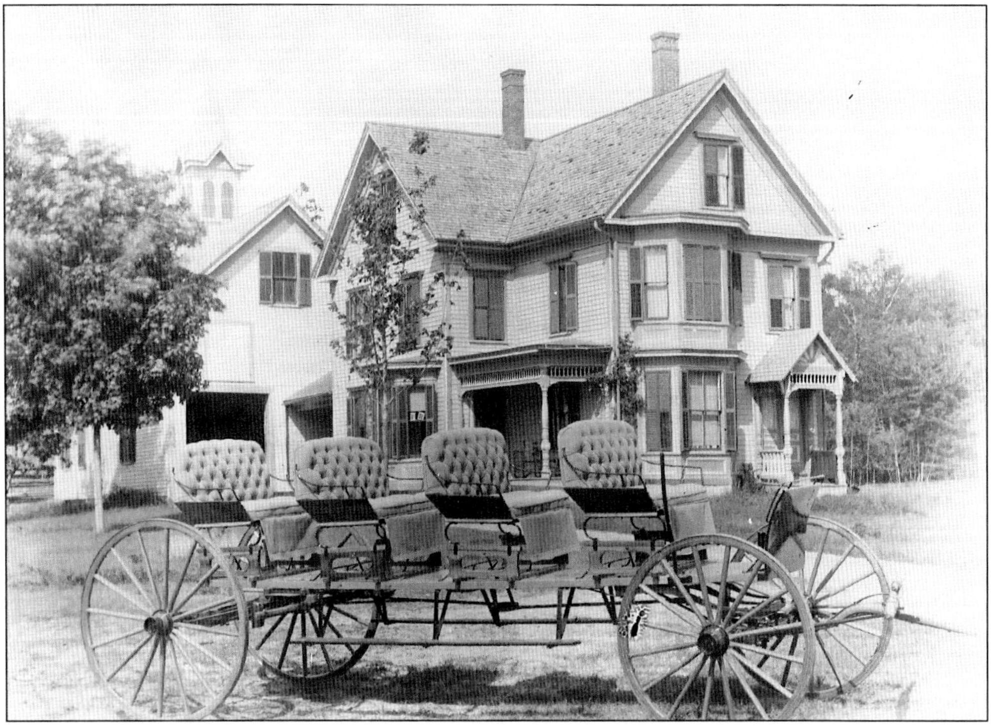

B.F. Perkins located his factory and residence on the banks of the Mad River where High (Route 11) and Central Streets intersect. He built wagons and custom-made vehicles and also served as an undertaker. The house pictured burned in 1910; Cameron's Garden Center today occupies the factory site.

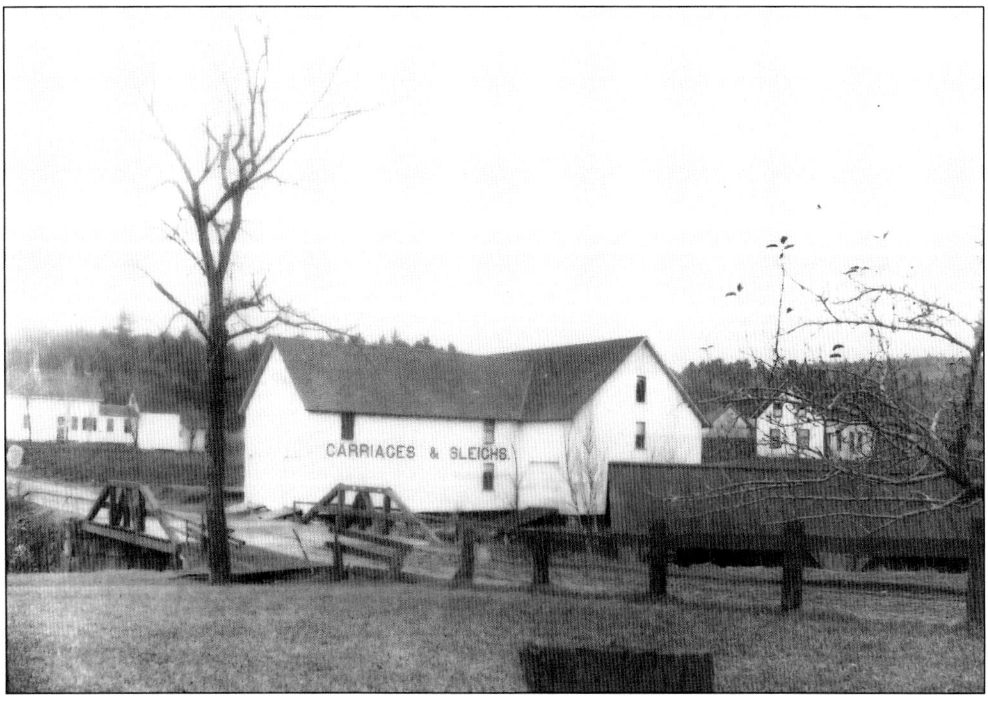

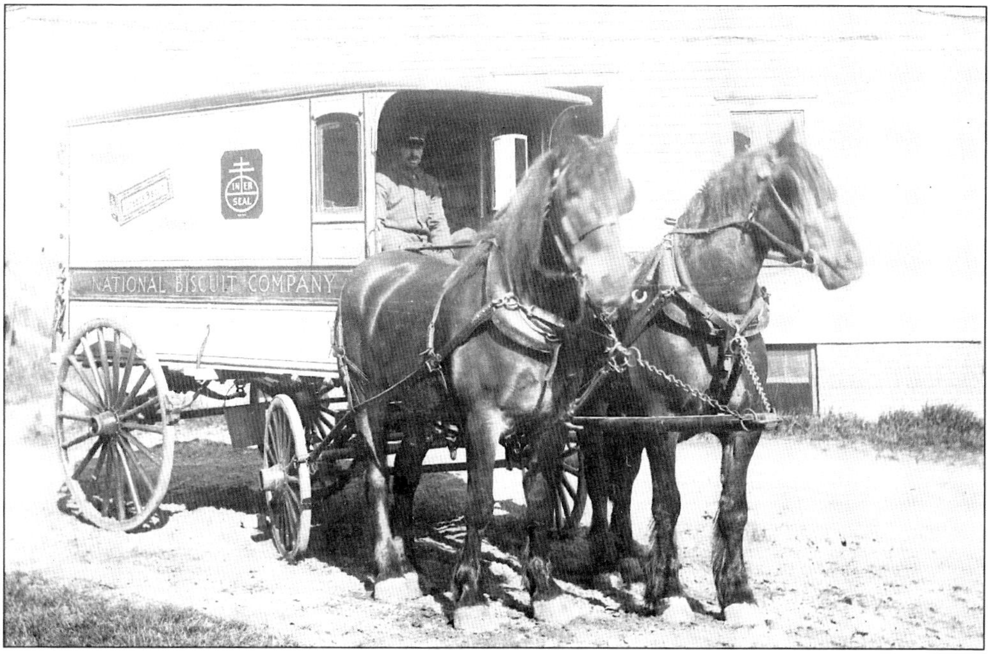

"Cracker" Horne was a local delivery man around 1900 who resided on Lone Star Avenue.

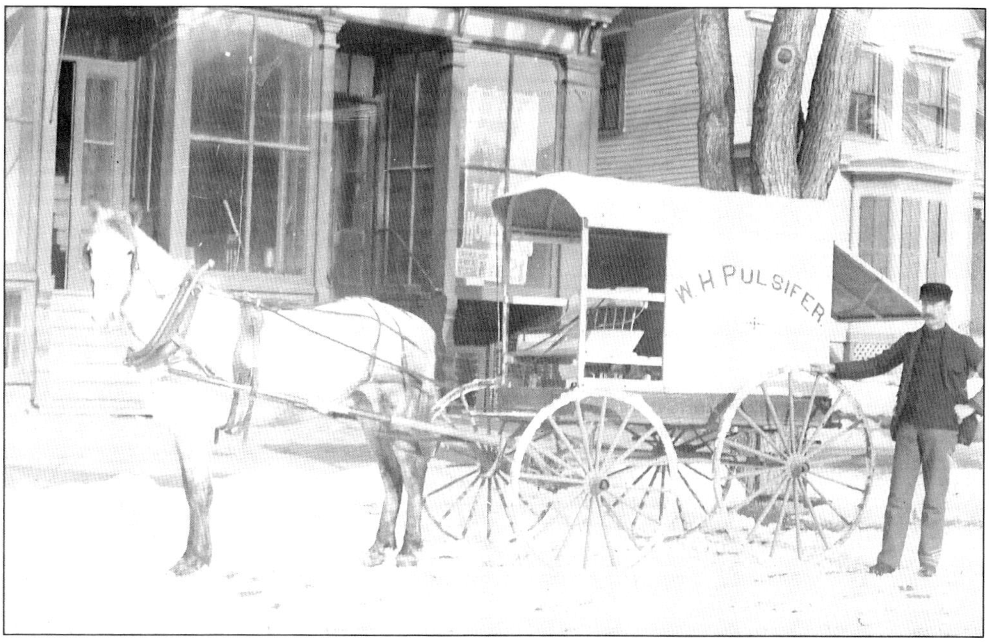

Walter Pulsifer stands with his horse-drawn delivery wagon in front of the Shackford Block on Central Street.

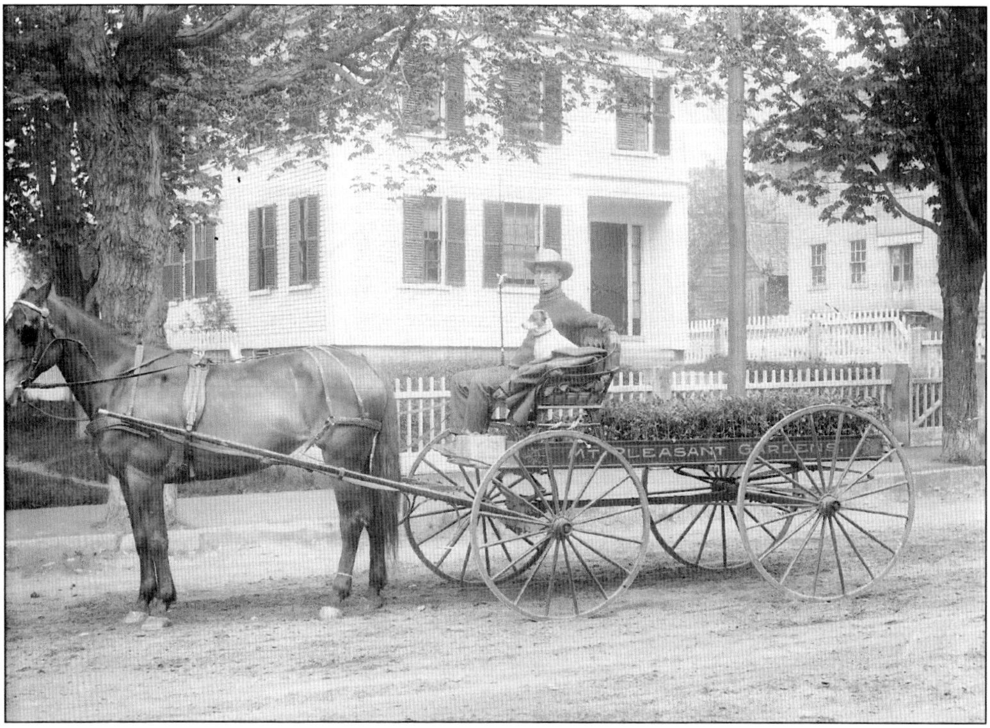

James Fletcher's wagon made frequent deliveries from the greenhouse near his home on Mt. Pleasant Street where he operated a market garden business.

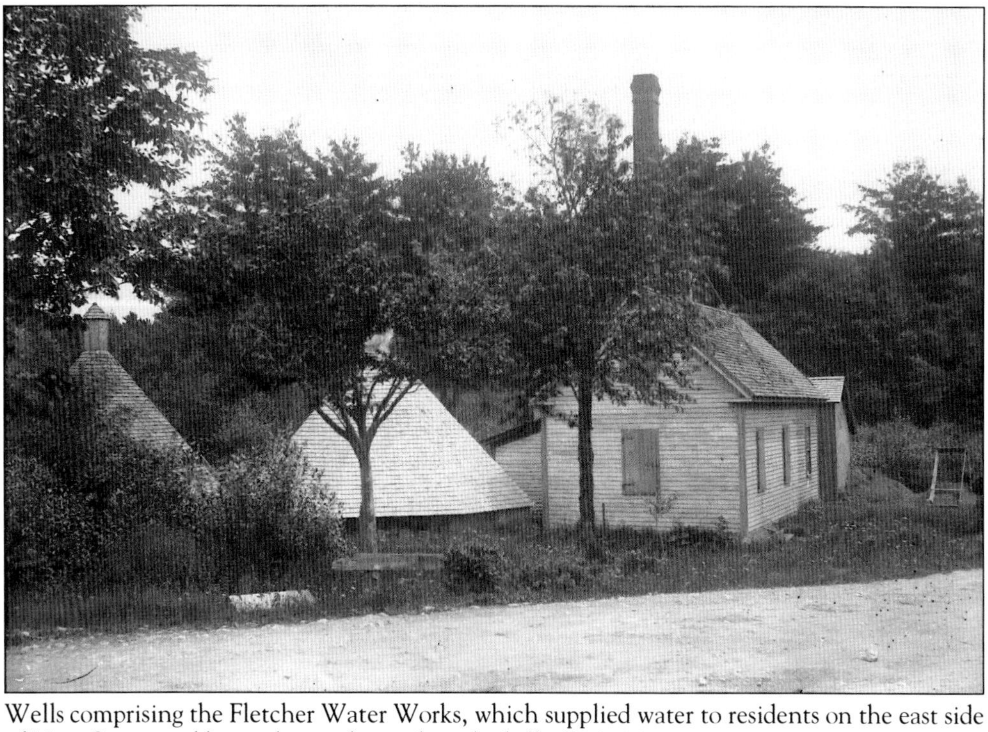

Wells comprising the Fletcher Water Works, which supplied water to residents on the east side of Main Street and beyond, were located on the hill off Mt. Vernon Street.

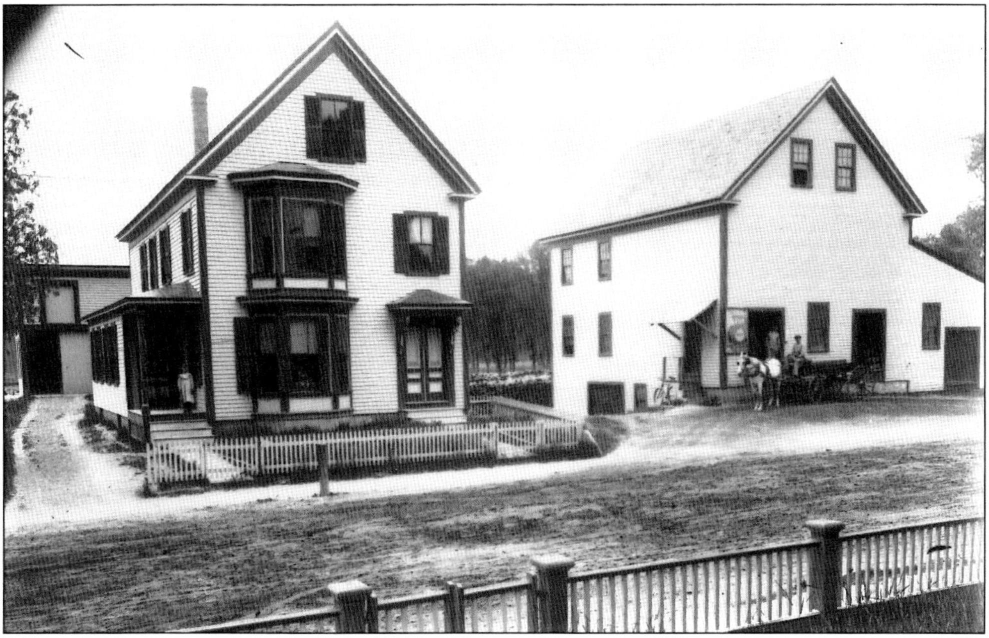

Beginning in 1899 H.W. Roberts operated a gristmill next to his home on Central Street. Using a 25-horsepower steam engine instead of water power to grind grain and flour, he was able to operate his mill year-round.

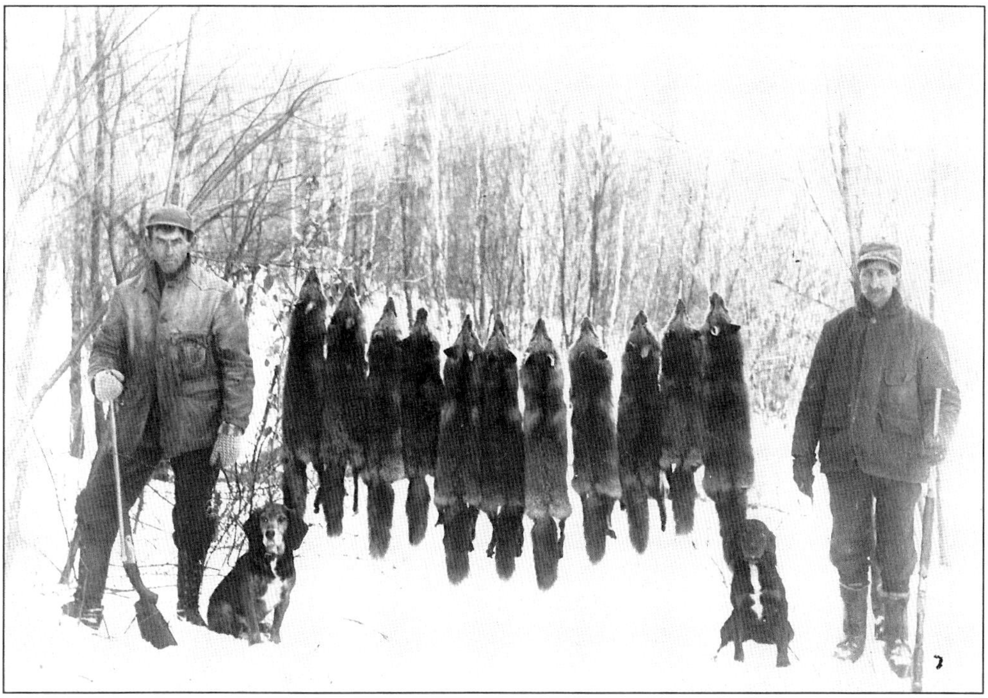

Back when fur coats were a popular item of apparel, the trapping and hunting of animals such as these foxes shot by Charles Wyatt (on right) and friend provided a seasonal means of income.

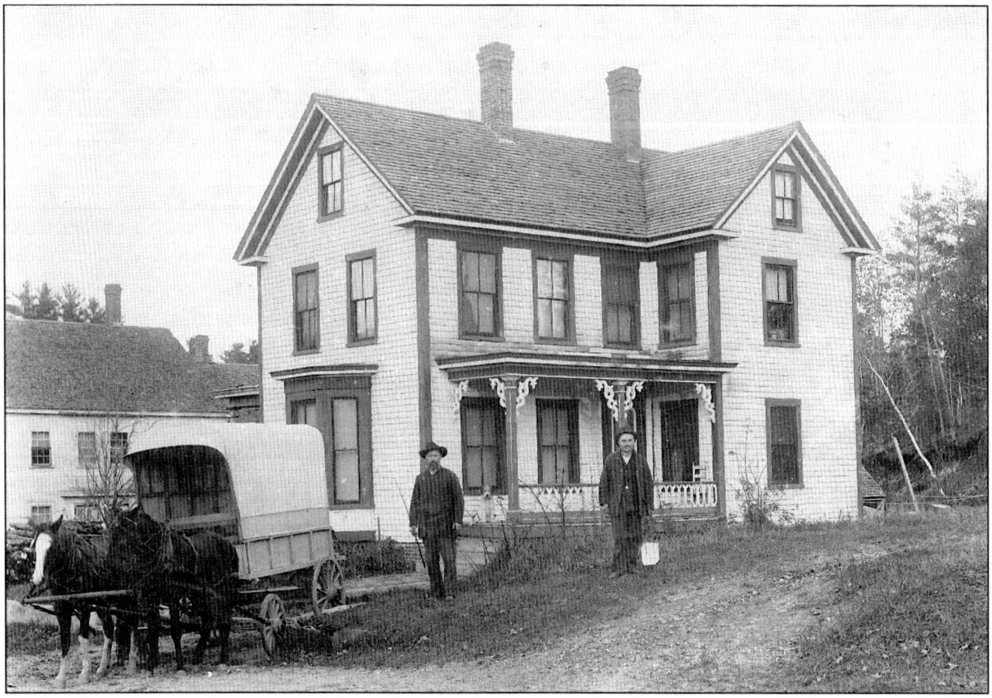

Before the days of mechanical refrigeration, food was preserved in "ice boxes," insulated containers that could hold a large block of ice. In winter, cakes of ice were cut, packed in sawdust, and stored in ice houses to keep all year. Freeman Johnson operated such an ice house on Beaver Pond off Spring Street, and his horse-drawn cart delivered ice to the homes in town.

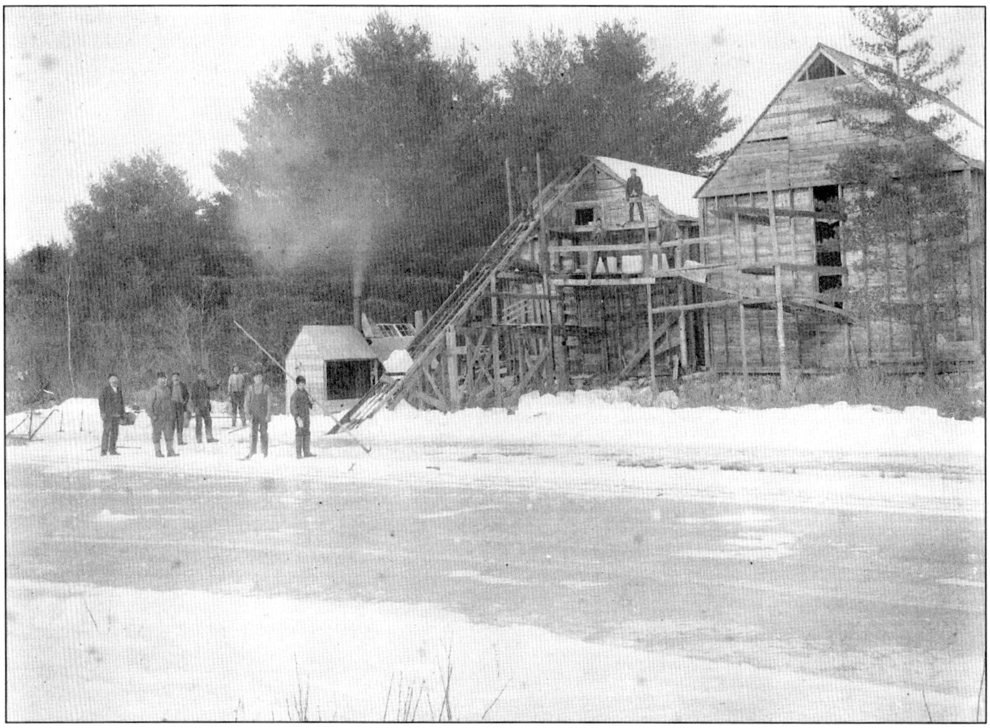

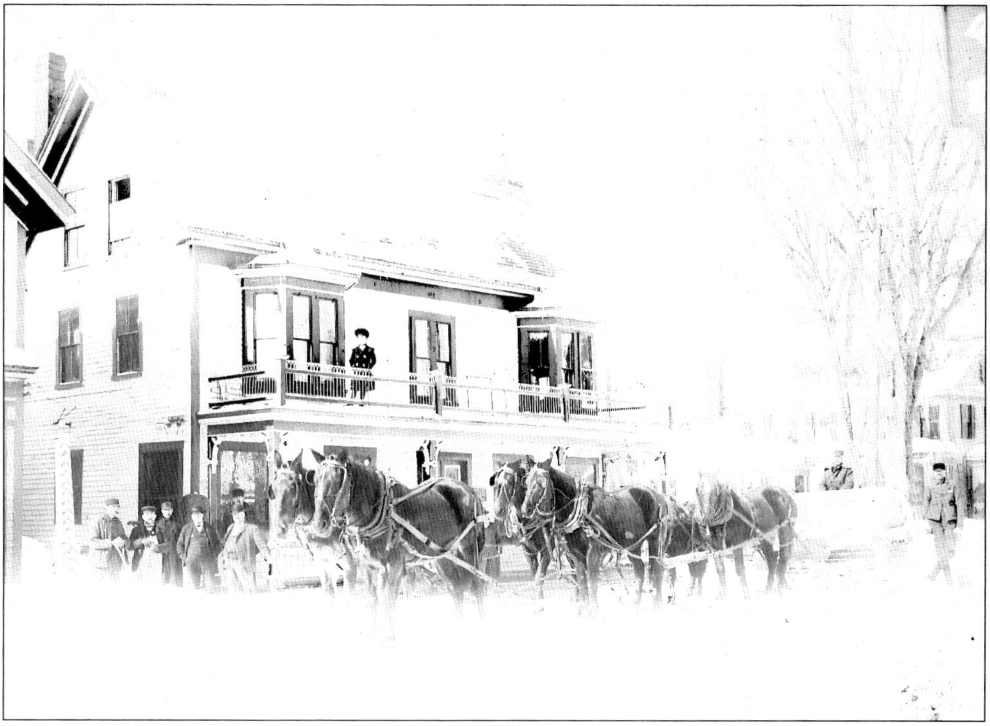

Six of Wes Locke's finest pull a snow roller along Main Street in front of Nutter's Saloon, thus packing down the road for the passage of sleighs, the common mode of winter travel.

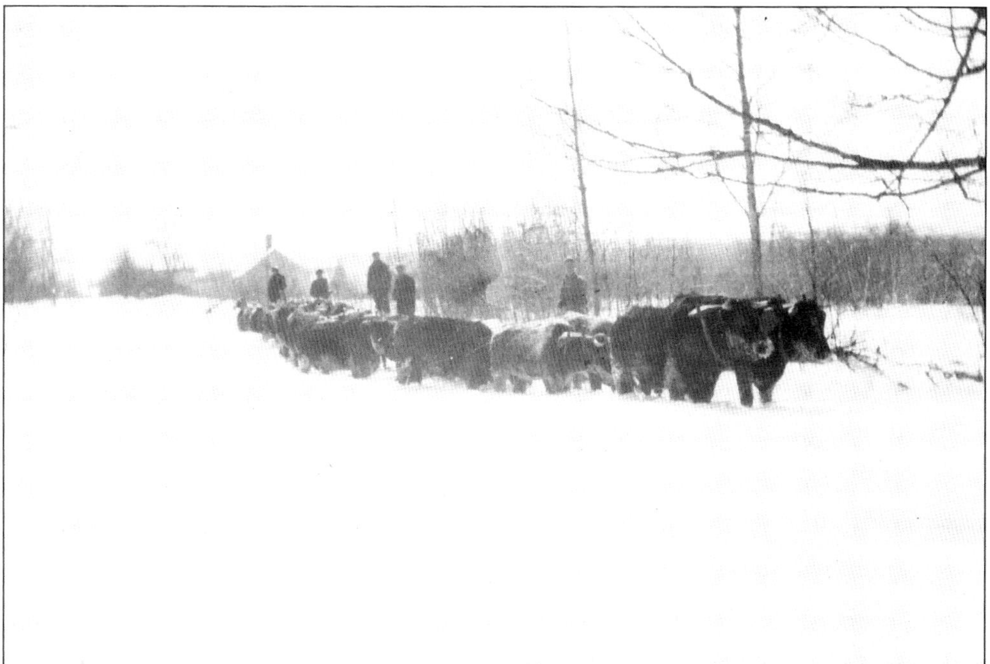

On country roads, such as this scene of the Meaderboro Road near Merrill's Corner, teams of oxen "broke the road" after a deep snowfall so that horses could travel.

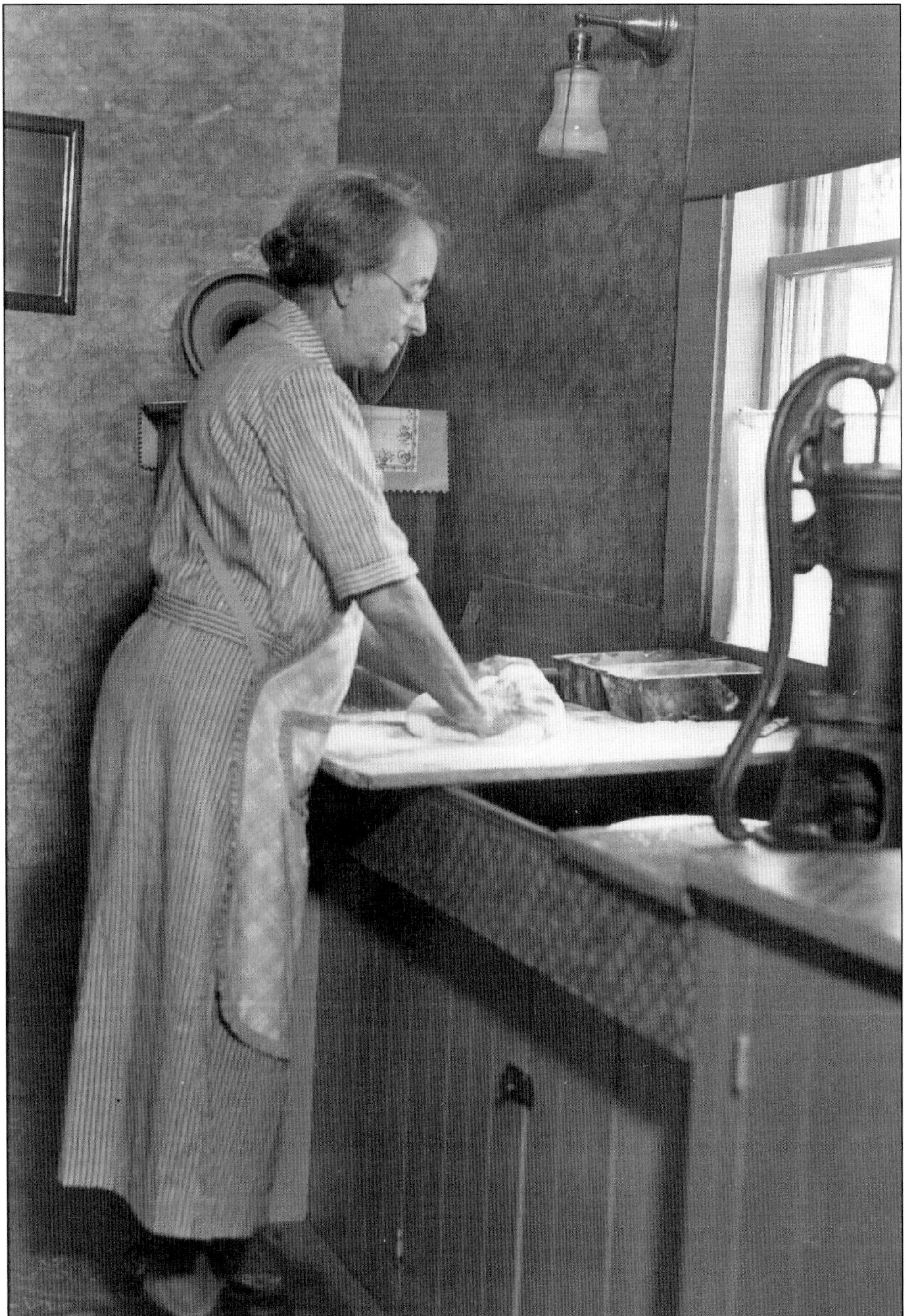

With no supermarkets on which to depend, a woman's work was never truly done in earlier times. Each morning she had to bake bread for the day in a wood-fired stove, no pleasant task in the heat of summer!

Farm women such as Ida Bean raised all their own fruit and vegetables, spending many days canning and drying produce for winter use.

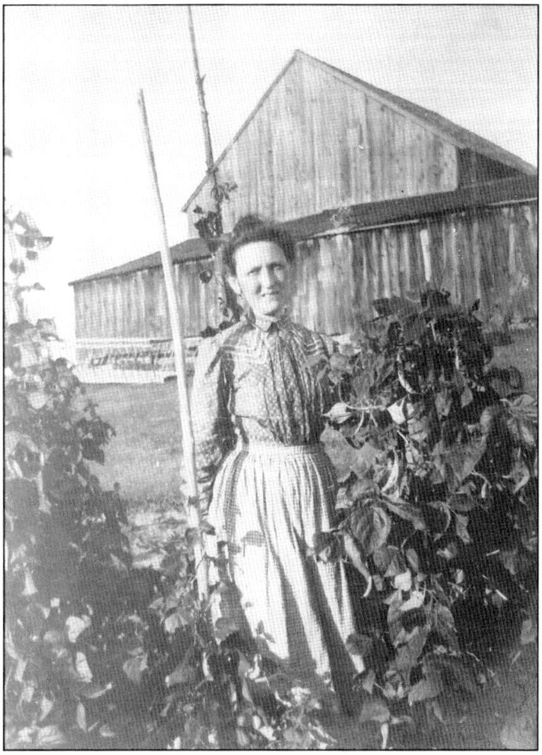

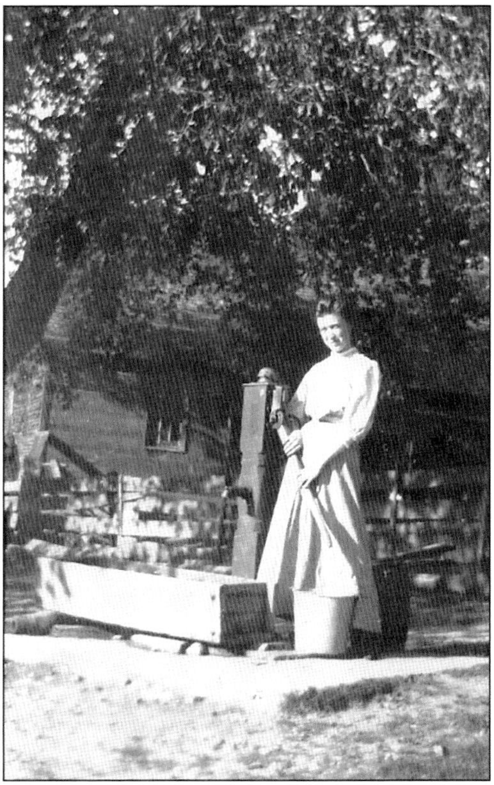

Before the days of running water in the home, a hand pump in the dooryard was a necessity. Beulah Wyatt is shown drawing water on the Demeritt farm from a well which is still operable today.

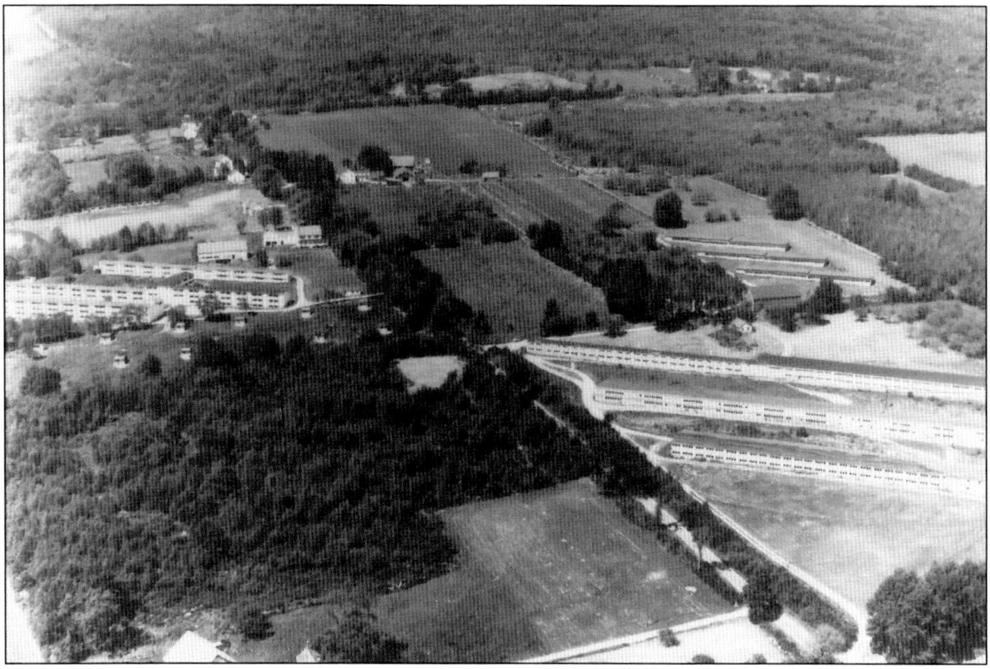

An aerial view of "The Hensnest" on Meaderboro Road. One of the largest privately owned poultry farms east of the Mississippi River, it was operated by Ralph W. Canney from 1926 to 1963. Although enduring fires both in the 1950s and 1960s, some of these buildings remain and are used today.

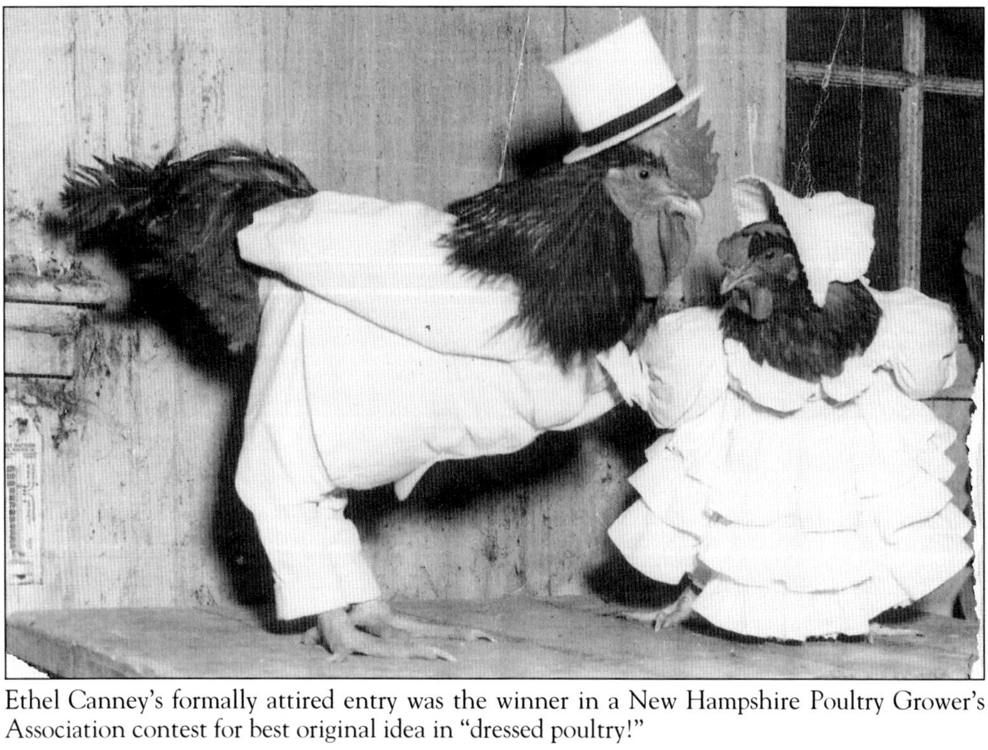

Ethel Canney's formally attired entry was the winner in a New Hampshire Poultry Grower's Association contest for best original idea in "dressed poultry!"

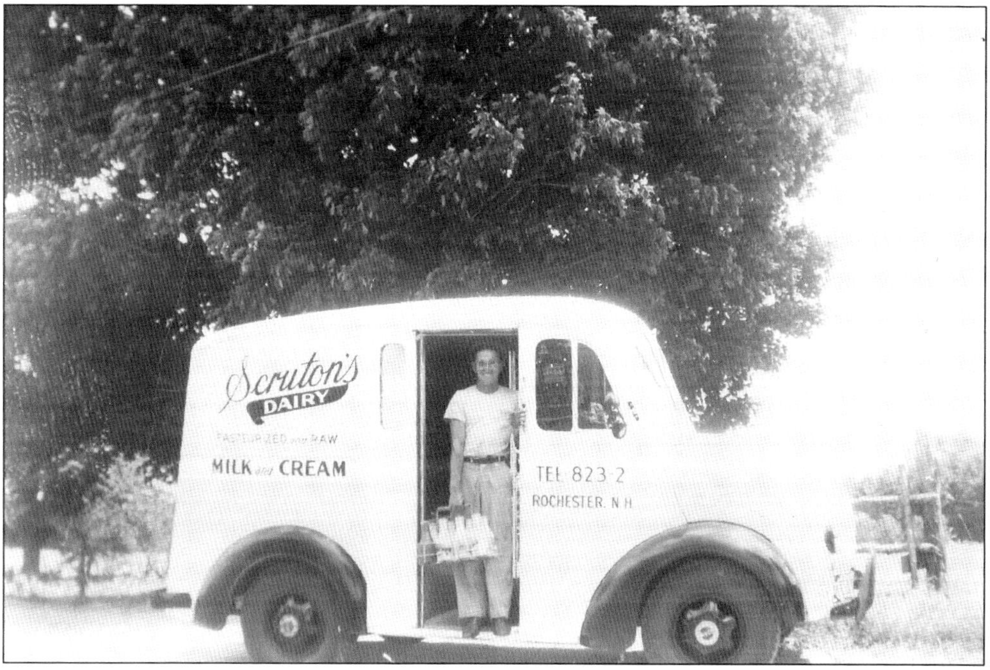

With a herd of over two hundred Holsteins, the Scruton Dairy on Meaderboro Road was the largest and last producer-handler of milk in the state. Established in 1942 by Arthur Scruton and his son Frank (the milkman in the 1948 picture above), the farm still raises and milks prize-winning cows but no longer processes and delivers.

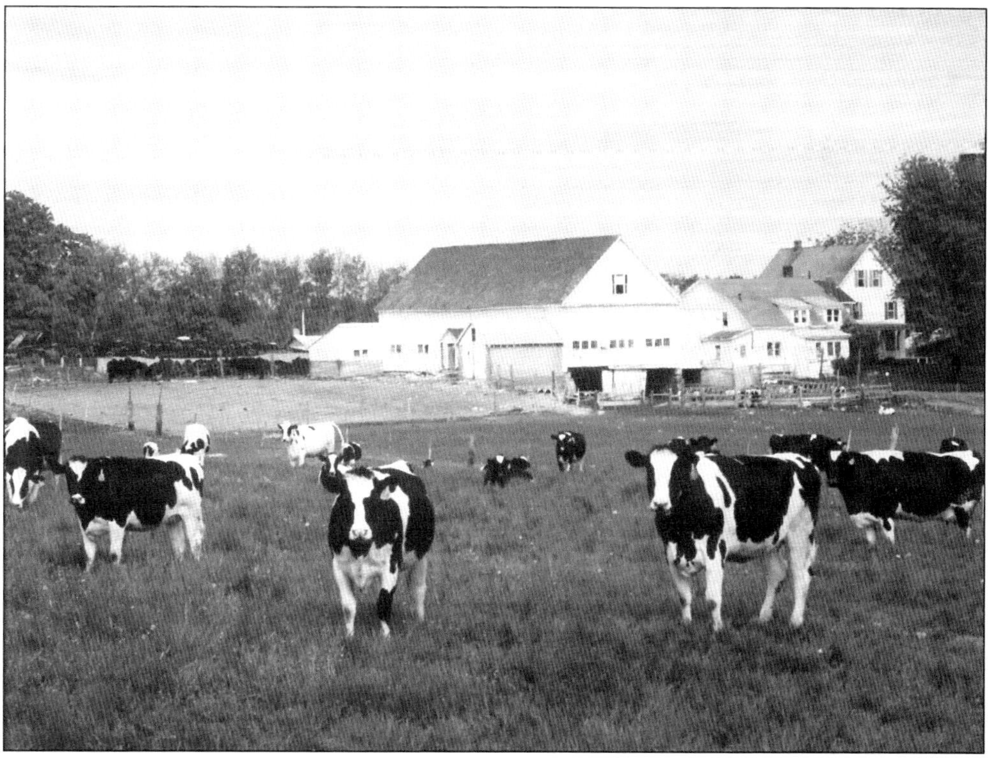

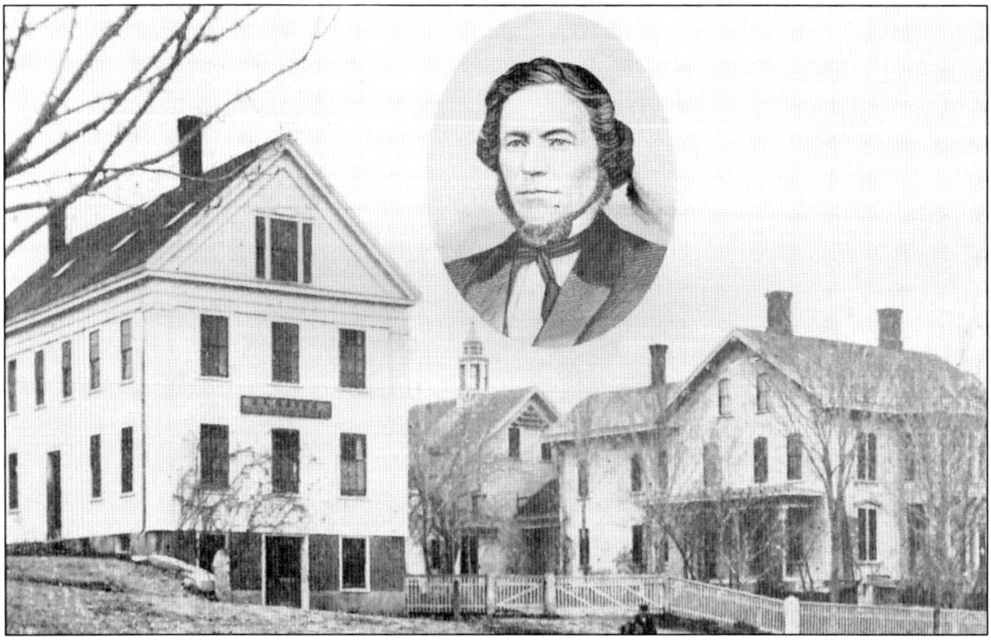

Farmington began its long legacy as a shoe manufacturing center in 1836 when E.H. Badger opened a shoe shop on Spring Street. Martin Luther Hayes soon took over the business and prospered. He is shown here with his enlarged factory and home, both of which still exist, the latter currently the residence of Dr. and Mrs. Quinn.

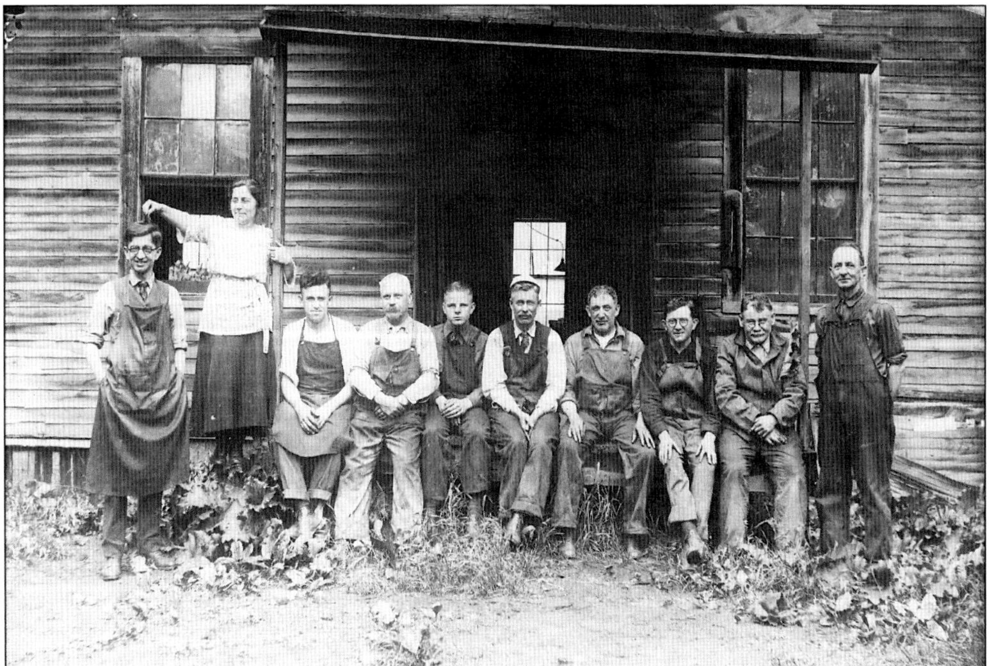

In 1905 the M.L. Hayes factory became the Fred Browne Wire Brush Company, manufacturing twenty-nine types of brushes. Fred Browne stands on the left with his workers. The business remained in the family until 1964; today the building houses an antique shop.

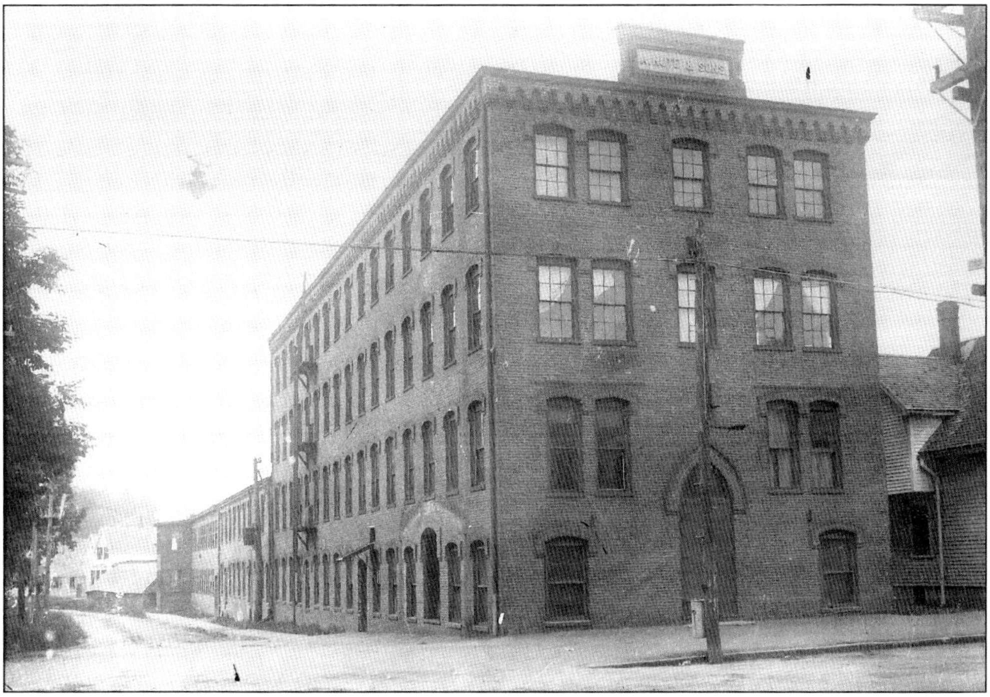

Another pioneer in the shoe business was Alonzo Nute of Milton, who in 1849 located a wooden factory at the corner of Grove and North Main Streets. After a disastrous fire in 1874, the brick building shown here was erected, and it has lasted through the years.

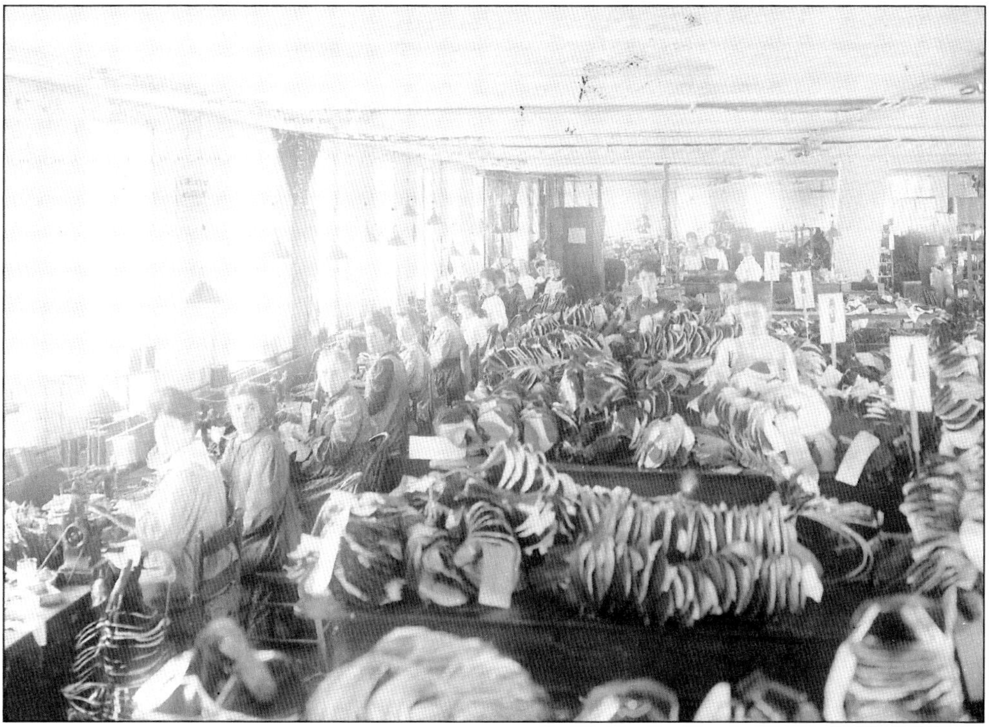

The stitching room of the Nute factory.

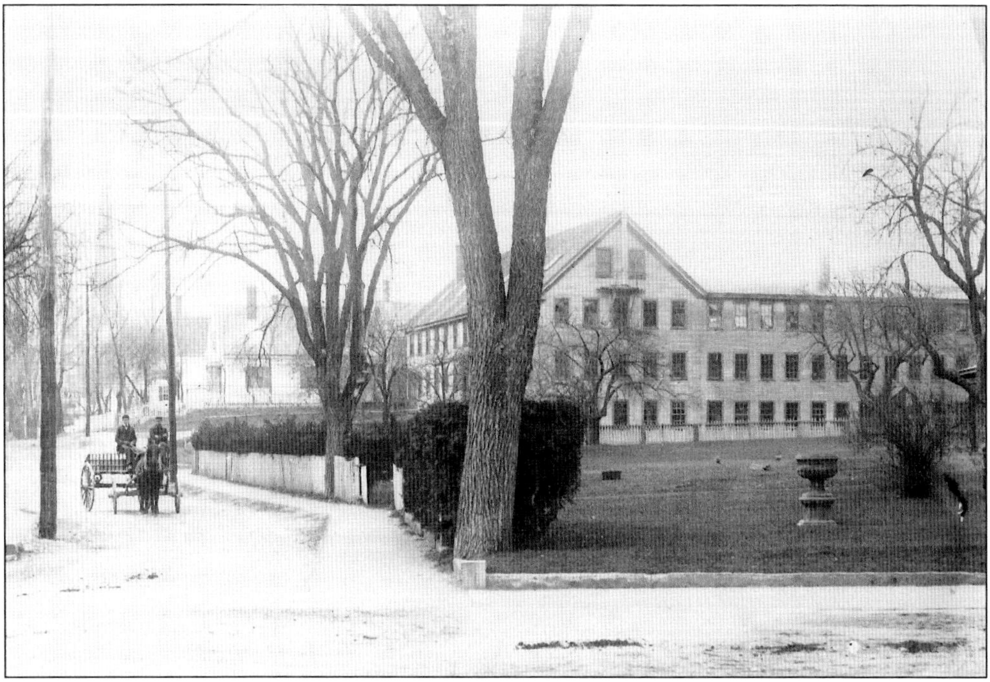

On the corner of Grove and Orange Streets Israel Hayes and sons manufactured shoes in this large factory employing over two hundred people. After the destruction of its rear ell, the building was turned on its foundation and today houses apartments.

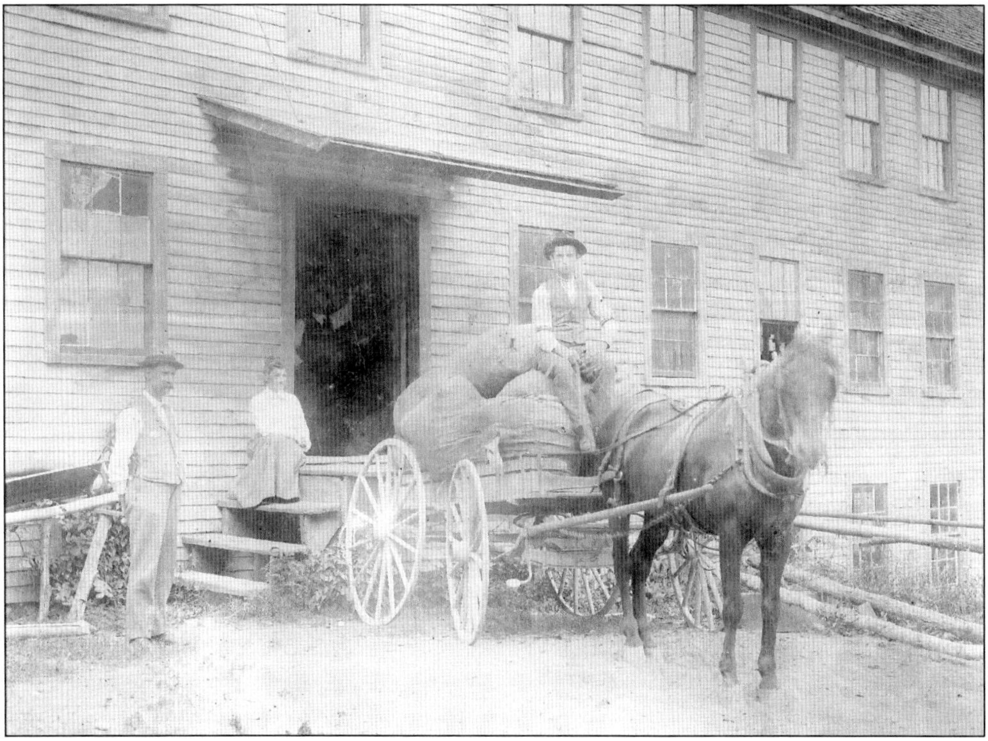

A delivery cart leaving the Hayes factory.

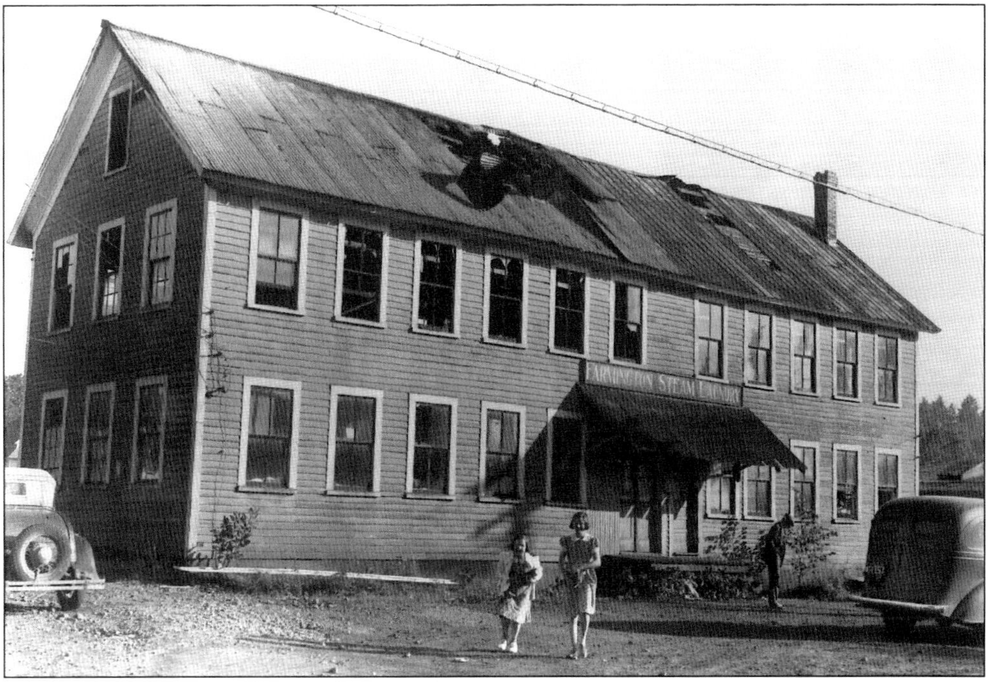

After the shoe last and sole pattern company operated by L.S. Flanders went out of business, its building on East Grove Street became a steam laundry. It is shown here after fire destroyed the interior.

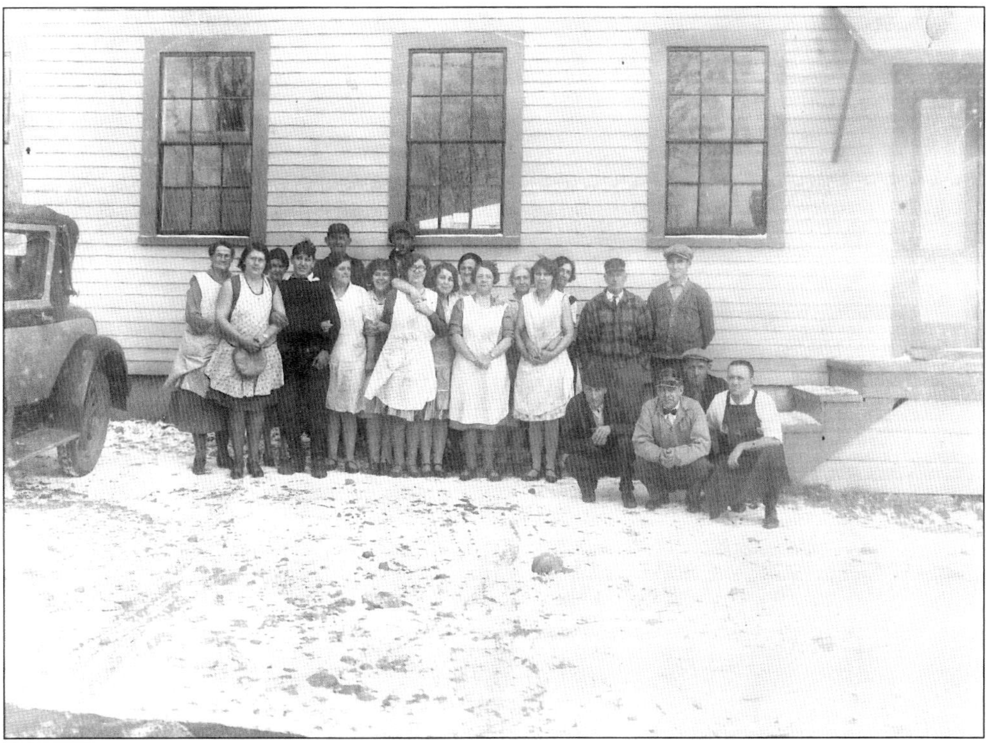

Employees of the steam laundry pose for the photographer on a winter day.

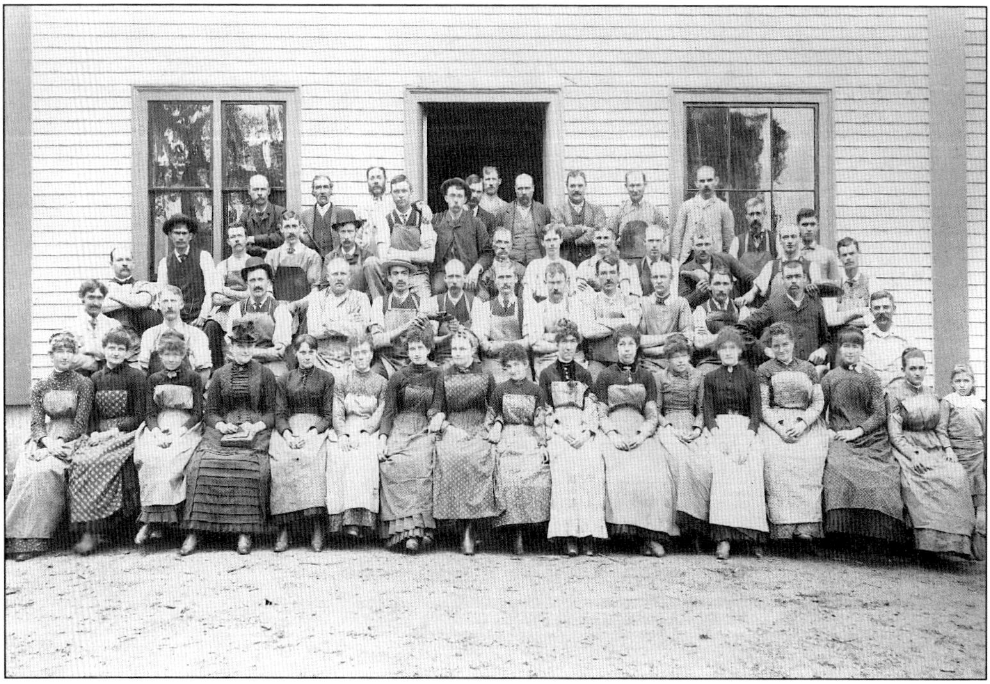

Personnel of the Edgerly Shoe Company in front of the South Main Street factory in 1887.

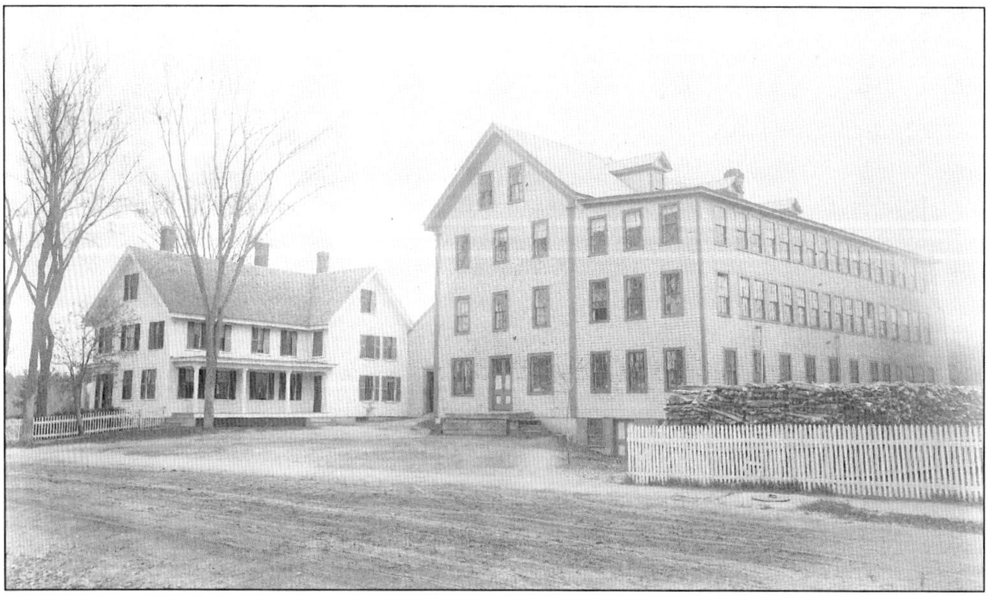

Built in 1880 for the shoe company founded by Hosea B. Edgerly and continued by his son Frank, this building has held many businesses. The adjoining home was later occupied by Frank's daughter, Beatrice E. Ellison, who gave to the town the Summer Street playground.

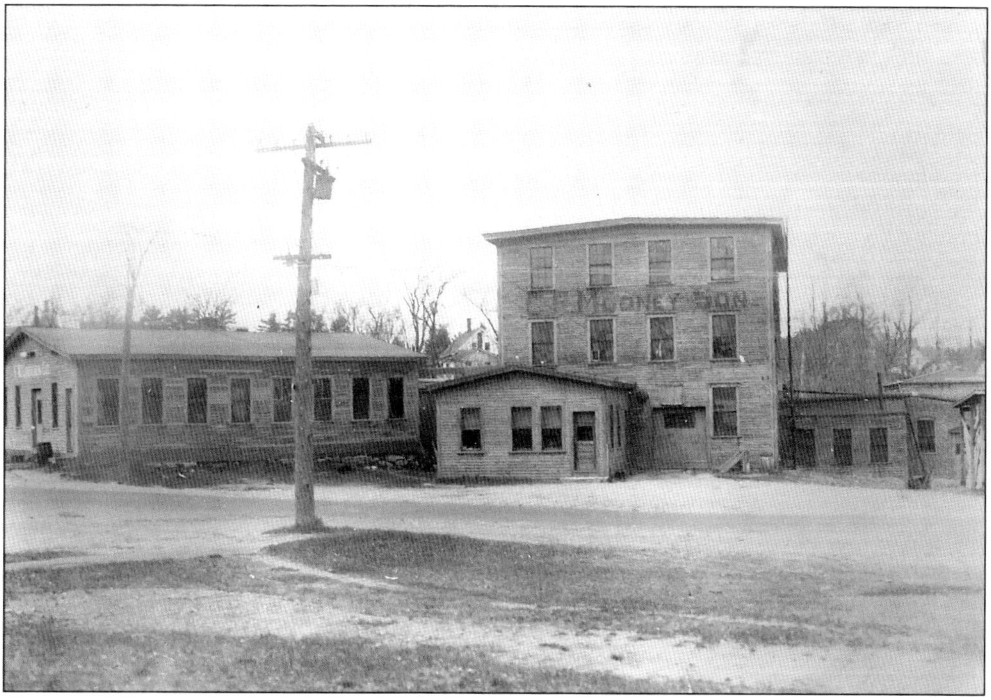

What was originally the William Hayes sawmill became Mooney's Mill, a wood-turning plant, in 1916. Locally it was referred to as the "handle factory," for it produced all sizes and shapes of wooden handles for tools.

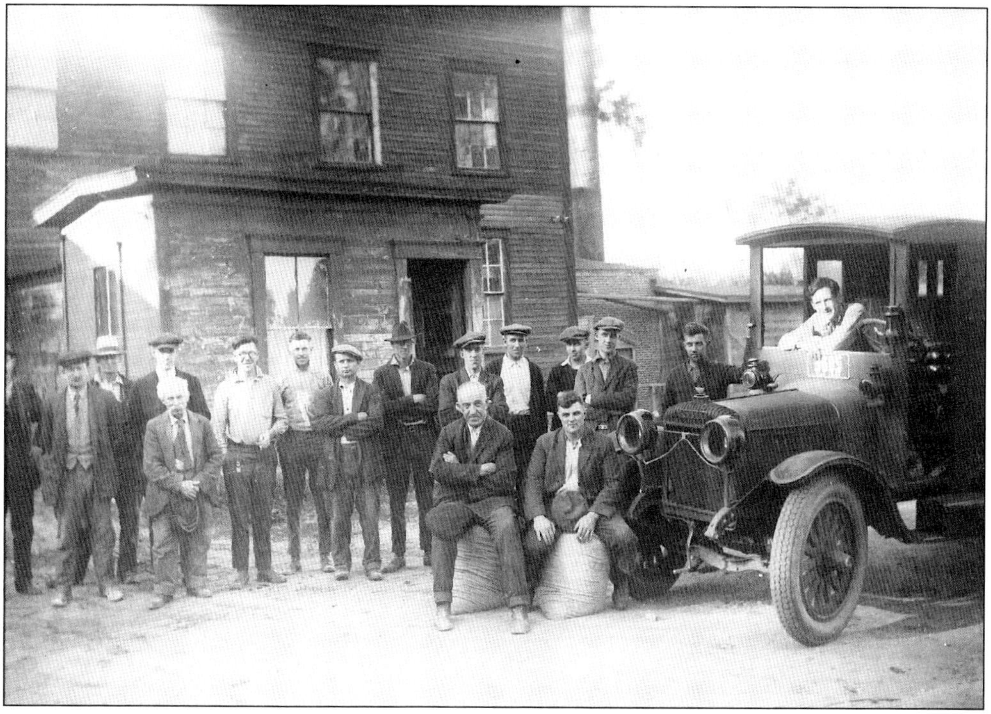

Many a Farmington man was employed by Mooney's Mill during its fifty years of operation.

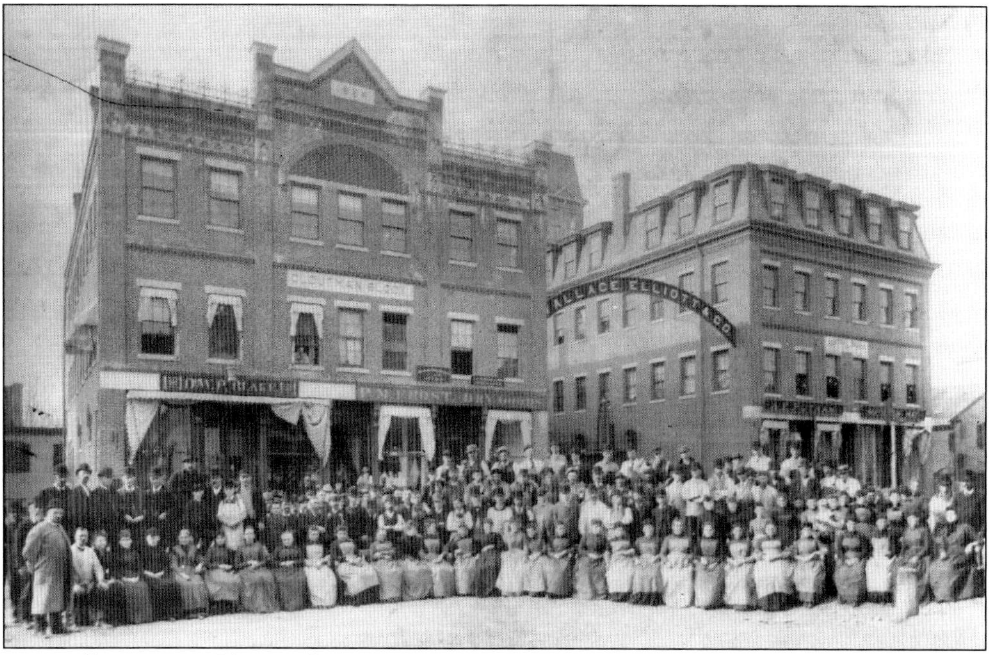

Originally connected by a walkway and always referred to as "The Twin Factories," the Central Block was built in 1877 and the Cloutman in 1884. Wallace, Elliott & Co., manufacturers of fine boots, was an early occupant. Extensively damaged by fire in 1971, one block is now apartments and the other houses the Union Telephone Co.

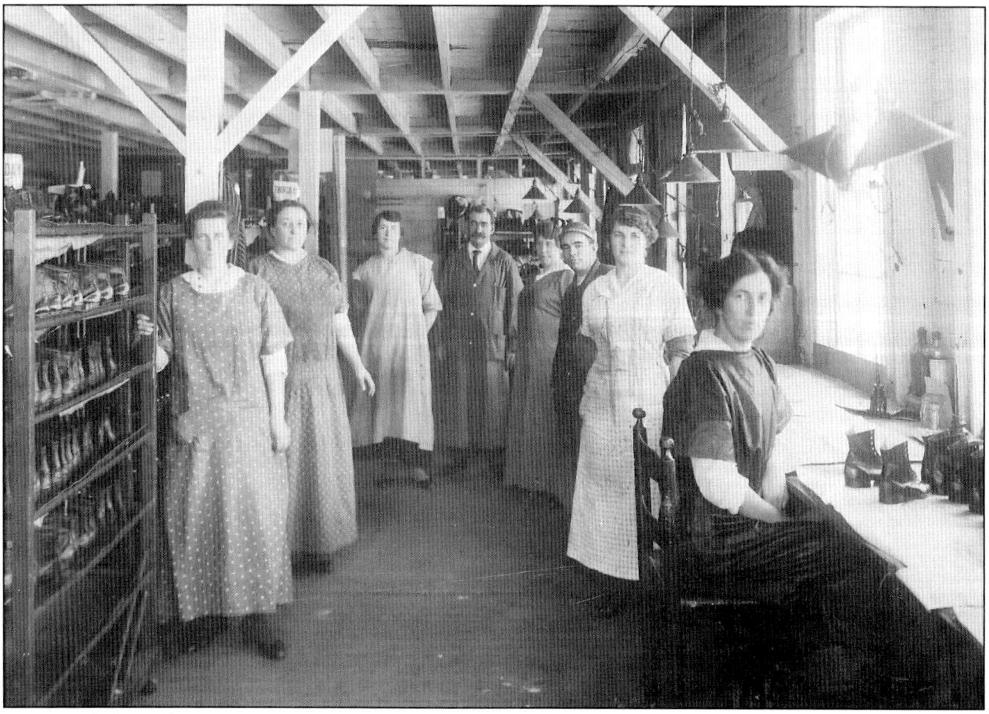

A typical shoe shop interior. Hattie White (on the far right) donated a large collection of town photographs to the library.

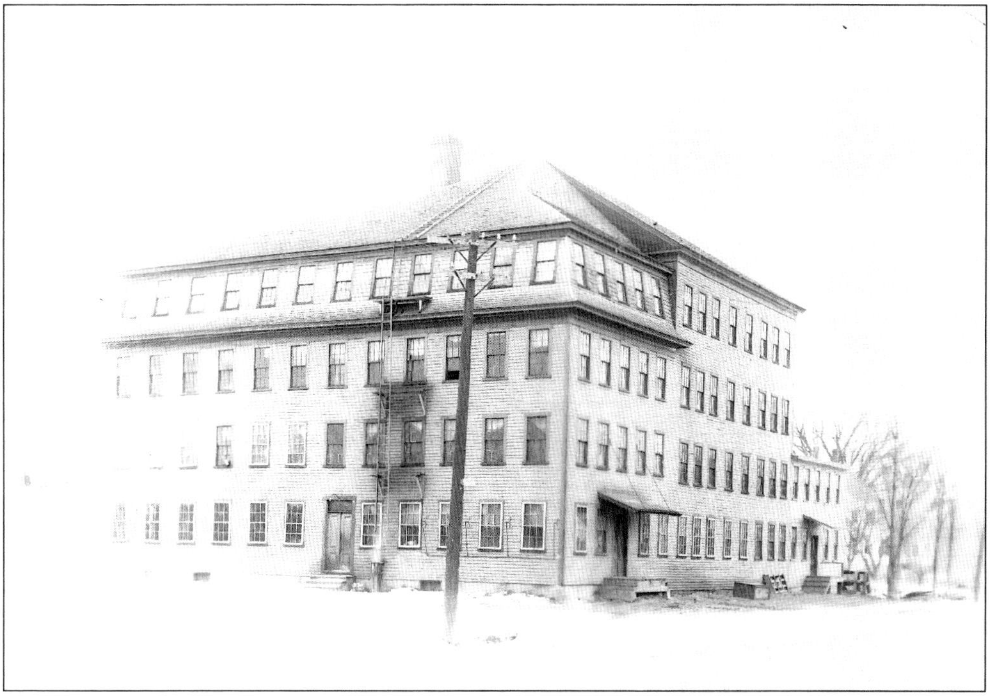

Located opposite the site of Main Street School, this impressive four-story factory for the production of mens and boys shoes was erected in 1873 by Arthur Berry. Purchased by John Cloutman in 1896, it burned to the ground in 1918.

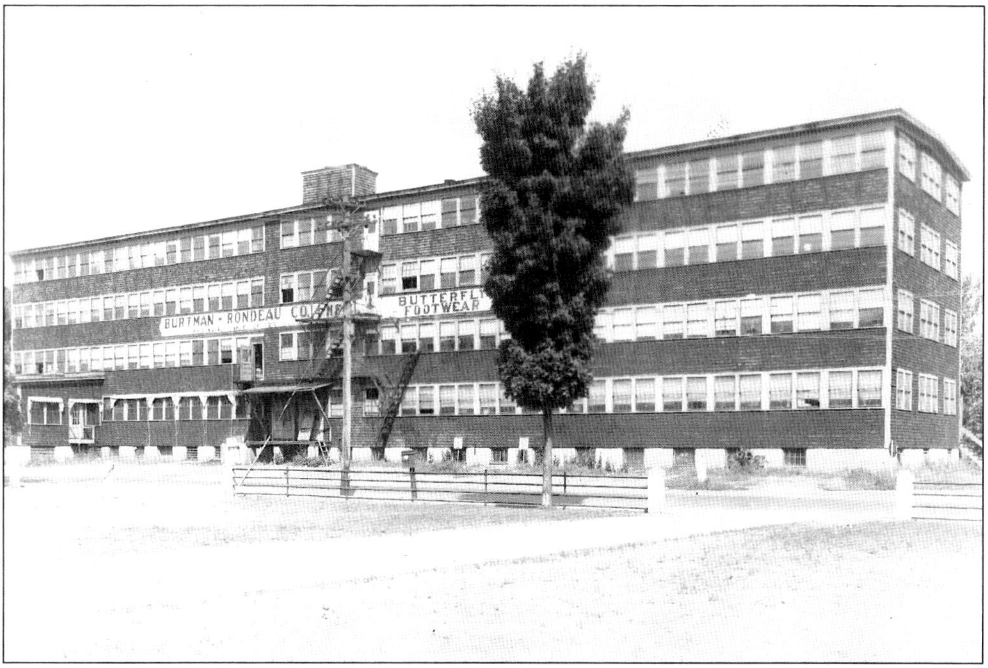

A new Cloutman Factory rose from the ashes of the old and was back in production that same year. Eventually this building became the property of Abe Burtman and Omer Rondeau, philanthropic businessmen who provided funds for the former high school's gymnasium.

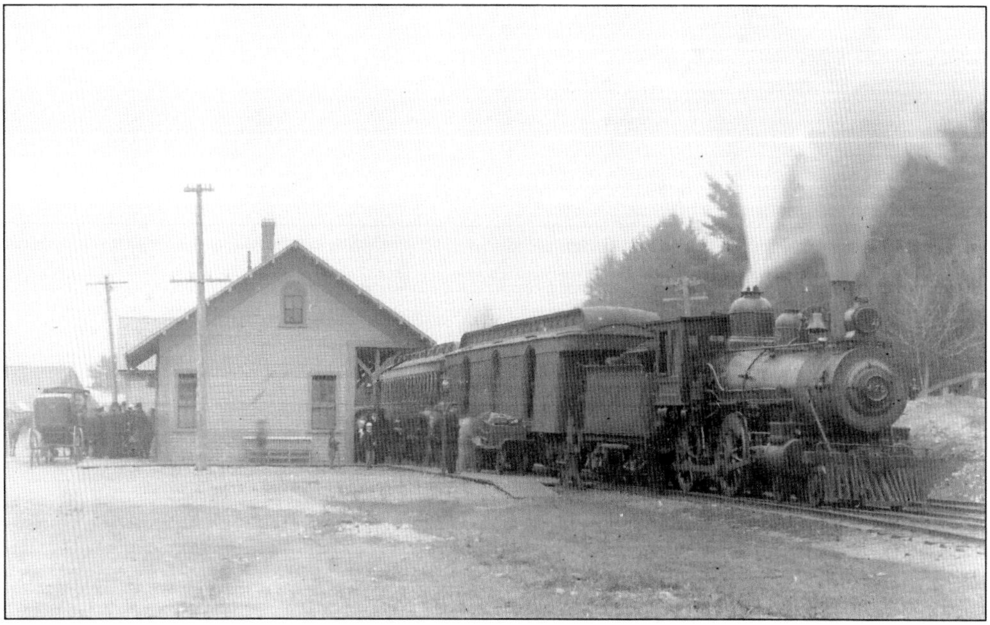

The extension of the railroad from Dover to Farmington in 1849 brought both passenger and freight service. The Boston and Maine Railroad purchased the line in 1892, operating this station until 1953.

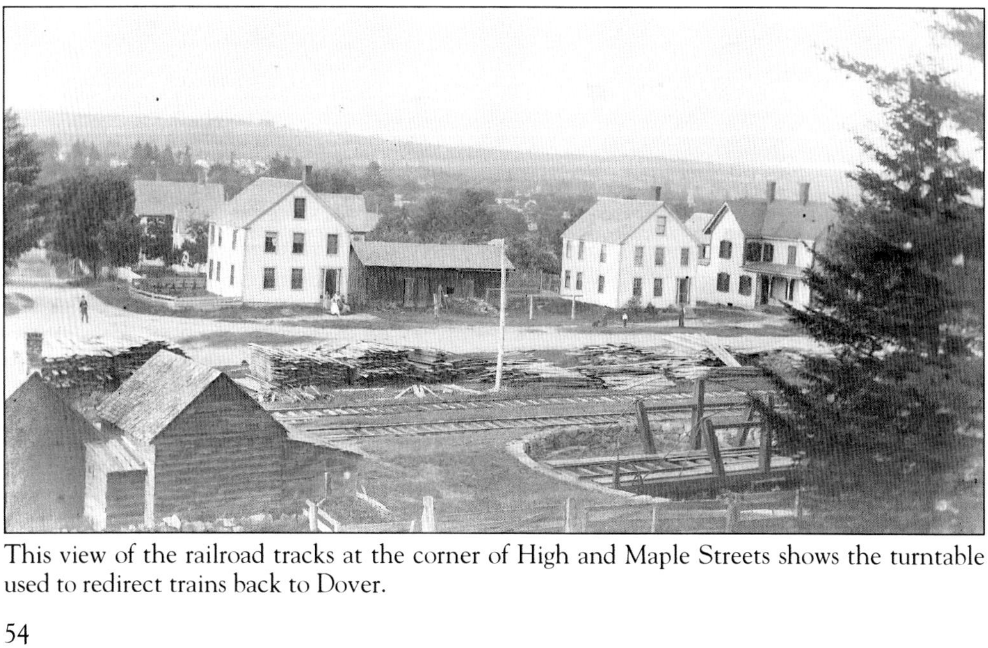

This view of the railroad tracks at the corner of High and Maple Streets shows the turntable used to redirect trains back to Dover.

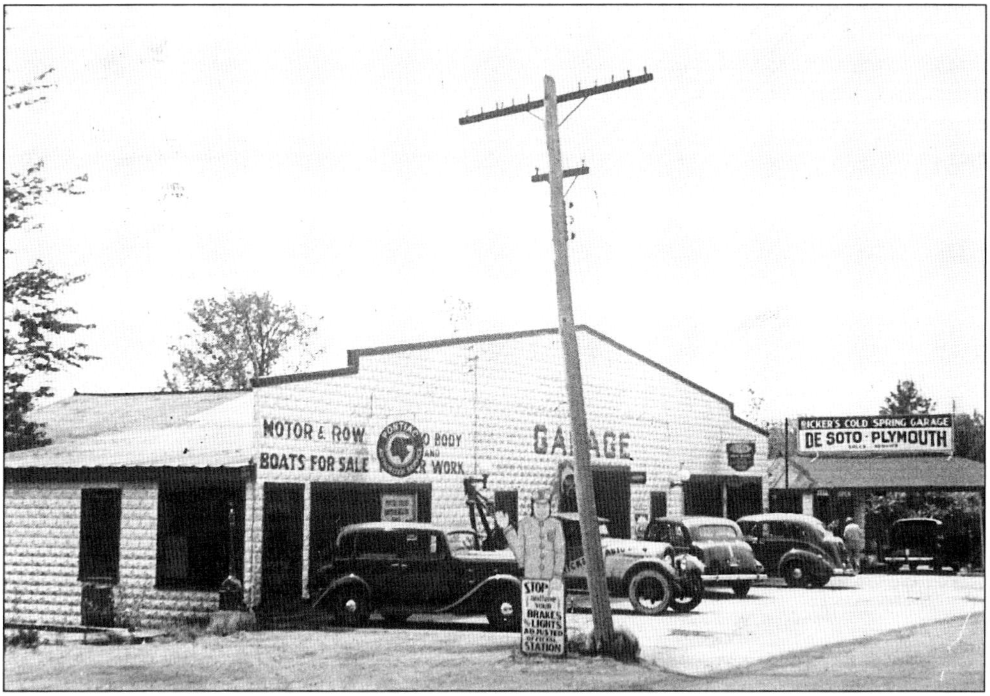

Prosperity arrived with the establishment of an auto dealership operated by John Ricker on Spring Street.

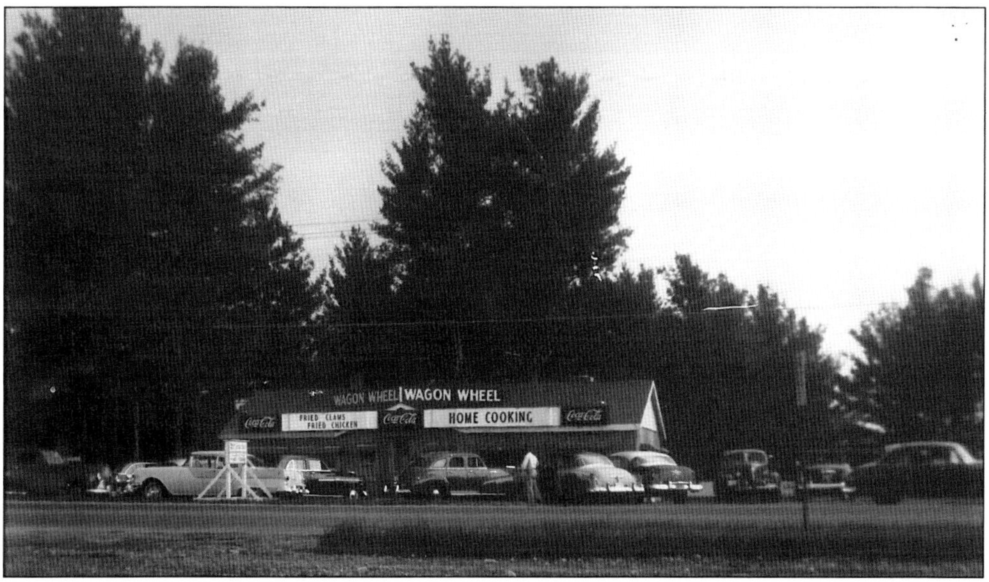

With a "car in every garage," dining out became a common occurrence. A popular place was the Wagon Wheel Restaurant on the Farmington Road. Started in 1930 by Jack and Helen Cardinal, its home cooking was famous for thirty years.

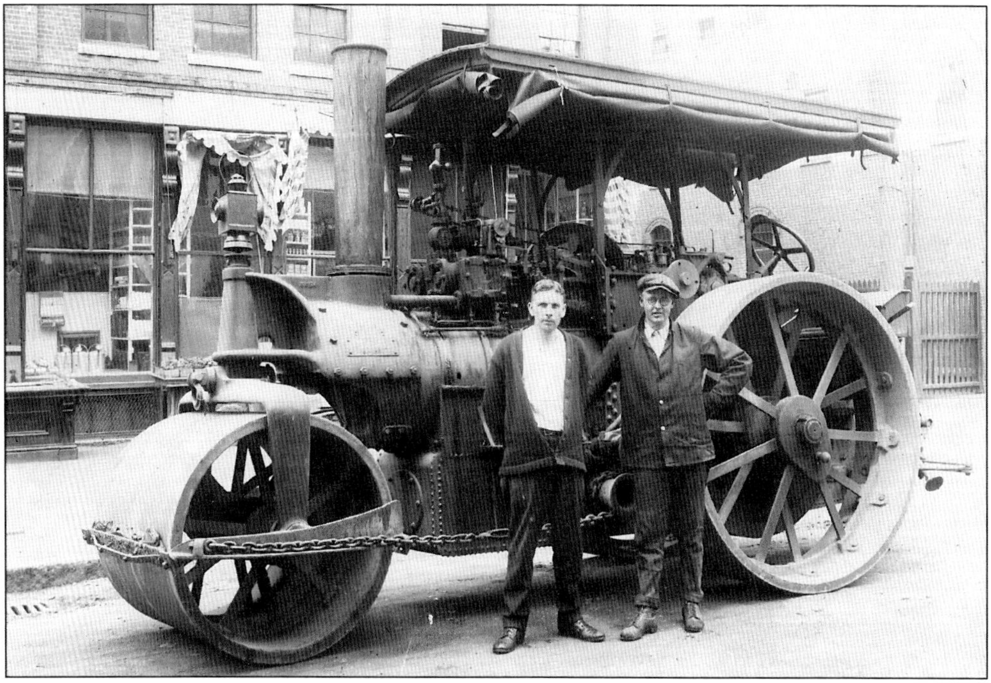

This noisy and cumbersome steam roller used for road maintenance was operated by Harry Knox (in hat).

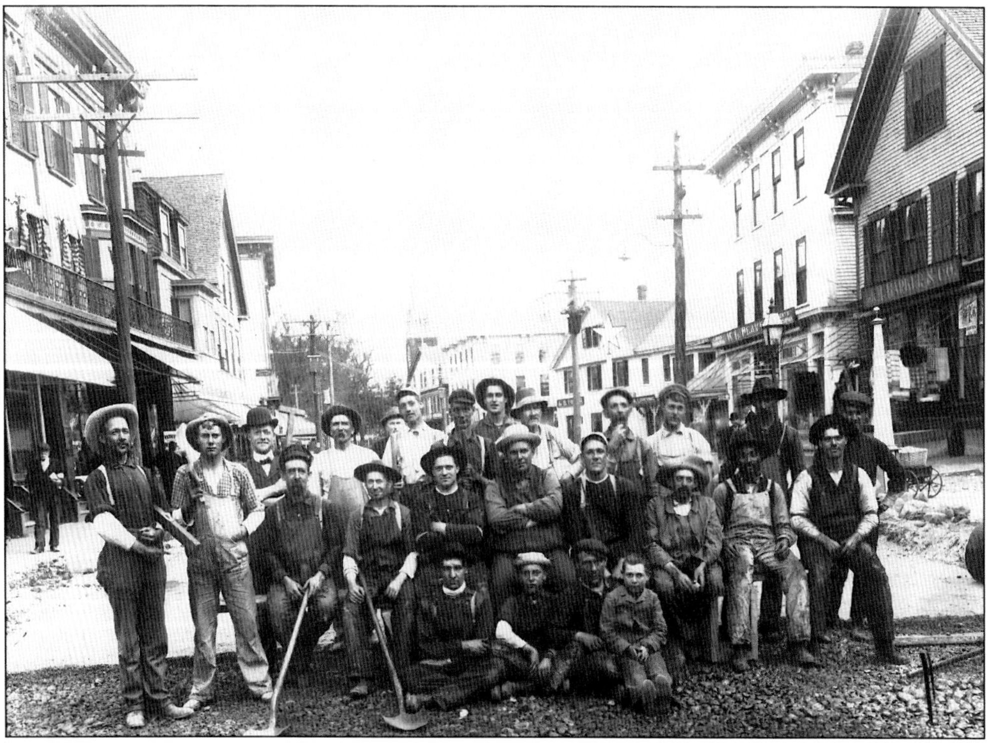

Progress comes to town! Main Street is paved at last by Harry Howard of Rochester and his road crew.

Three

Homes

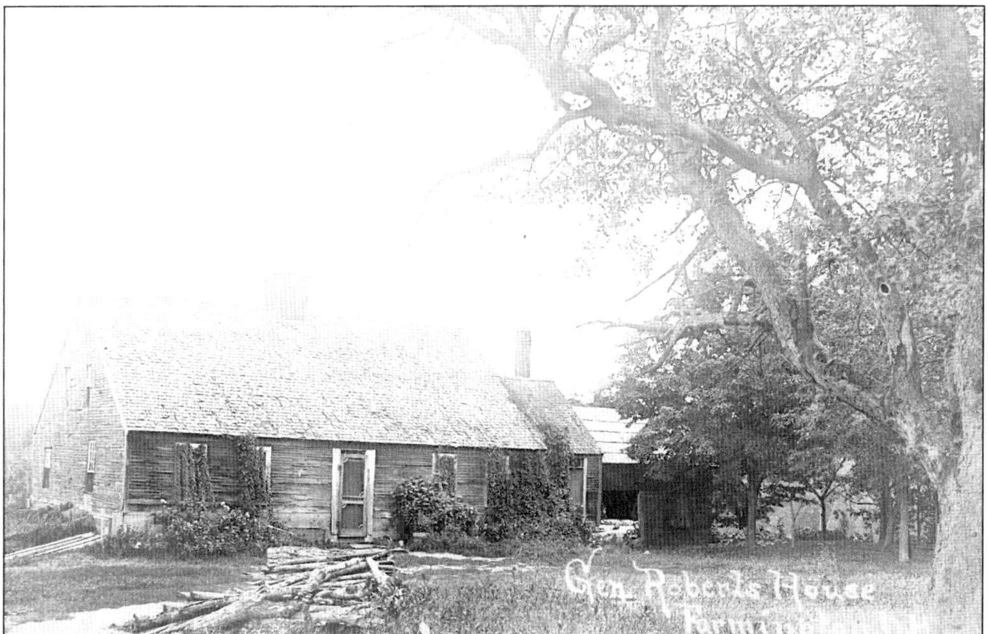

One of the earlier homes, the Roberts House, was located on the Farmington Road near the Rochester line. General Jeremiah Roberts' sawmill on Rattlesnake Brook provided lumber for the construction of many nearby houses.

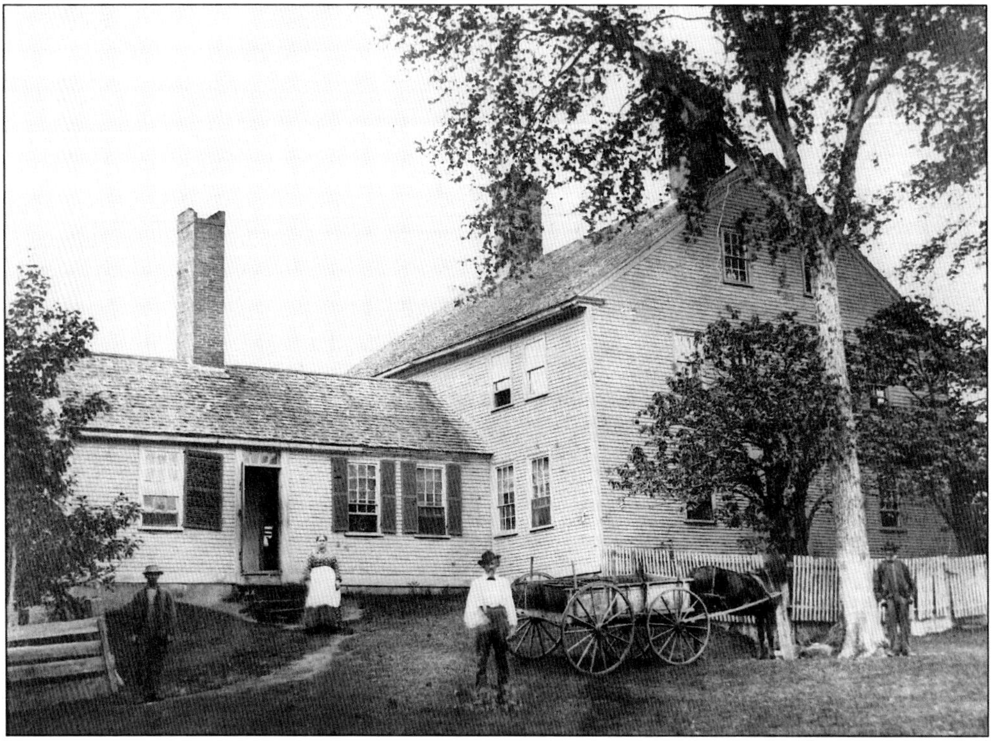

The Demeritt home on Meeting House Hill Road was built in 1818, the third dwelling on this property. The land was settled in 1775 by Paul Demeritt of Madbury, whose grandson Joseph is shown here. Upon Joseph's death in 1915, ownership passed to Ivory U. Bean.

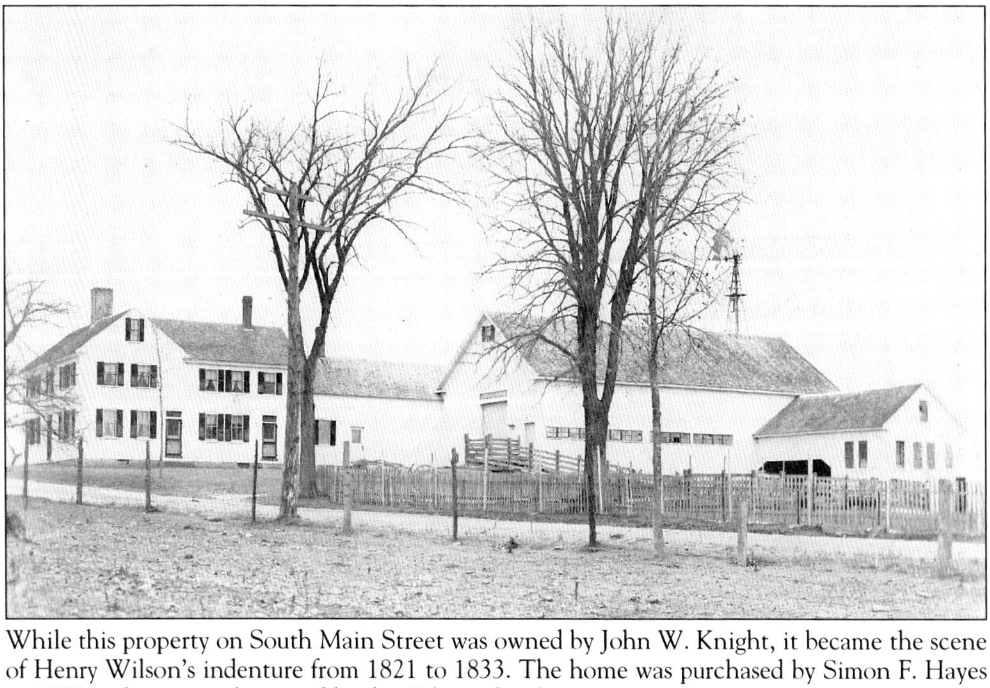

While this property on South Main Street was owned by John W. Knight, it became the scene of Henry Wilson's indenture from 1821 to 1833. The home was purchased by Simon F. Hayes in 1850 and is currently owned by the Gilman family.

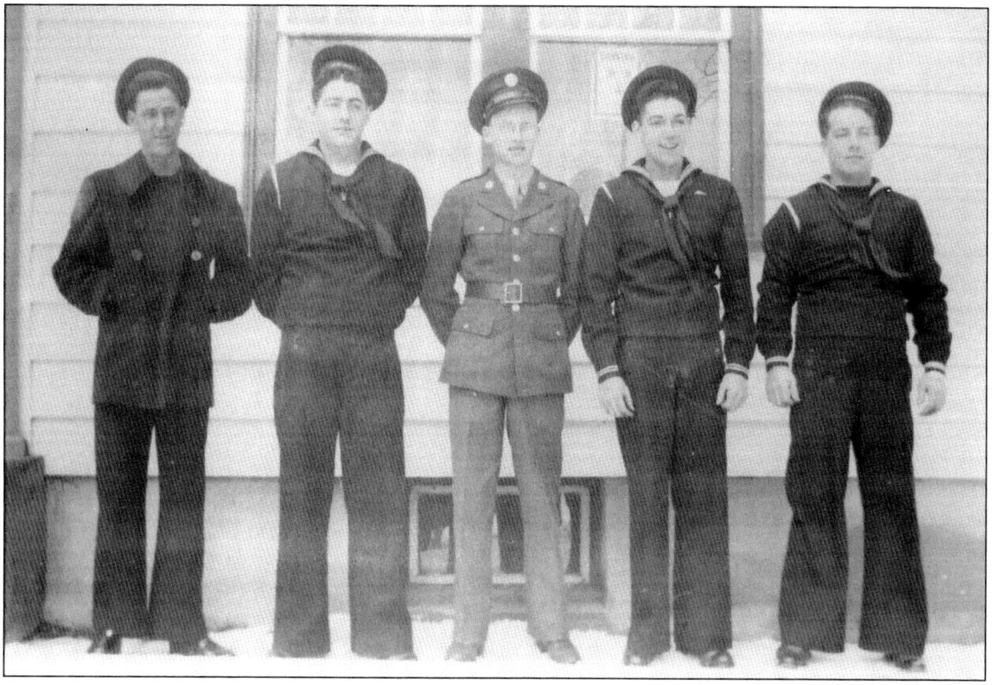

Many families in town sent men to battle during World War II. Shown here are "Meat" Merrill, Carl Worster, Eddy Gray, and George and Bob Worster.

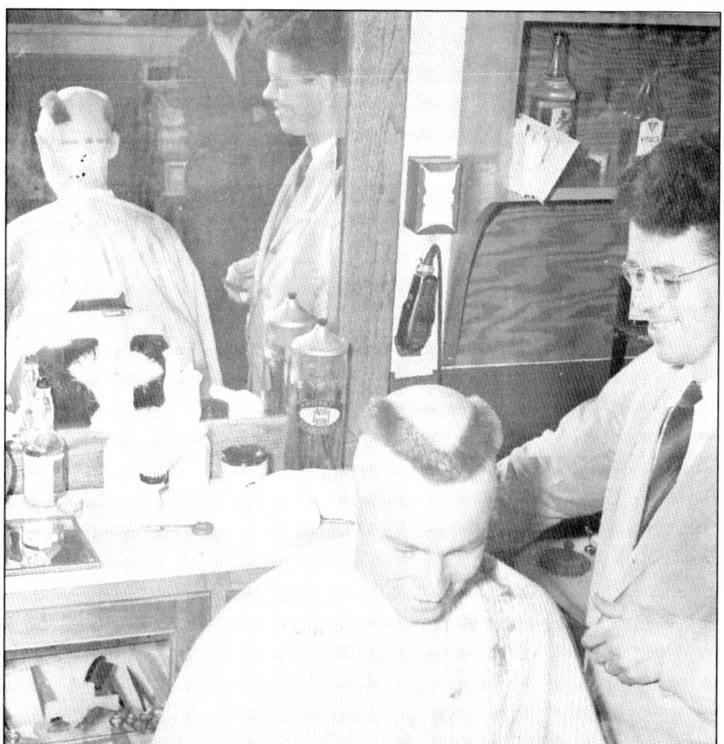

Lee Russell celebrated the end of World War II with a "V for Victory" haircut by barber Rufus Rundlett.

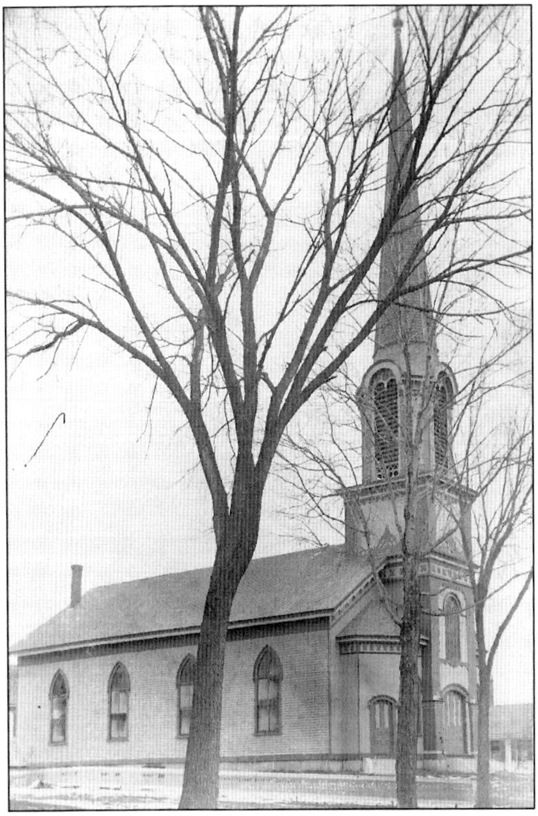

The oldest church building in town is the First Baptist, dedicated in 1857. This 1904 picture shows it with its original steeple, which was destroyed in 1920 and replaced with an octagonal dome.

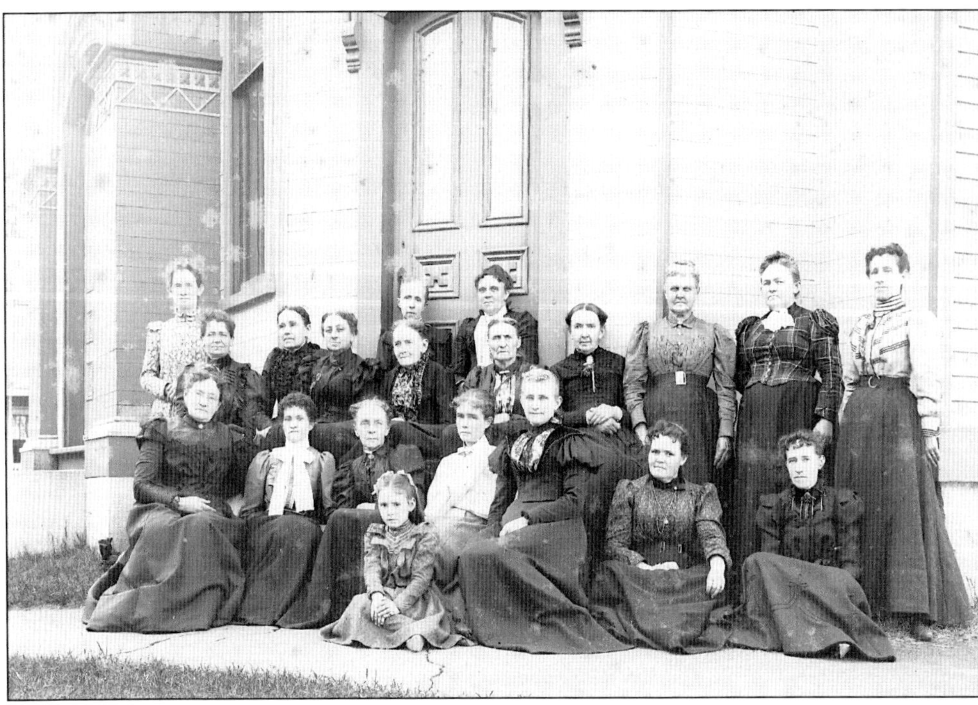

Ladies of the Baptist sewing circle pose on the church steps.

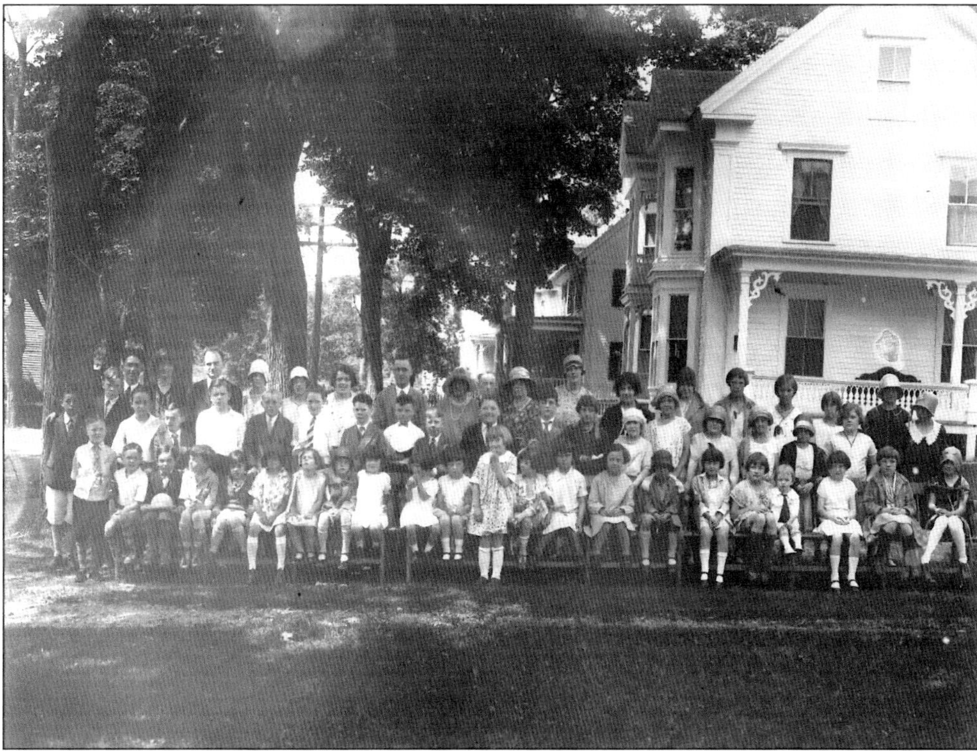

Baptist Bible School students in their Sunday best sit still for a portrait.

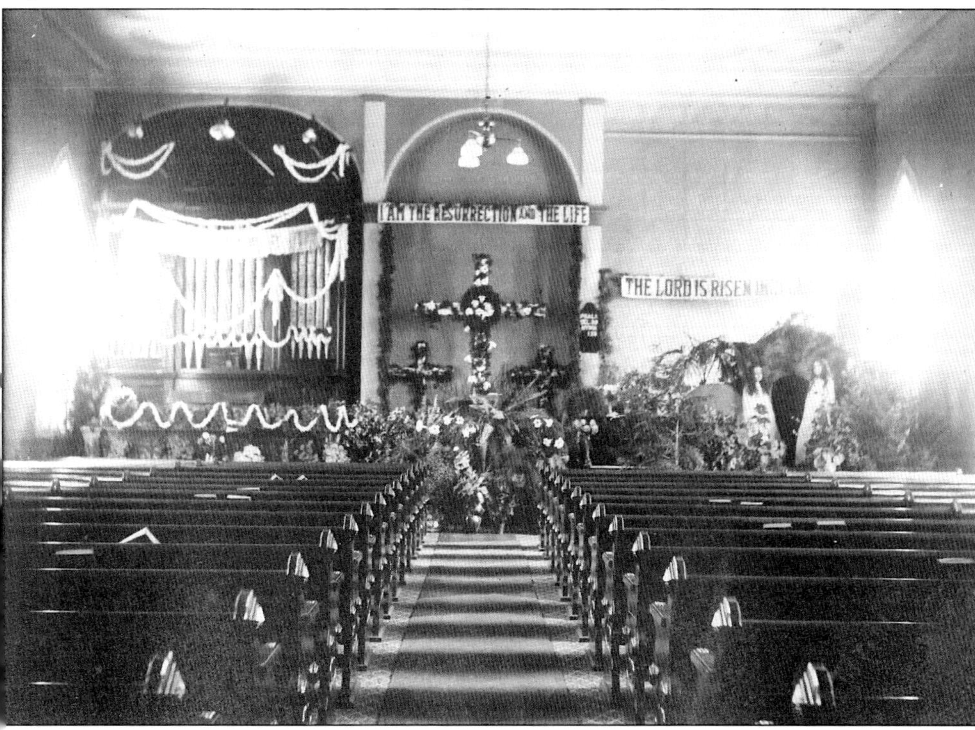

The interior of the Baptist church is shown at Easter time.

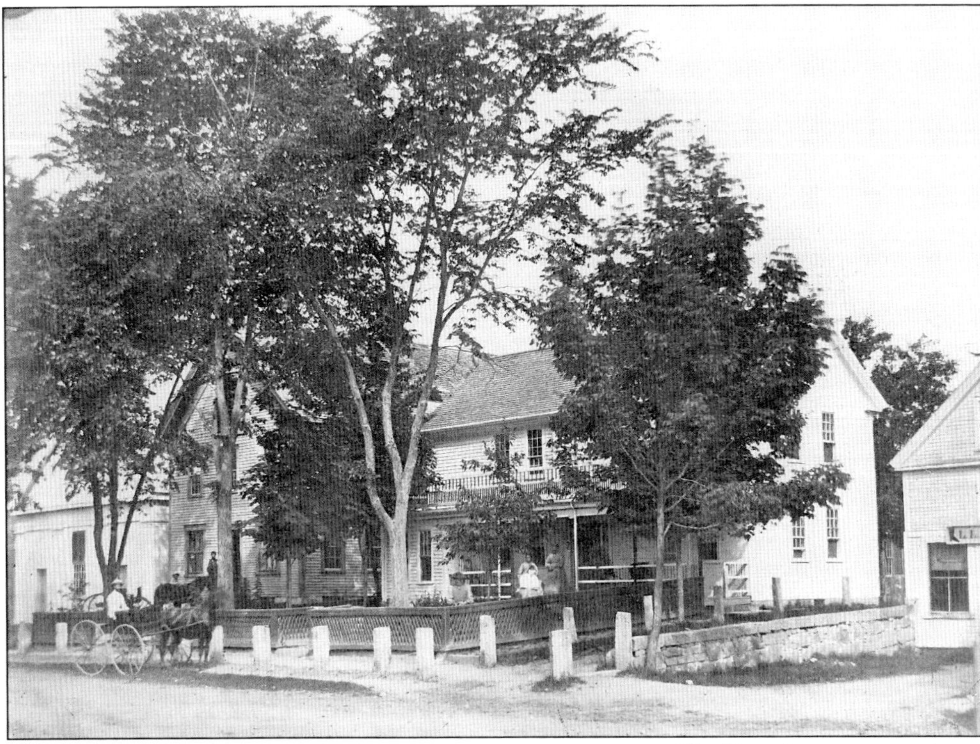

The First Congregational Church and parsonage occupied these buildings, constructed in 1844 on Central Street land donated by Judge George Whitehouse.

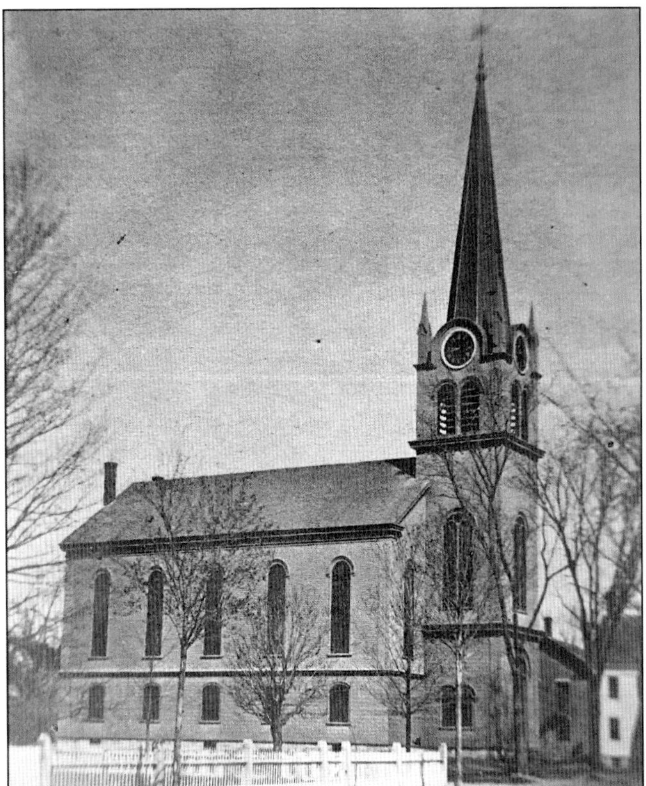

In 1870, this two-story wooden Congregational church was erected on Main Street. It was in use only five years before being reduced to ashes in the terrible fire of February 10, 1875.

One year later, in 1876, the brick church in use today was dedicated. Its steeple holds the Town Clock and a large bell engraved with the words, "Ring to the Memory of Henry Wilson, Farmington's Honored Son."

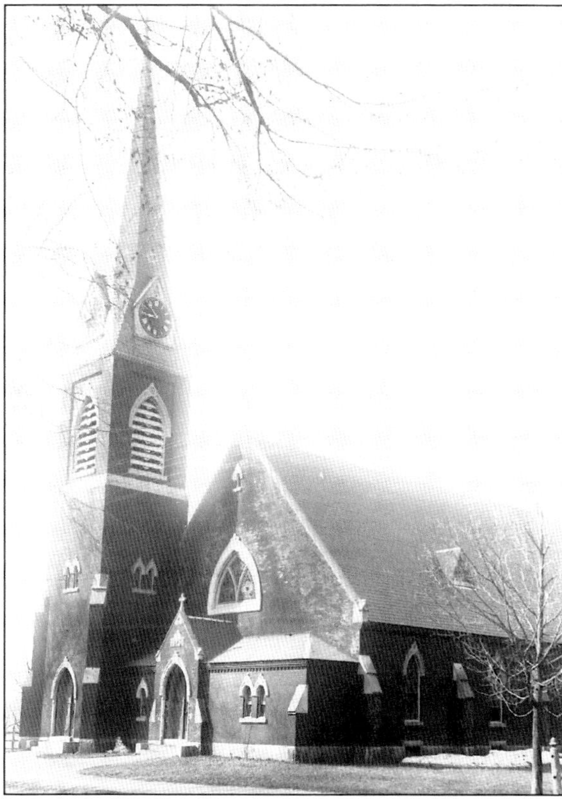

These beautiful chandeliers and massive organ pipes have been replaced since this picture was taken of the present Congregational church interior.

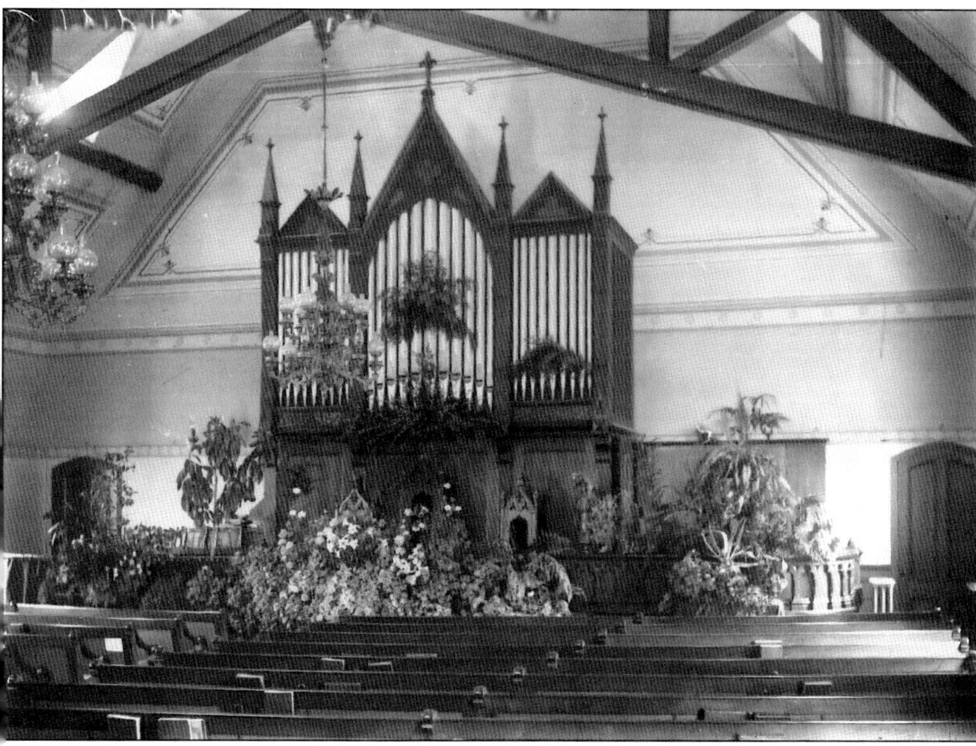

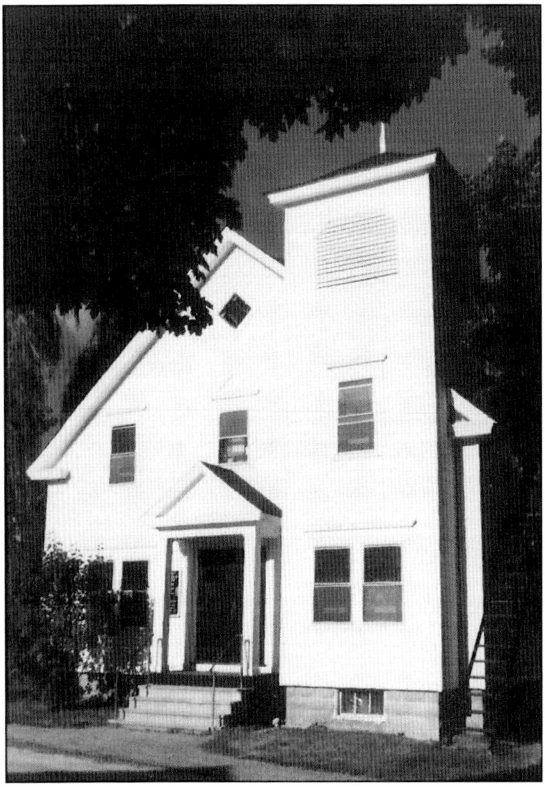

The Advent Christian Church on Orange Street had its beginnings in Farmington in 1869. Its parsonage and parish hall are located nearby.

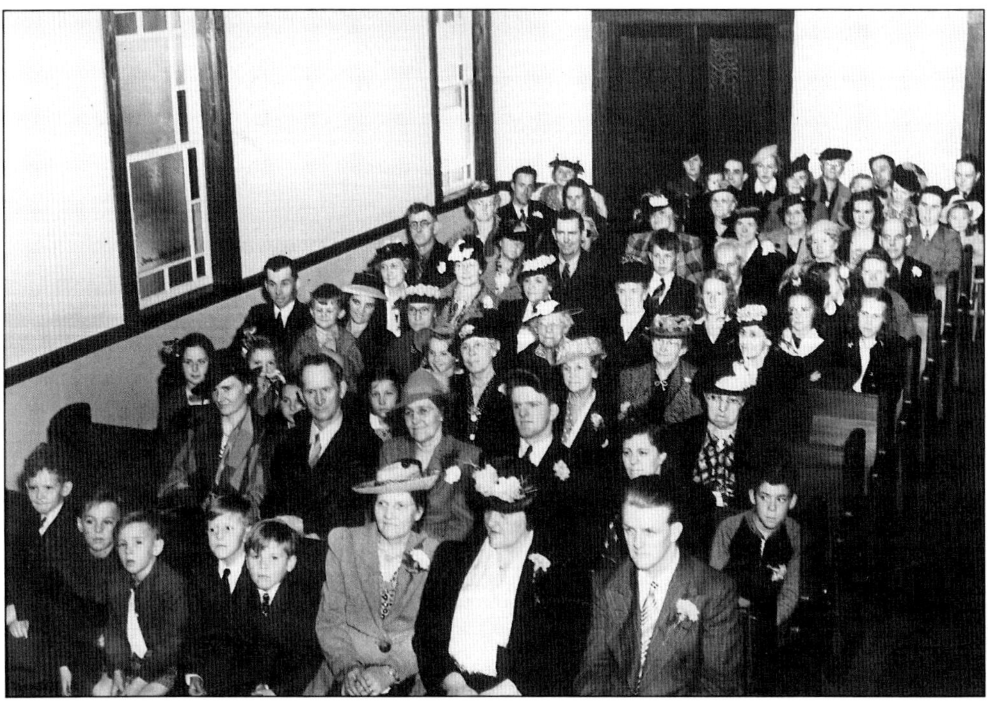

This 1941 photograph shows many families worshiping together during a Mother's Day service at the Advent Church.

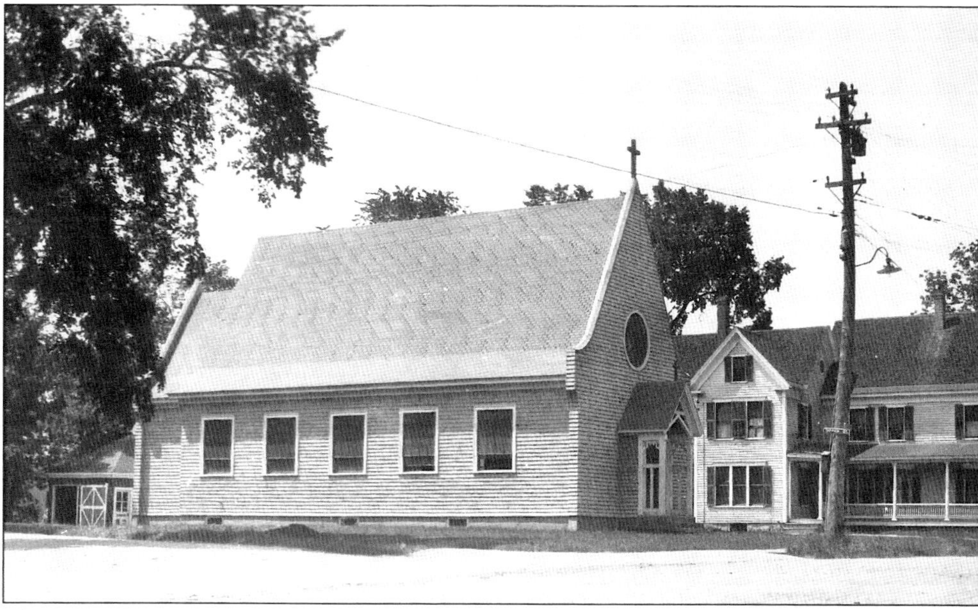

This original building of St. Peter's Catholic Church was erected in 1923 at the corner of Central and Tappan Streets. The expanding parish made necessary a larger building, which was constructed in 1955.

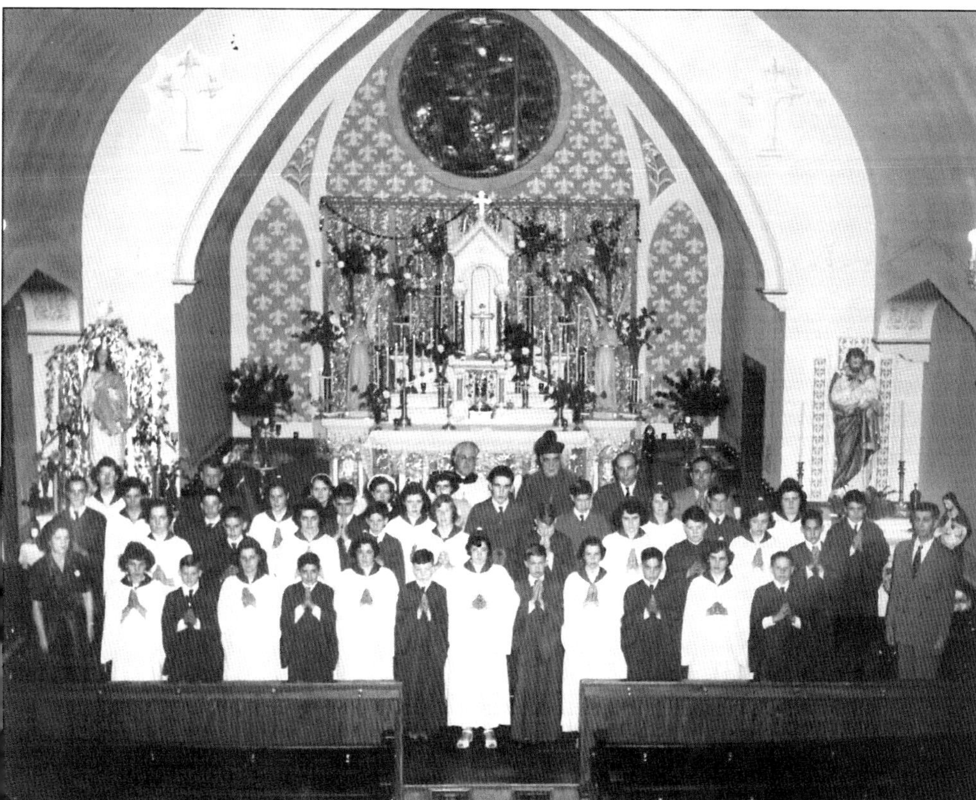

The 1953 Confirmation class of St. Peter's stands before the altar in the first church building.

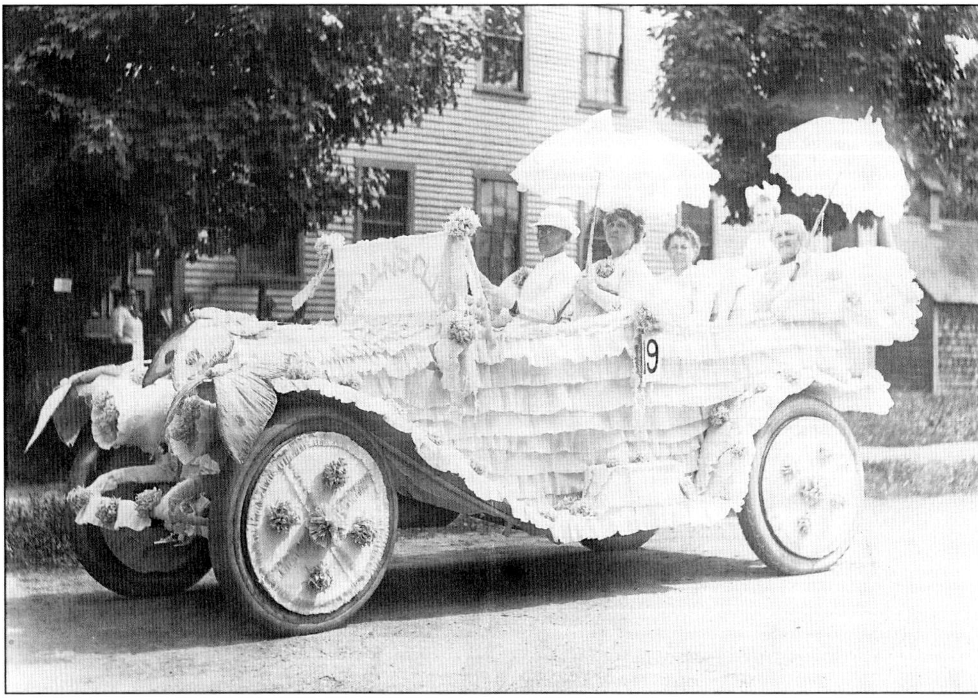

The Farmington Woman's Club was represented by this prize-winning float in the 1934 Old Home Day Parade.

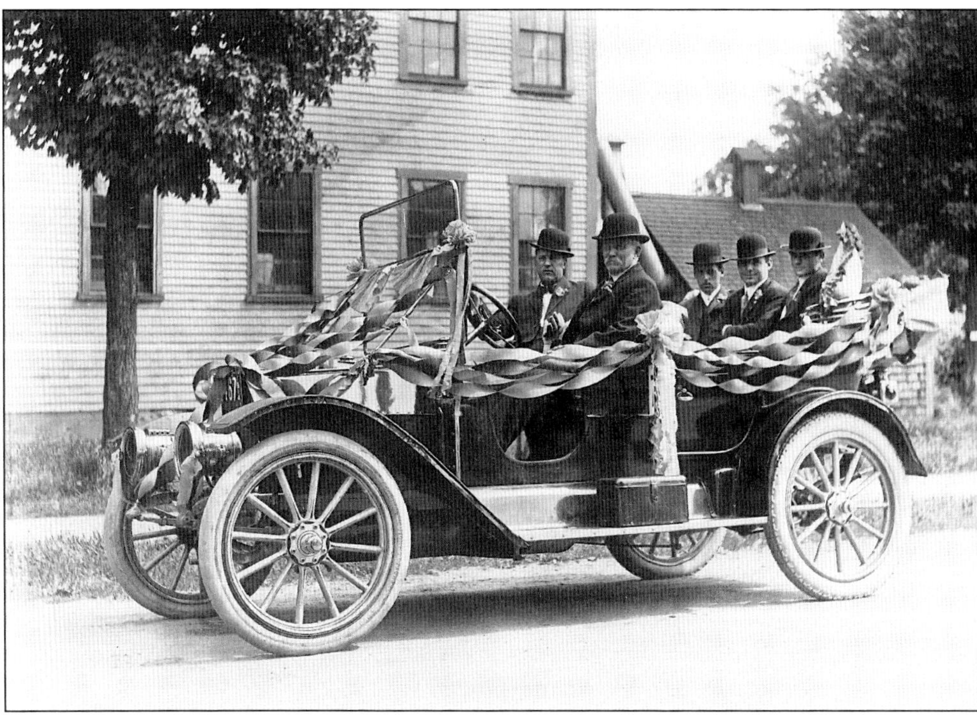

Five "dapper Dans" also participated in the parade. Old Home Week was established by gubernatorial proclamation in 1898 to encourage hometown reunions.

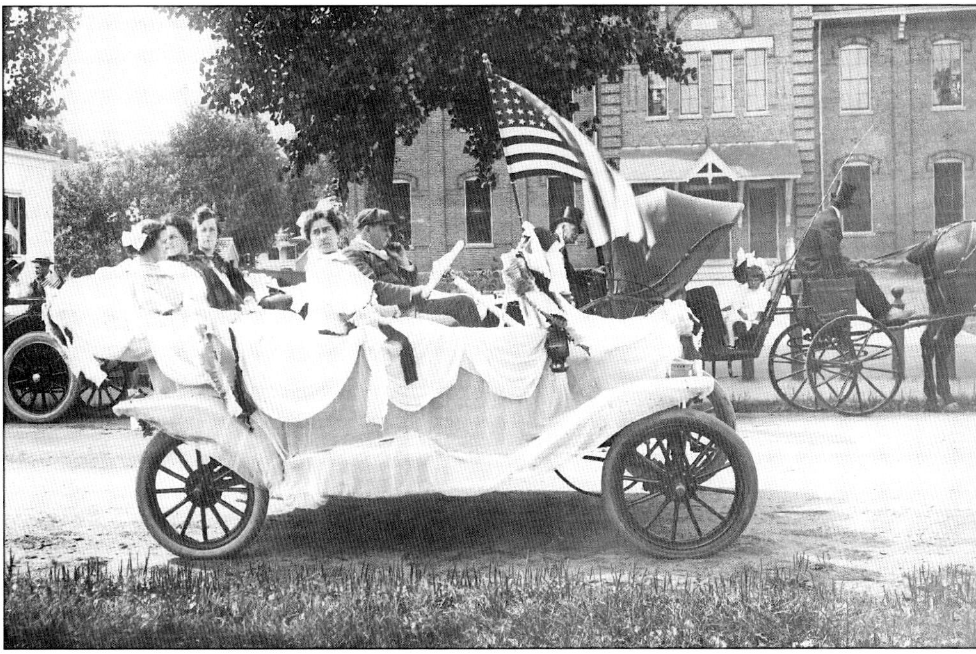

Will Nute drove members of the Pythian Sisterhood in this parade car. Mrs. Ella Chandler sits beside him.

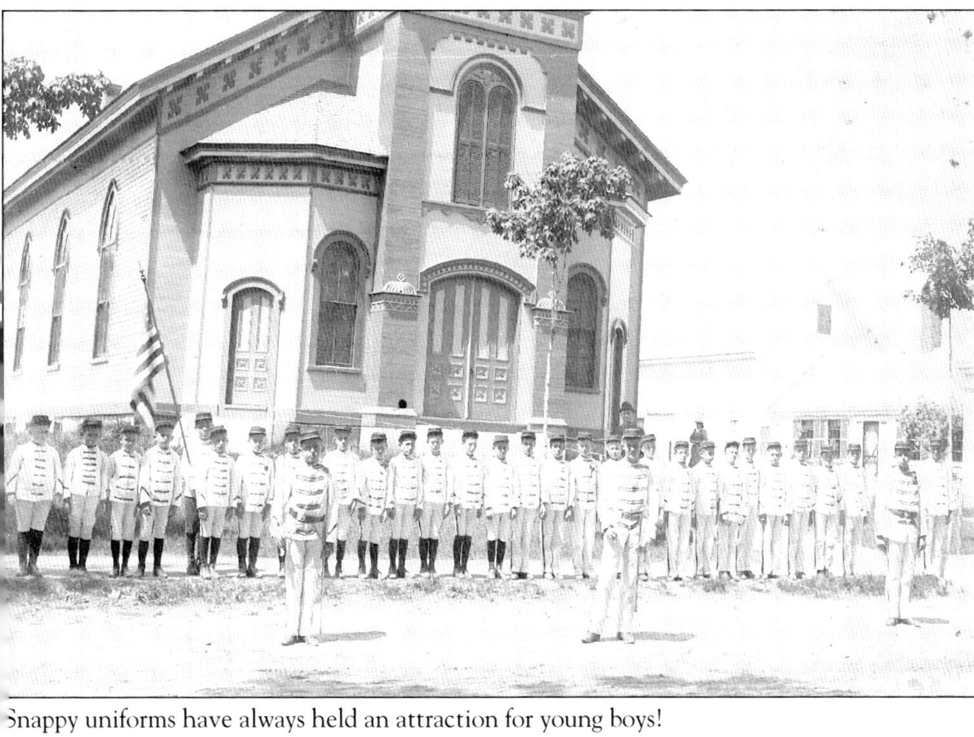

Snappy uniforms have always held an attraction for young boys!

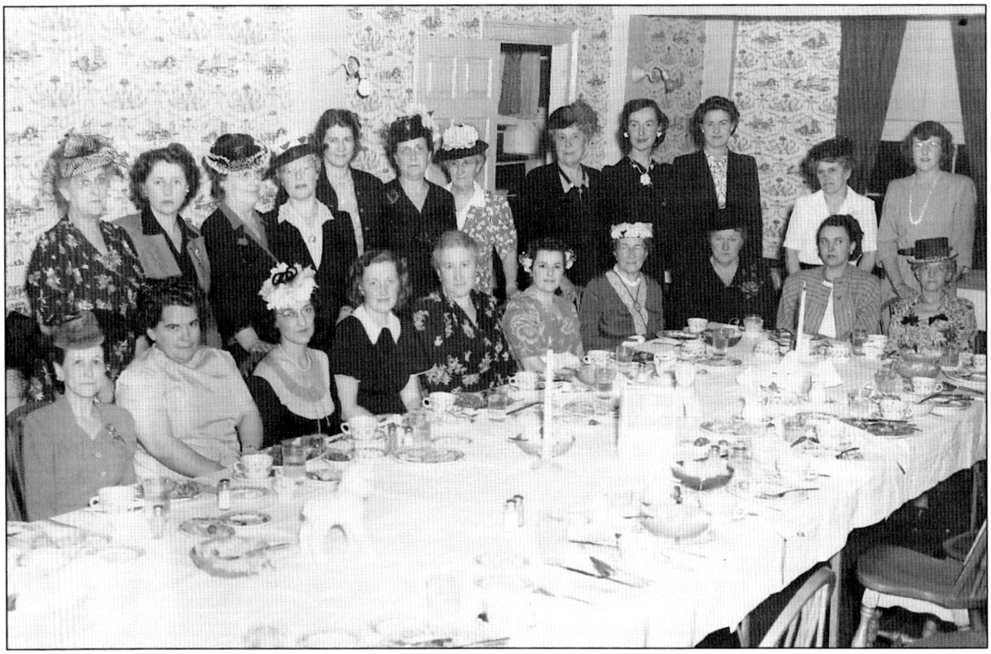

Ladies of the Farmington Woman's Club gather for luncheon. The club was organized in 1910 as a community service and social group. Its clubroom is on the second floor of the Goodwin Library.

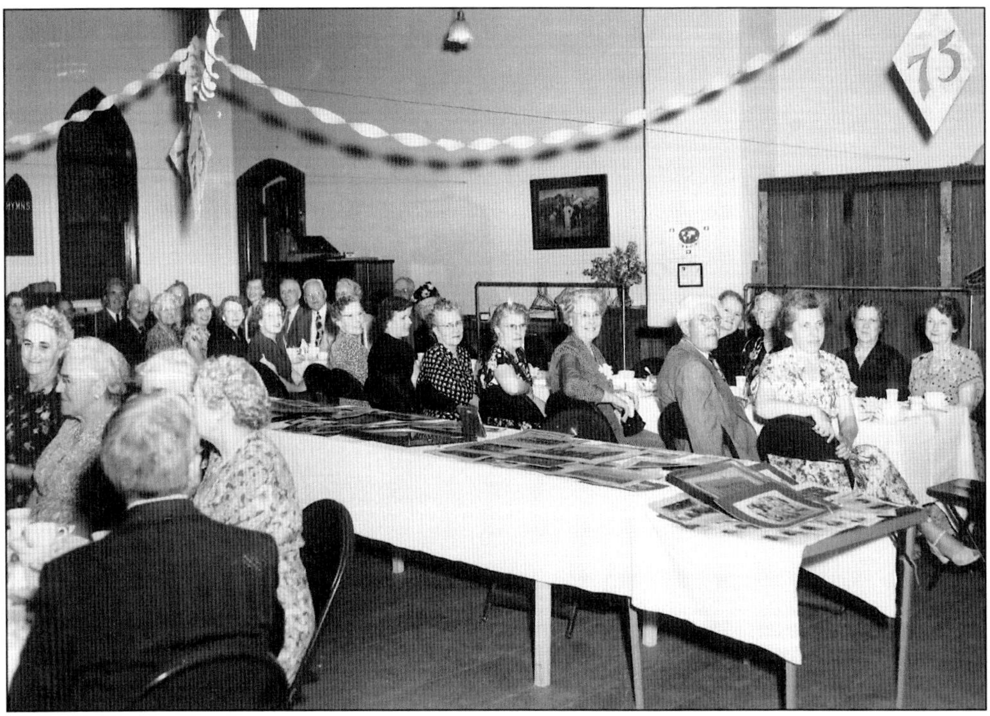

A dinner meeting in 1951 of the original Farmington-New Durham Historical Society. The Farmington Historical Society became independent in 1993; it meets monthly in the Goodwin Library's Henry Wilson Room.

Eight

Fun and Games

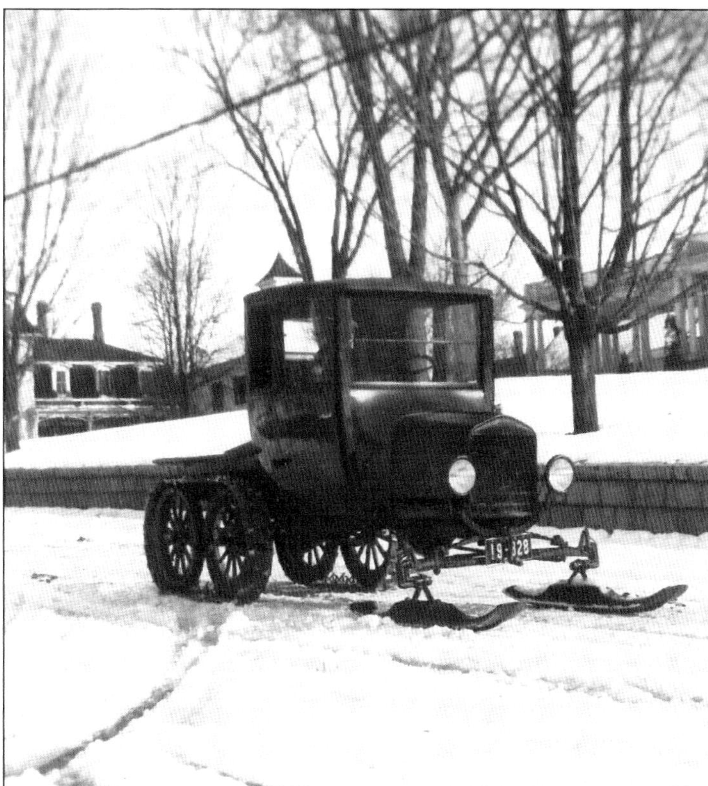

Walter Young bought this early snowmobile from its inventor, Virgil White of West Ossipee, who made his patented machine from a converted Model T Ford.

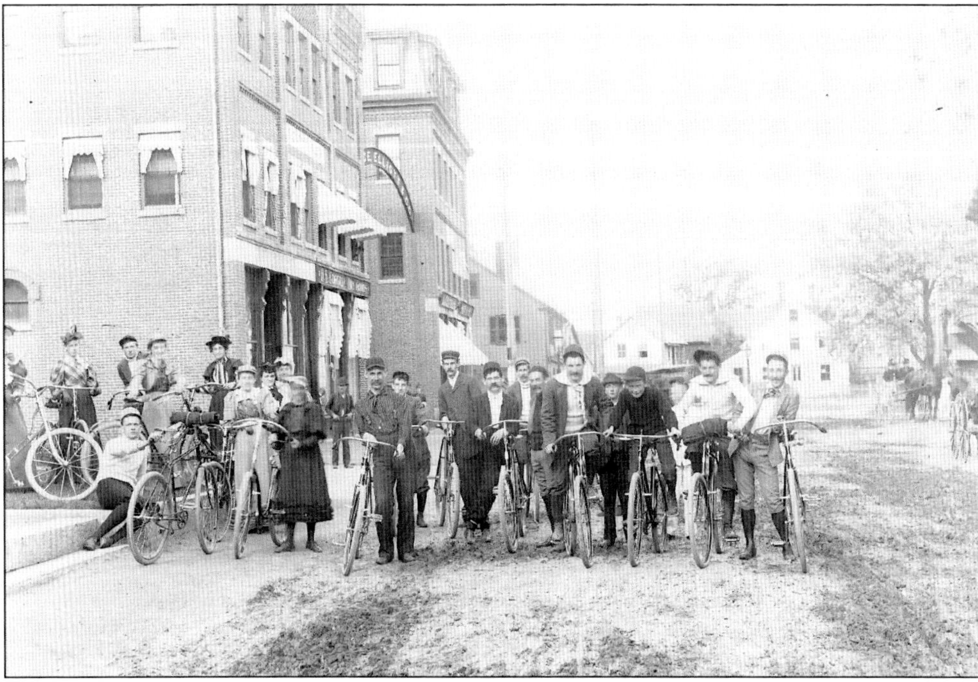

Bicyclists out for some fresh air and exercise pause for the photographer on Central Street.

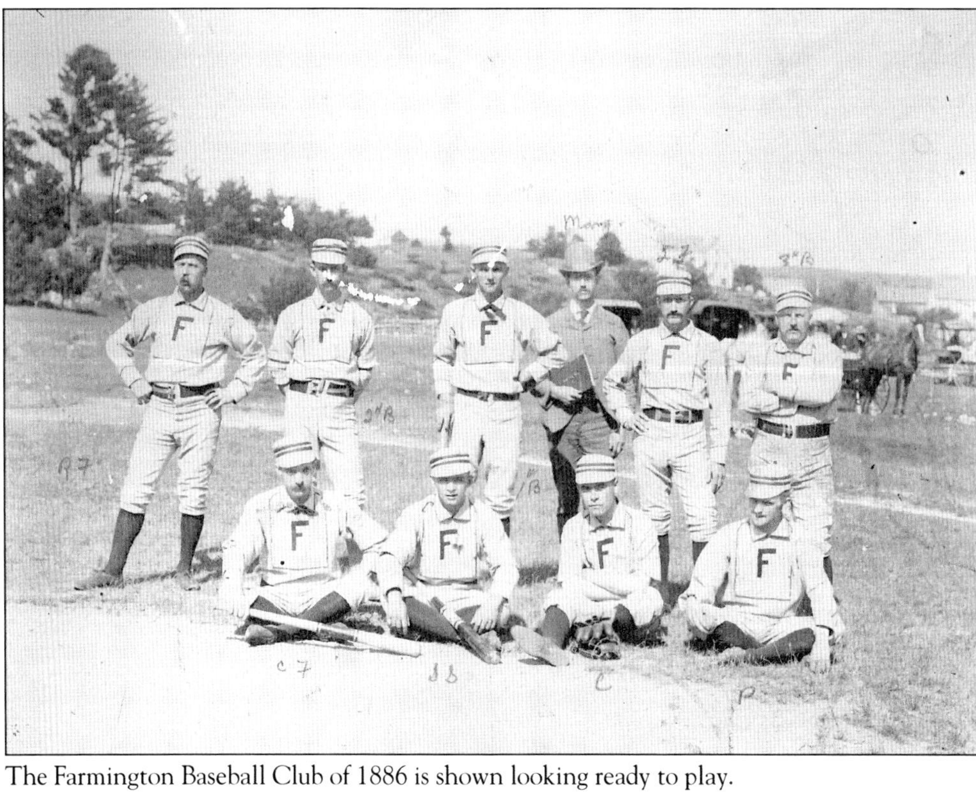

The Farmington Baseball Club of 1886 is shown looking ready to play.

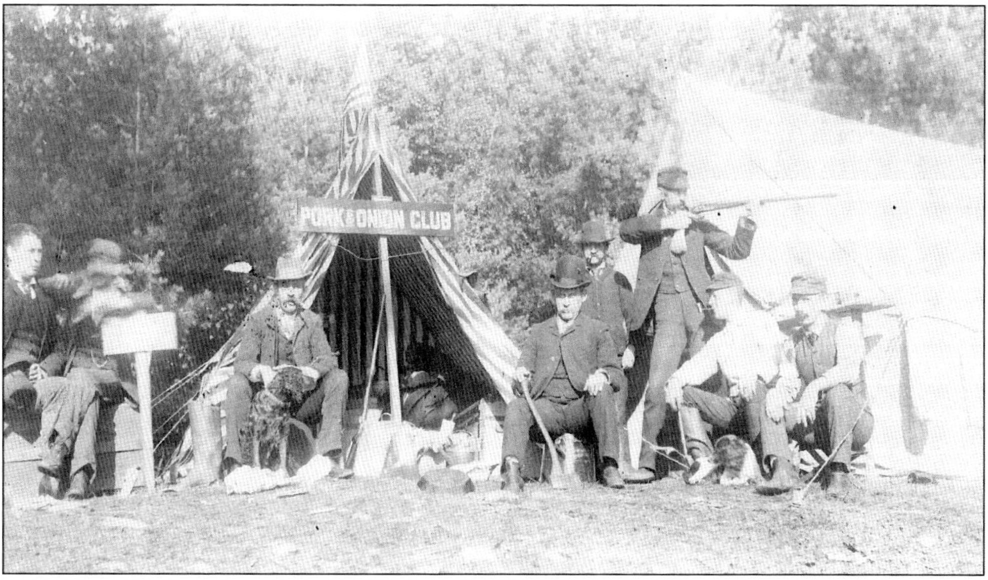

Was this jolly group an outdoor dining club or just well-dressed sportsmen-campers?

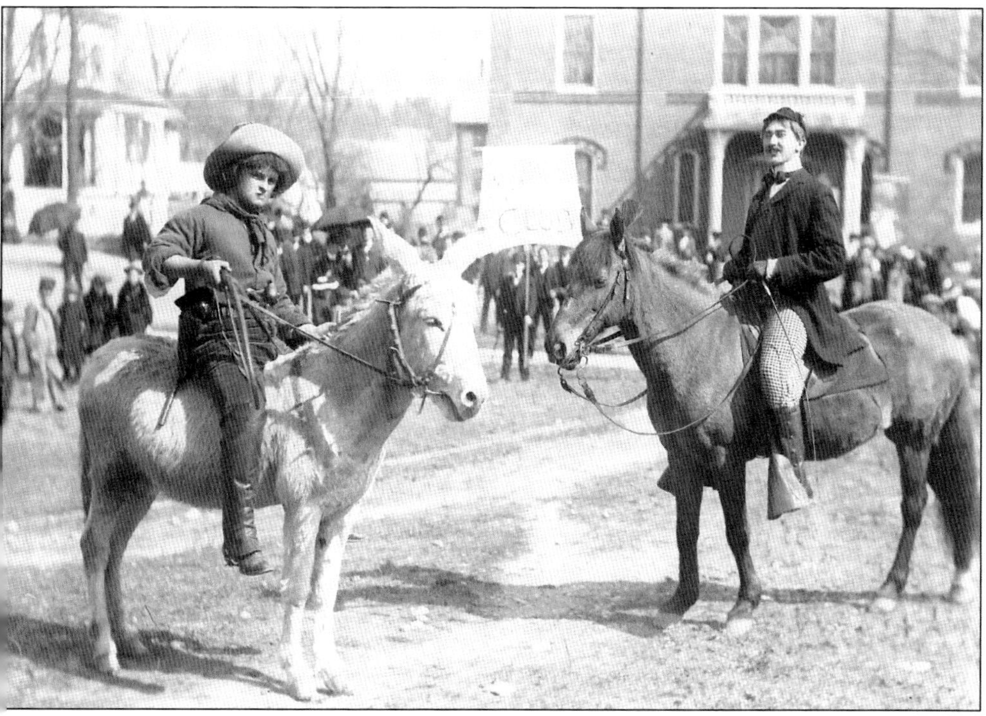

A great variety of clubs existed in the early 1900s as a focus of social life. Seen here are members of the Montauk Club in front of the Opera House.

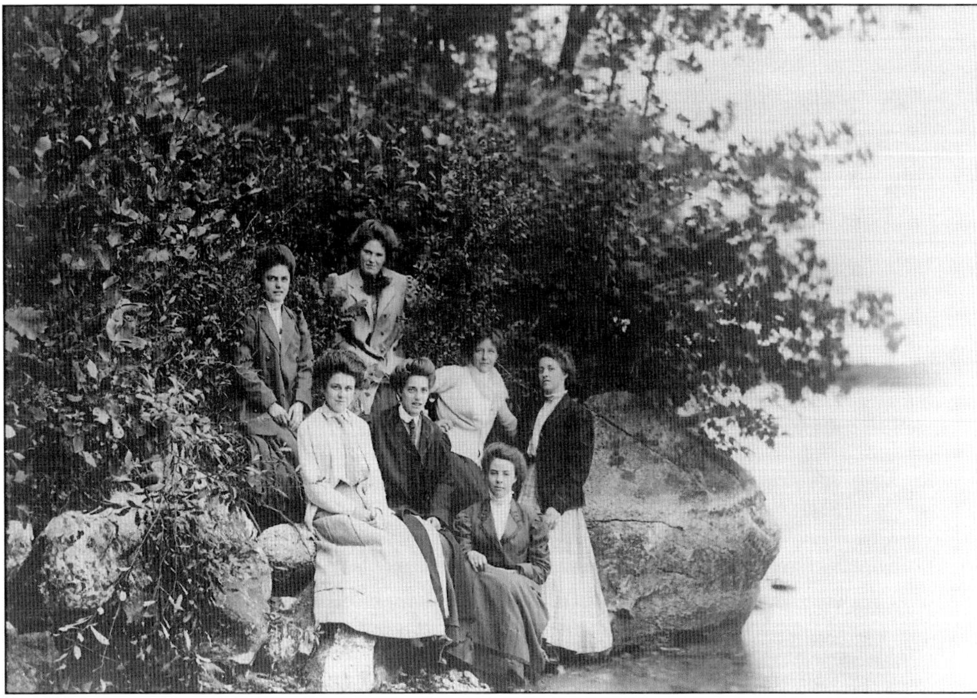

Among these ladies enjoying a lakeside outing are Hattie T. Lefavour, Edna H. Jewell, Maude McLean, Altire Corson, and Violet Jones.

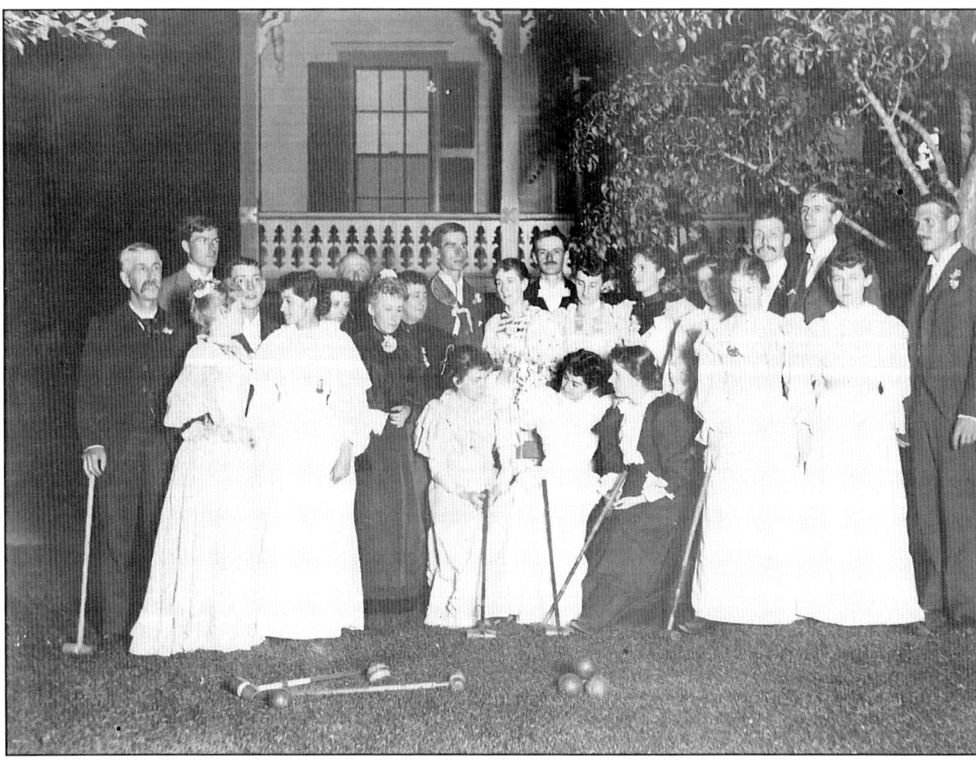

Shoe-dealer A.E. Putnam of Courtland Street entertains a group of friends at a croquet party.

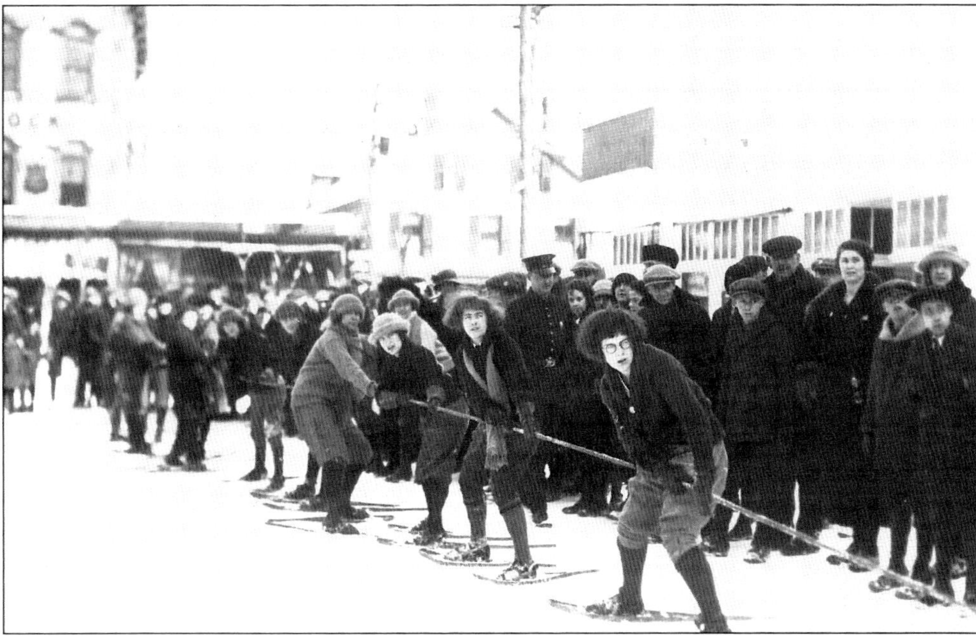

A tug-of-war on snowshoes! Winter fun took many forms before skiing became popular.

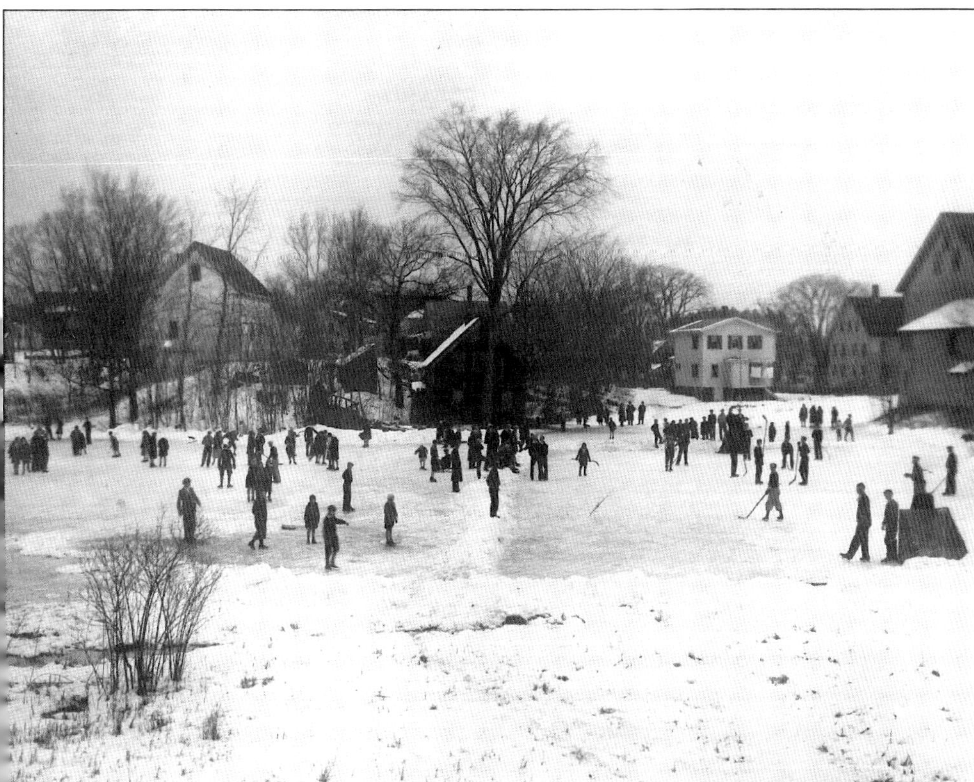

Another winter activity was skating on the Union Street pond, in use until 1963.

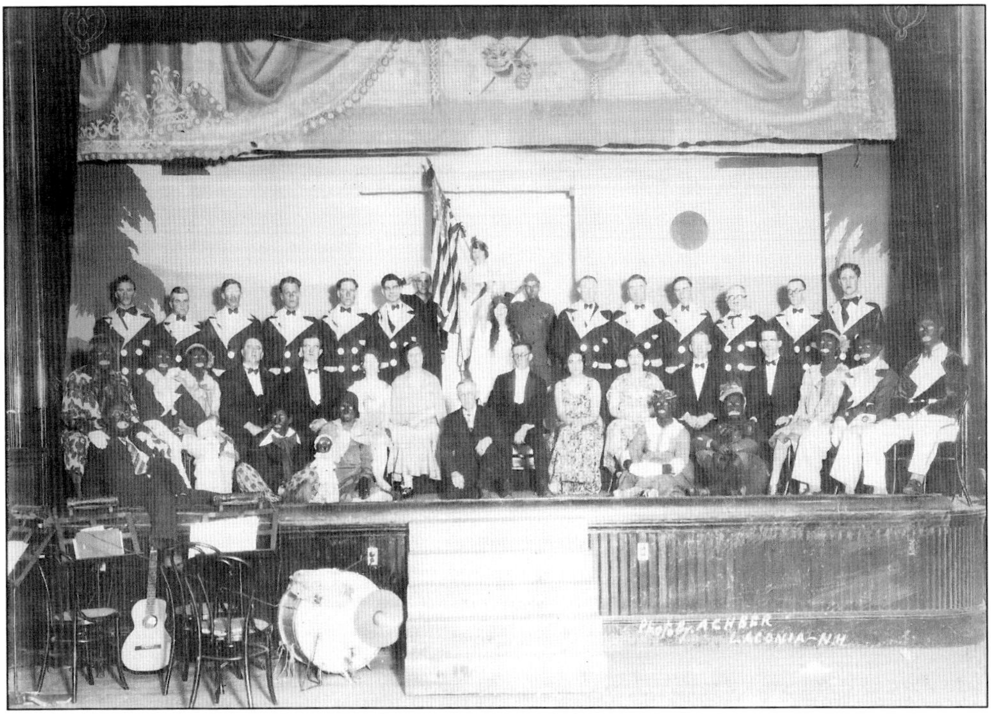

The Opera House was the scene of this early minstrel show.

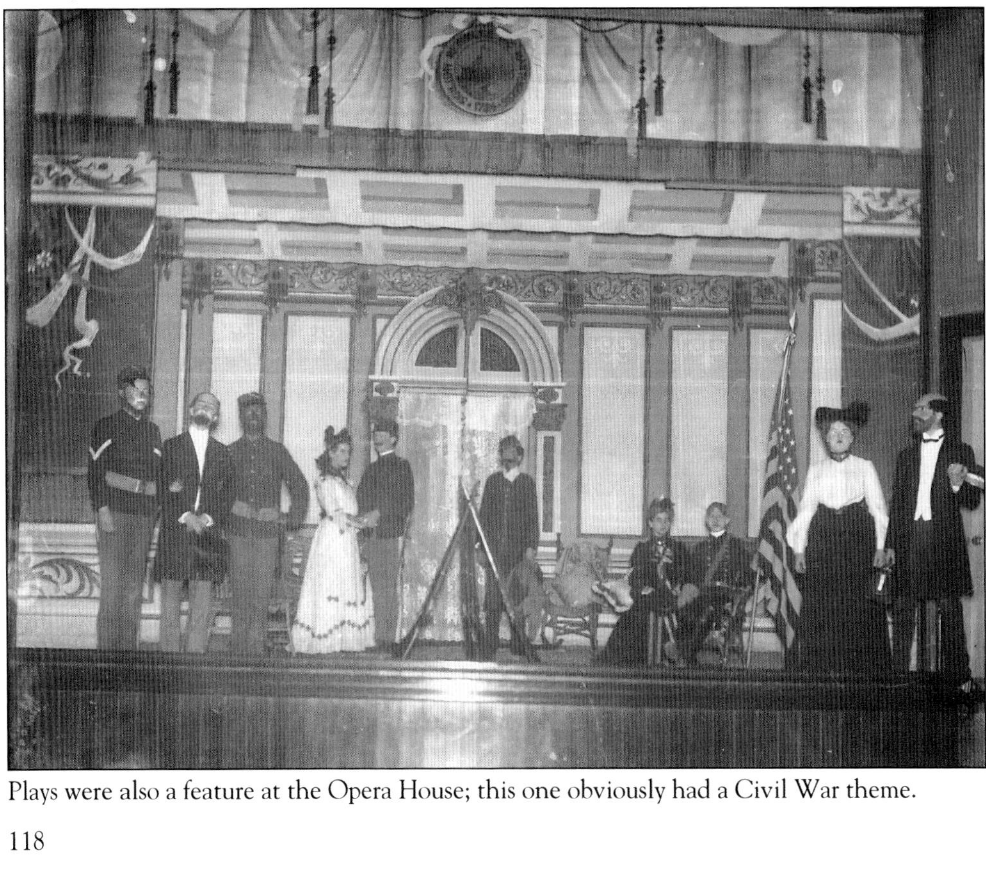
Plays were also a feature at the Opera House; this one obviously had a Civil War theme.

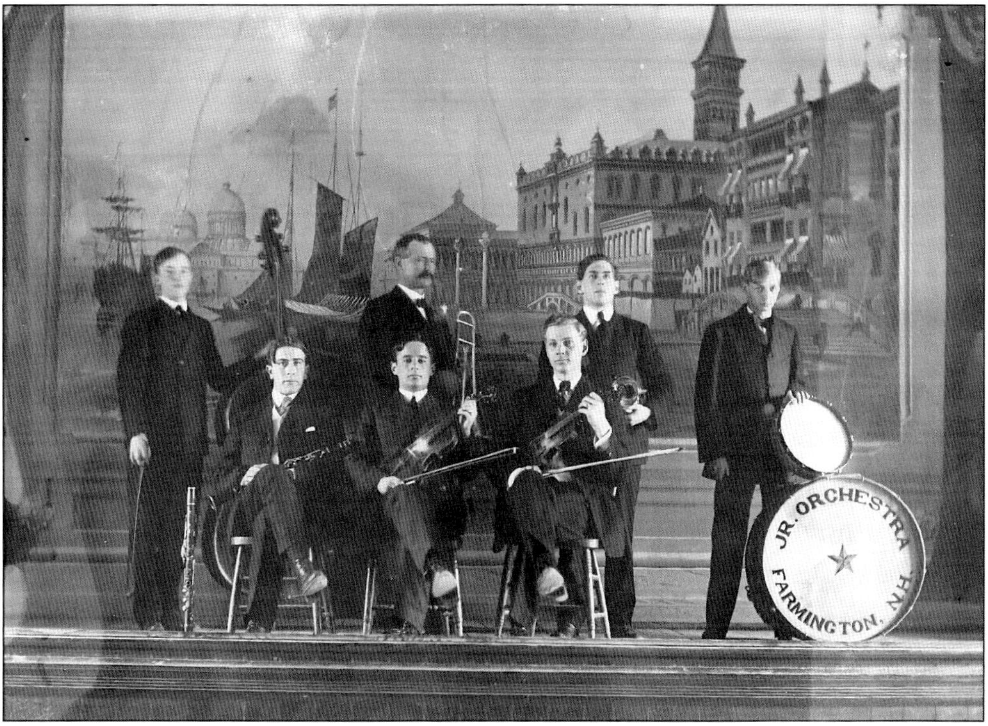

An elegant backdrop provides a classical tone for the town's Junior Orchestra. The cornet player is John Place.

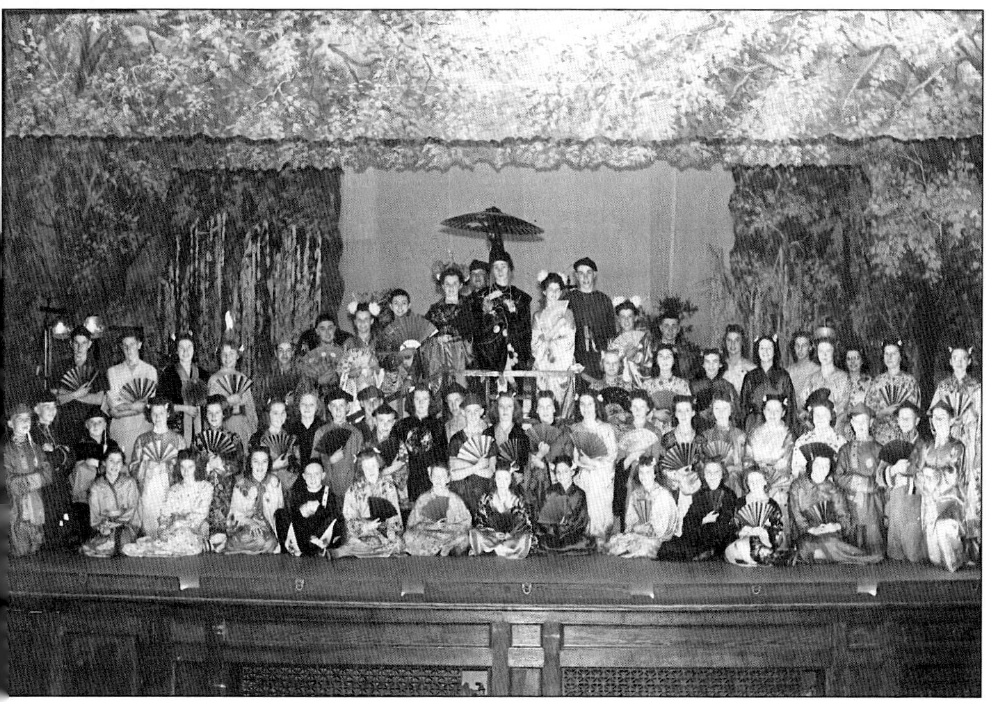

A spectacular production of *The Mikado* was presented by the Farmington High School students on April 15, 1941, at the Town Hall.

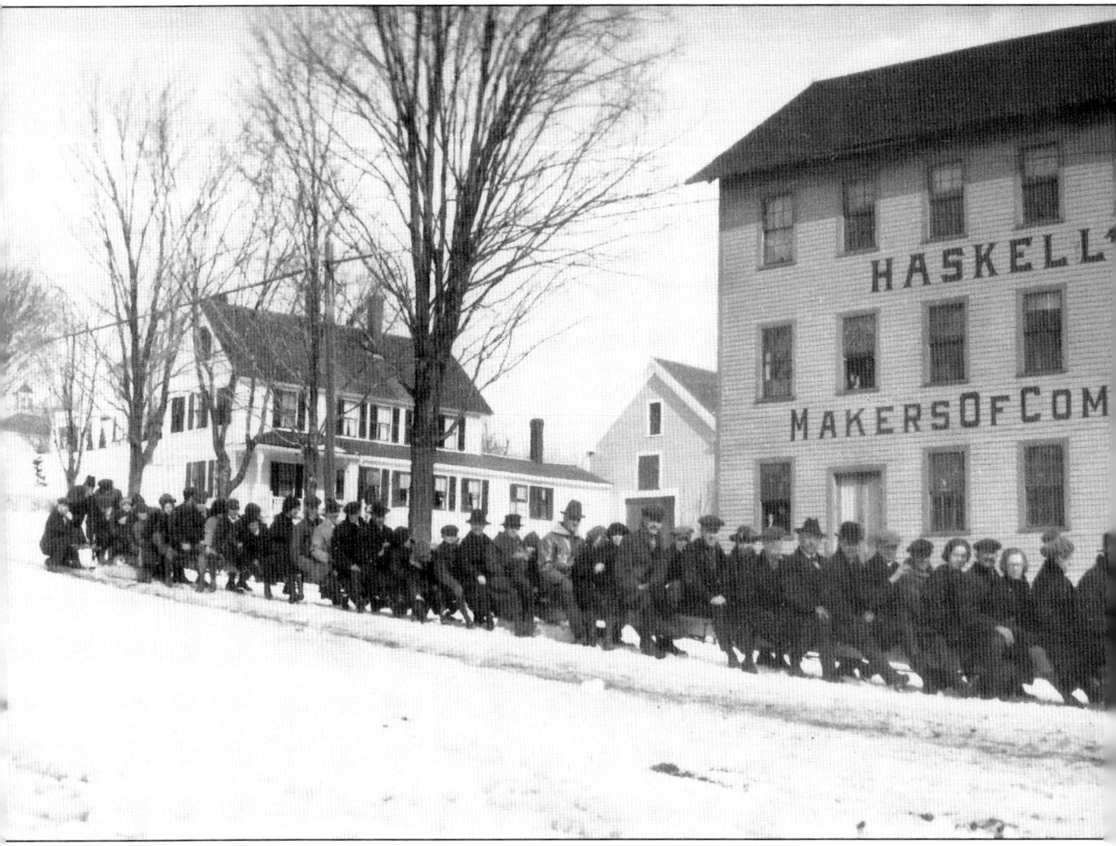

"Uncle Sam"—reputedly the world's largest bobsled at 90 feet in length—was designed and operated by Hervey Pearl. Built at the B.F. Perkins Carriage Shop in 1899, the sled weighed 6 tons loaded.

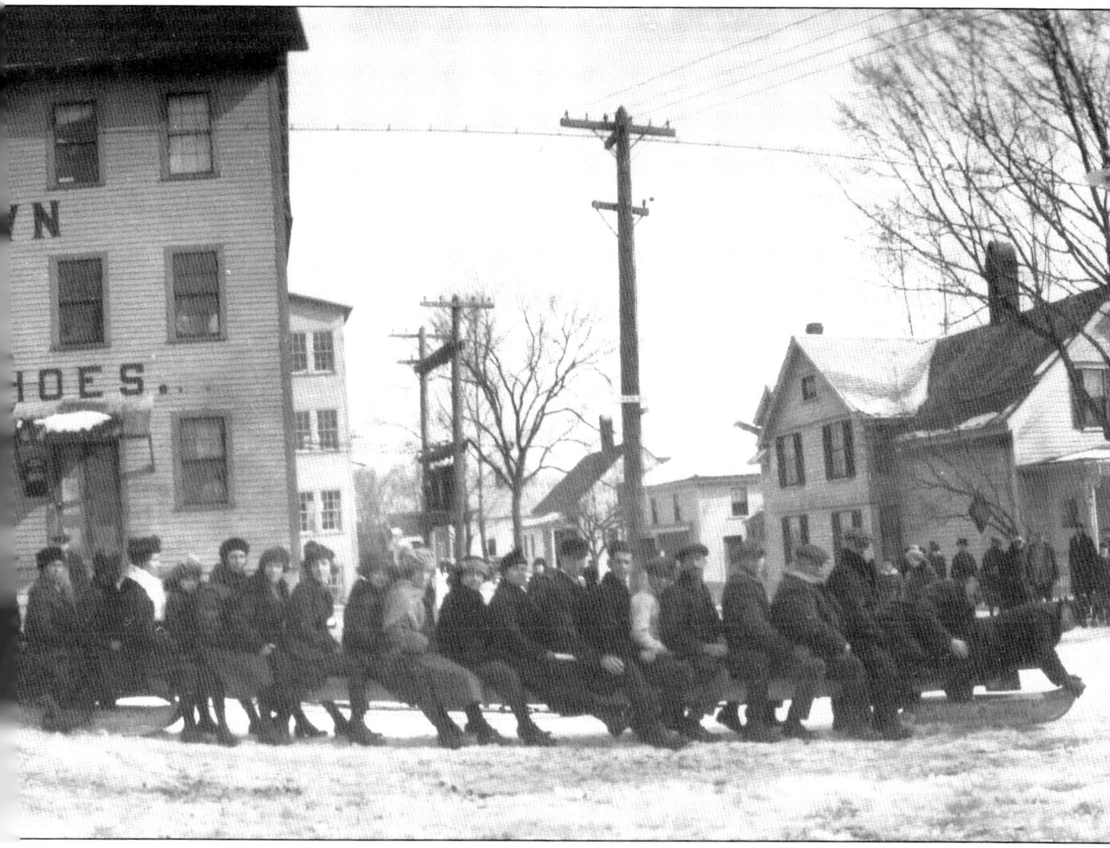

"Uncle Sam" could carry over one hundred riders as it traveled down icy Main Street at upwards of 60 miles per hour! Three of the four sections are preserved at Cameron's Garden Center.

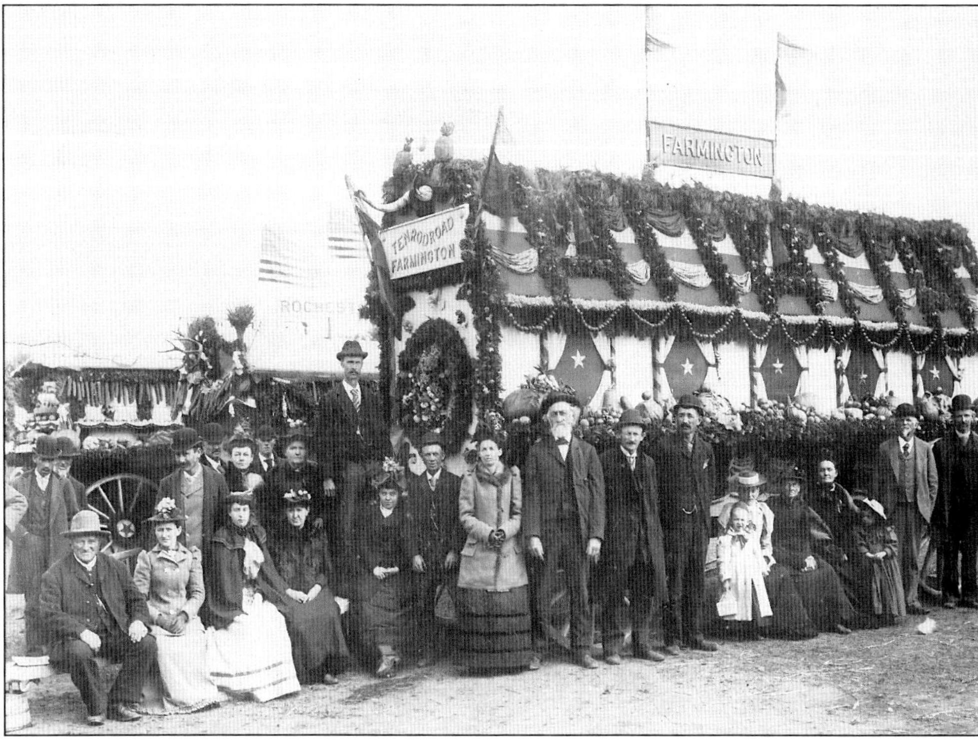

Lavishly decorated with home-grown produce by farmers of the Ten Rod Road section of Farmington, this float was awarded first place in the 1893 Rochester Fair Parade. Participation in the fair was the social highlight of the year—even the schools closed for the event.

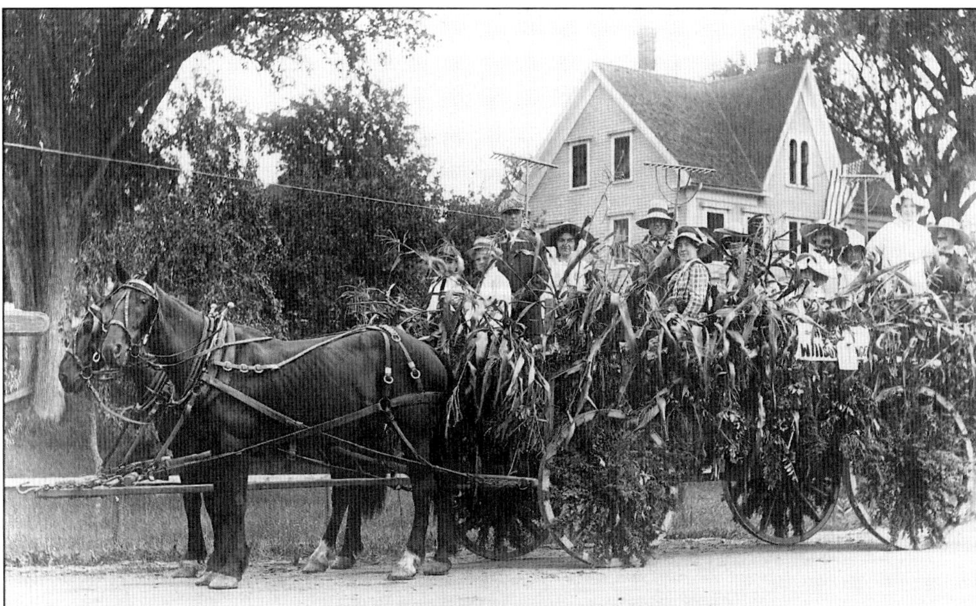

A horse-drawn parade float carries members of the Henry Wilson Grange. This order of the Patrons of Husbandry was organized in 1893, meeting first in the Odd Fellows Building and, since 1959, in its own building on Mechanic Street.

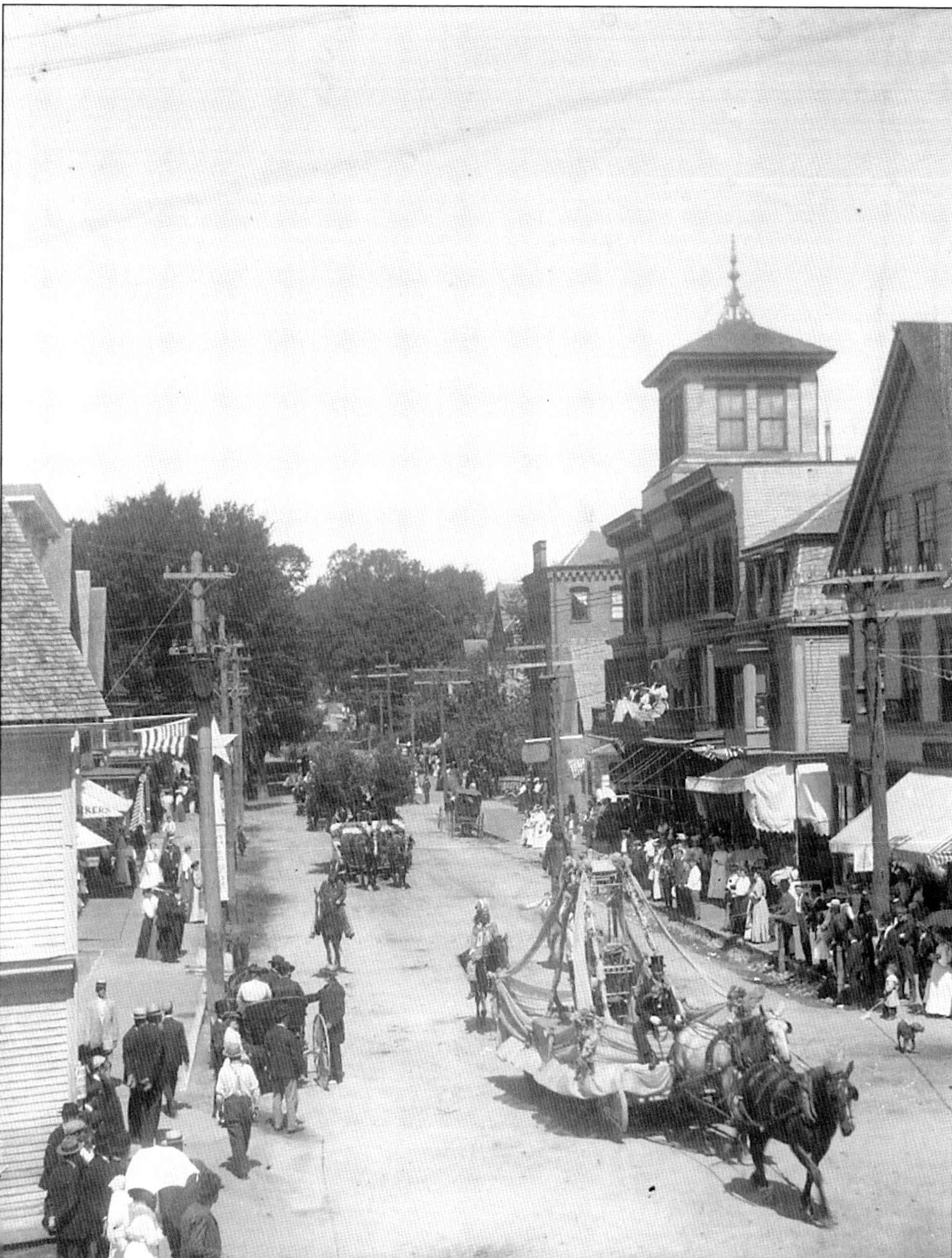

The Roberts Drug Store float in the foreground won first prize in this 1904 Old Home Day Parade on Main Street.

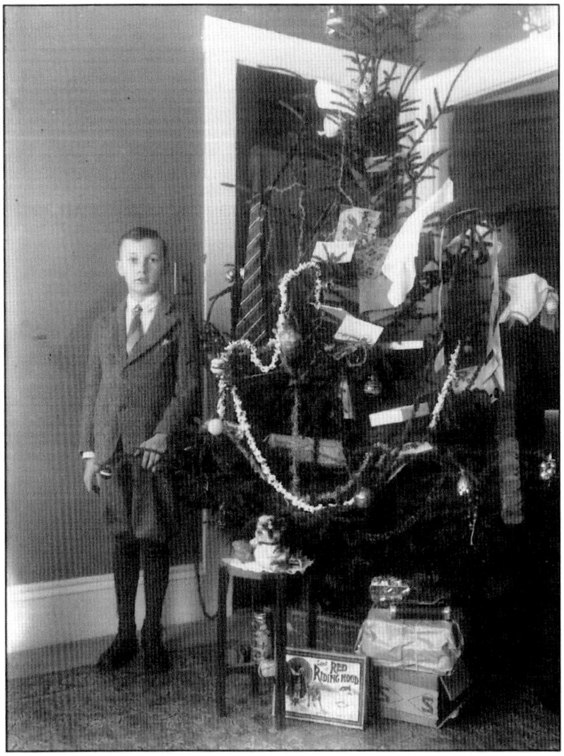

Sumner Evans is all dressed up to celebrate Christmas next to his gift-decorated tree.

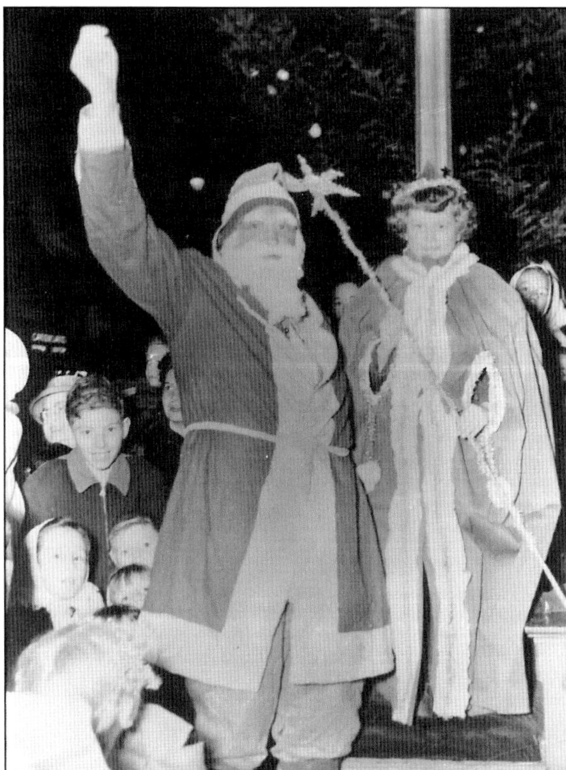

Santa and the "Spirit of Christmas" wish all the children a happy holiday.

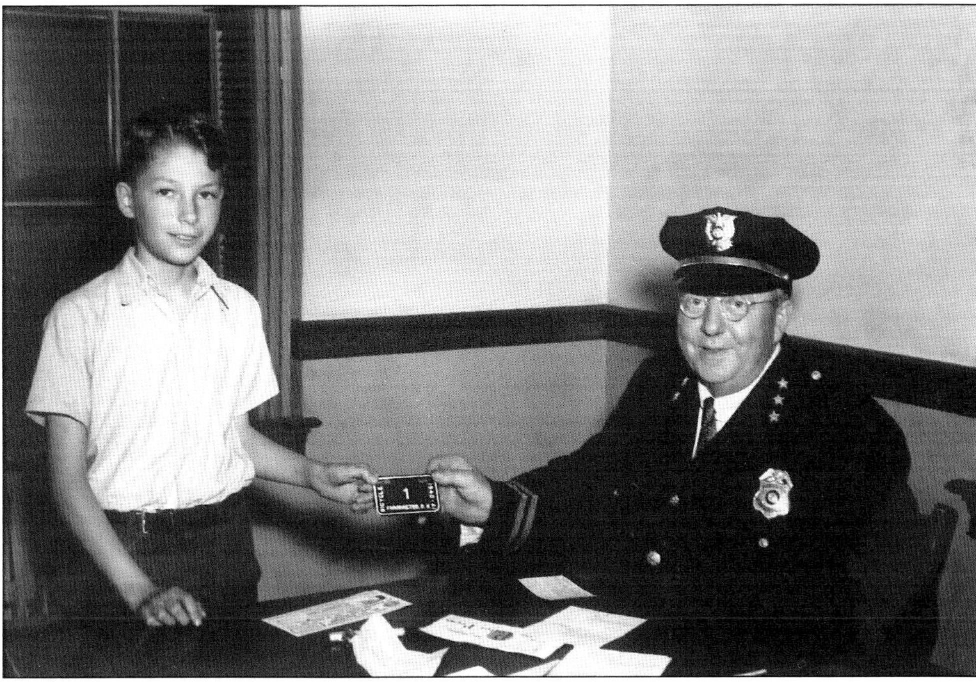

Chief Leon Furber presents the first bicycle license plate in 1940.

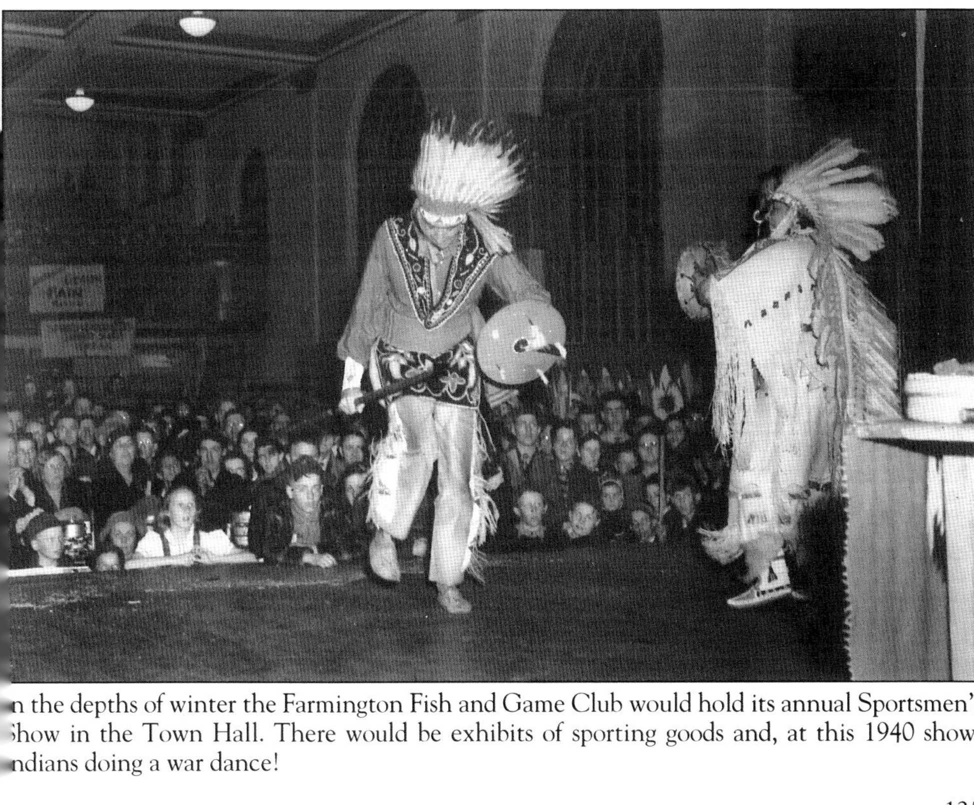

In the depths of winter the Farmington Fish and Game Club would hold its annual Sportsmen's Show in the Town Hall. There would be exhibits of sporting goods and, at this 1940 show, Indians doing a war dance!

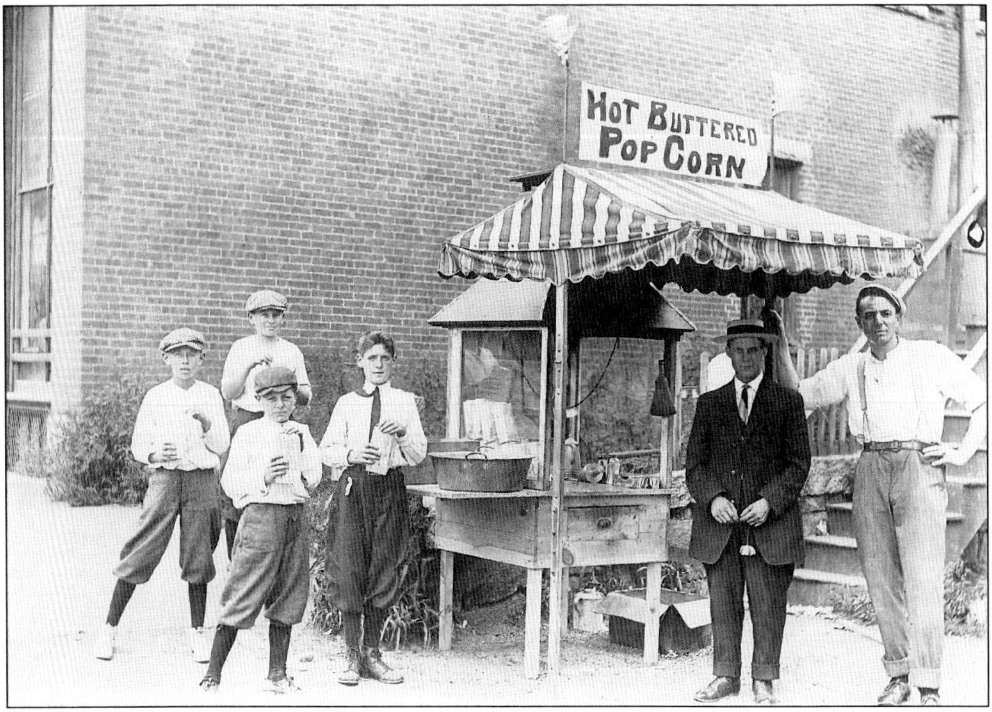

Some things never change!

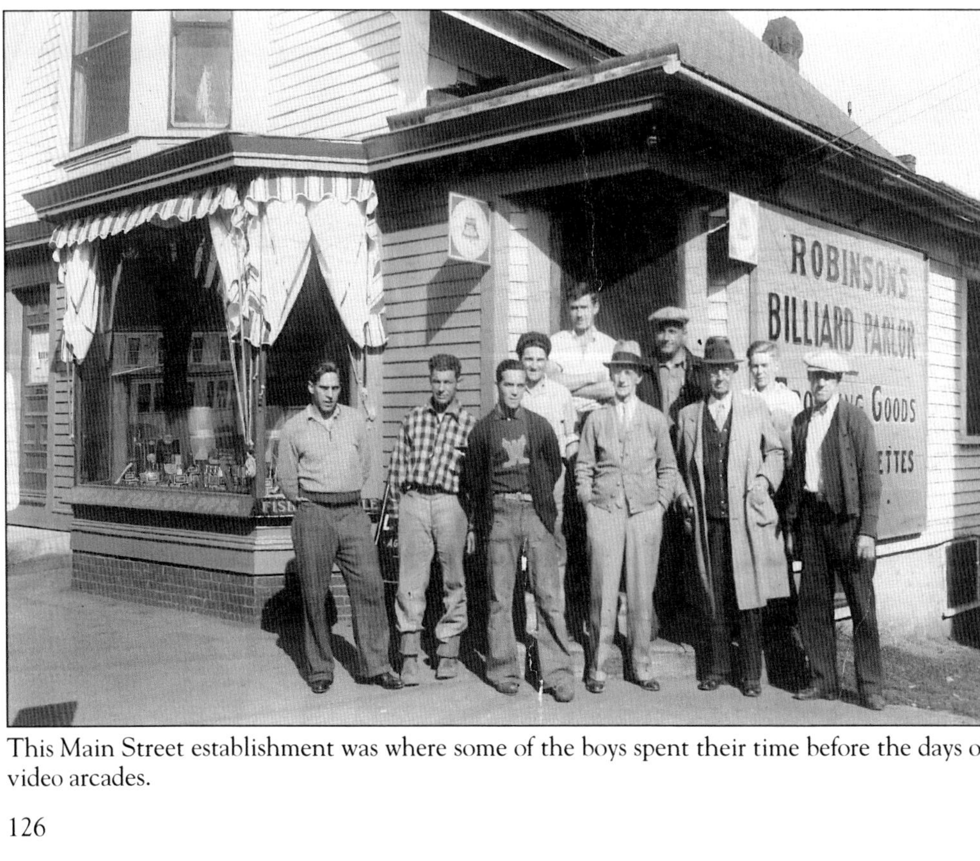

This Main Street establishment was where some of the boys spent their time before the days of video arcades.

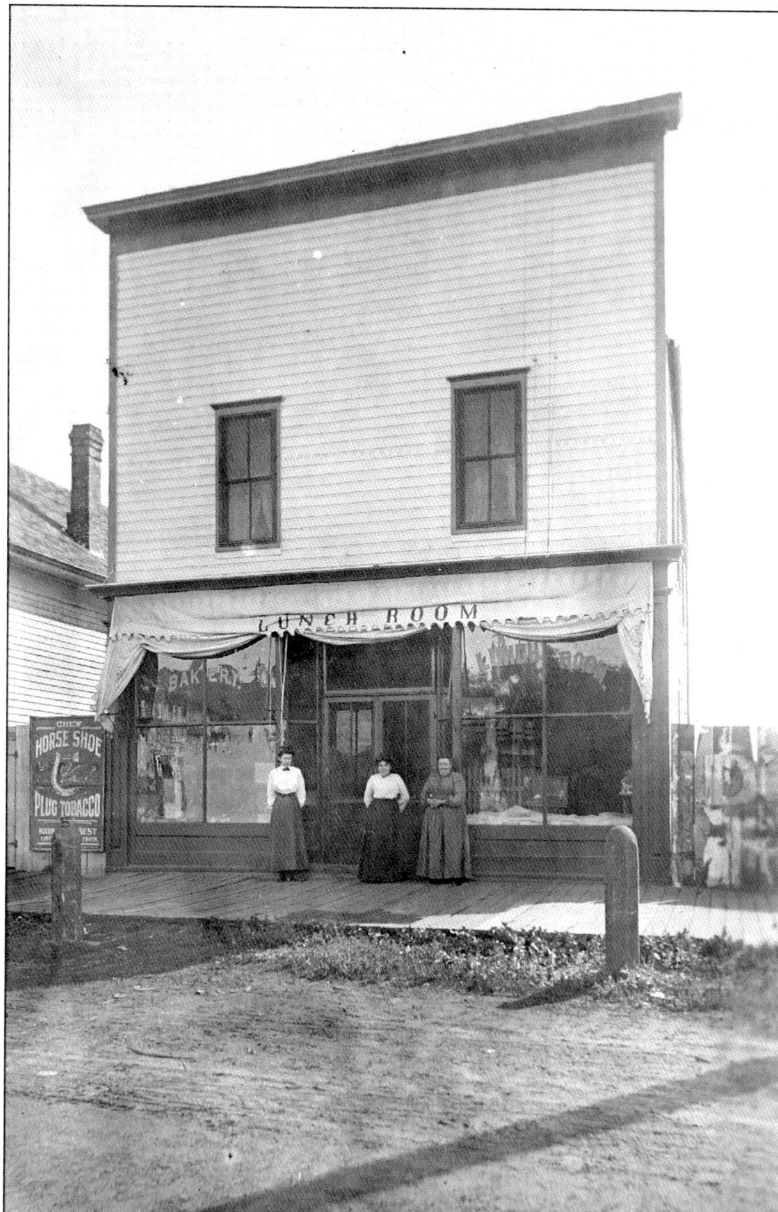

Millane's Store was a confectionery and lunch counter that was located on the north side of the Northern Pacific Railroad tracks at 611 Washington Avenue. The owner and operator, Mary Millane, came from Ireland in 1871 to settle in St. Cloud, Minnesota. She married Edward Millane in 1881, and the couple made their home in Sauk Rapids before coming to Detroit in 1894. It is unclear when the Millane Store opened, but it was sometime after they made their home here. They sold cigars, tobacco, and stationery and also rented out rooms when needed. In the photograph above are Mrs. Jim Keyes (Mary and Edward's daughter), Mary Cook, and Mary Millane. Mary passed away in 1910 from an automobile accident that was called the most distressing motor accident in Becker County. The car that Mary Millane was riding in flipped over, pinning her to the ground. The 12-year-old boy who was driving was protected by Mrs. Millane and survived the accident.

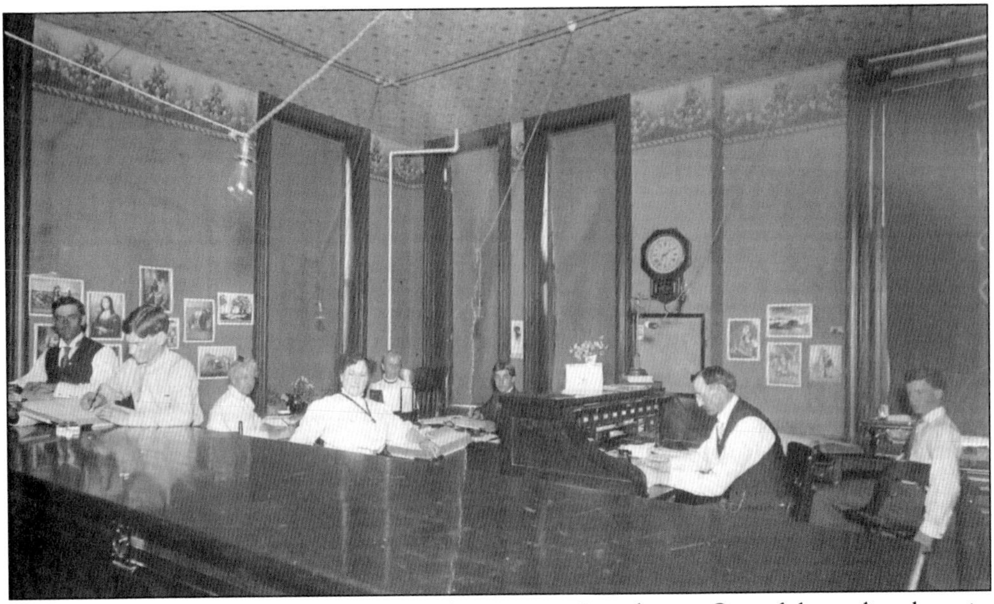

These images show the interior of the Becker County Courthouse. One of the earliest lawsuits held in the courthouse includes a case involving Harvey Jones, who was arrested for administrating family discipline with an ironwood sapling. He was tried before Squire McGrew and a jury of 12 men, who found him guilty. His sentence was 30 days in the Otter Tail City Jail. The commitment papers were given to Capt. F.K. Small, who made arrangements with John O. French, one of three constables. While en route to jail, Jones asked to consult with an attorney. French left his overcoat unattended when he went for a drink of water, and after a few miles down the road Jones argued that French had no authority to take him to jail. Upon finding that French did not have the papers in his coat anymore, he had no choice but to let him go.

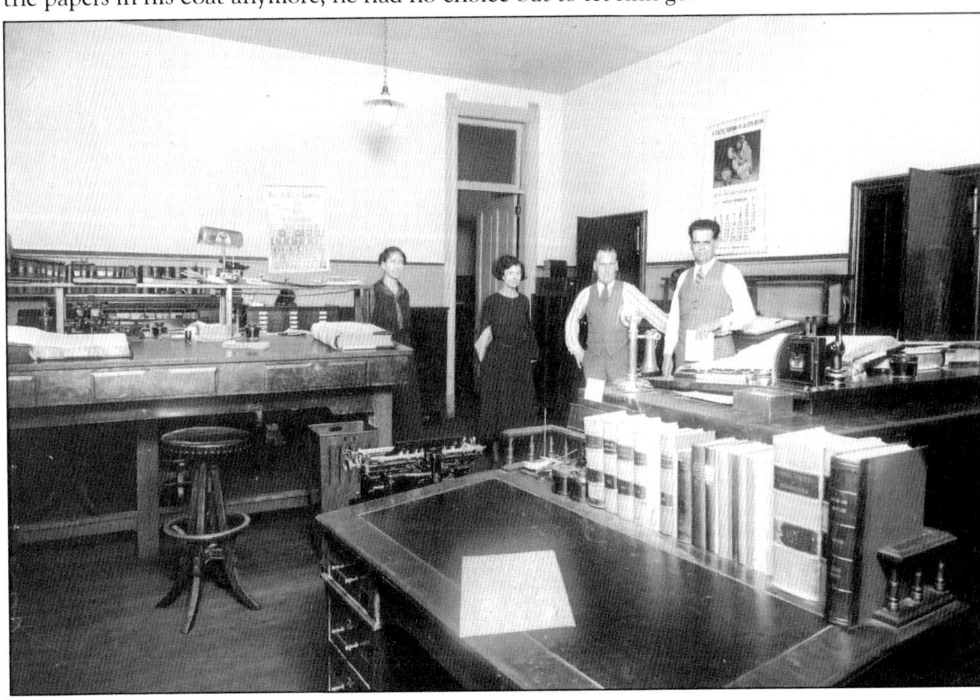

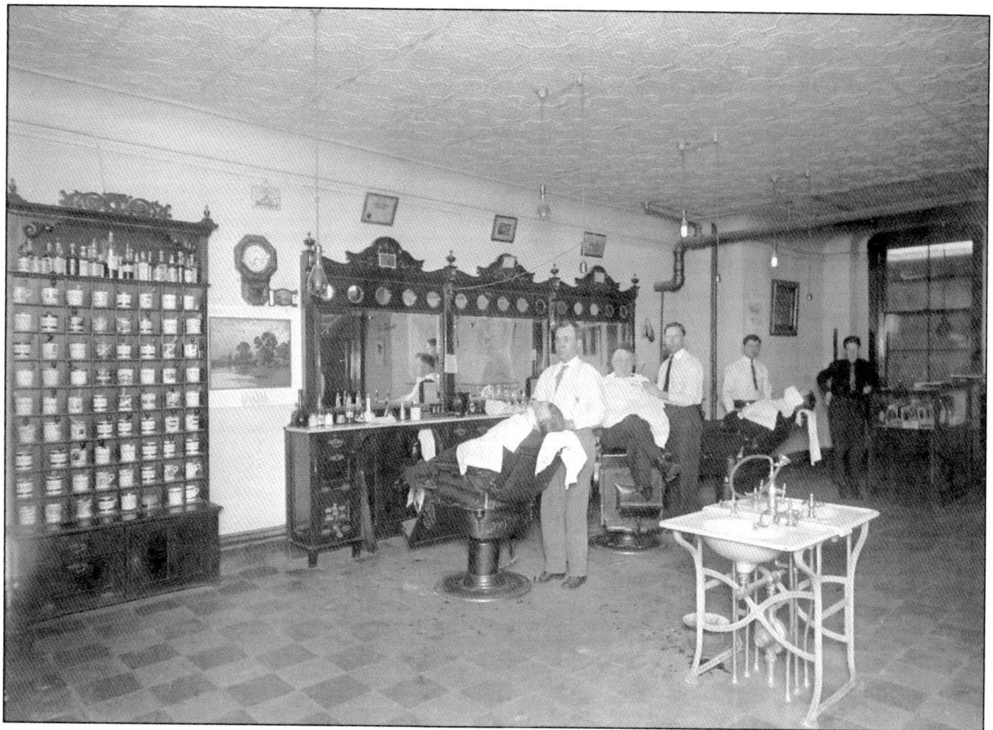

The best-known barber in the early days was George C. Bush. His shop was located on Washington Avenue, a block south of the opera house block. It was the place where one found out the "who's who" in the village of Detroit and the latest news on sports and politics. Bush served several terms as president of the village council and as county sheriff.

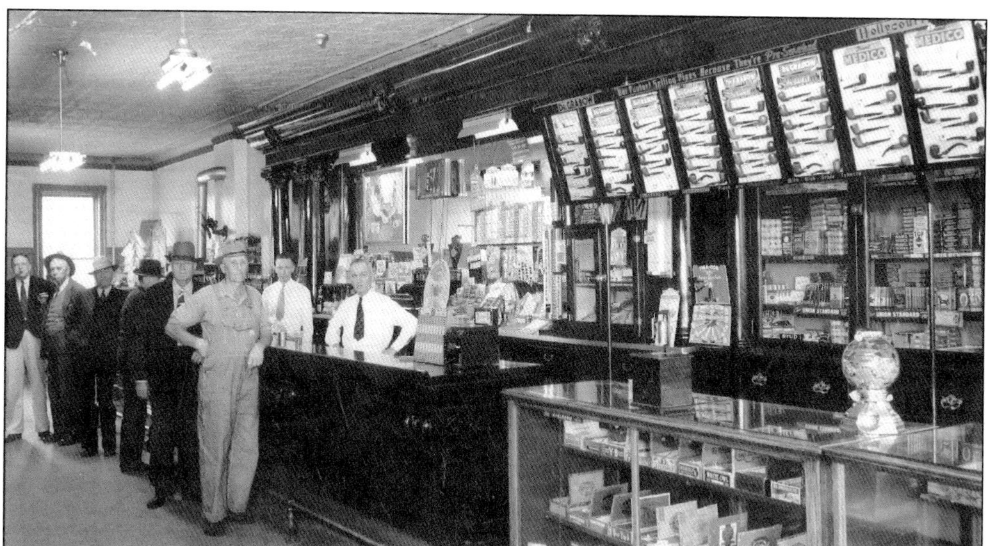

Courtright's, located at 713 Washington Avenue, was owned and operated by Frank S. Courtright. Advertising described the soft-drink parlor as an "up-to-date thirst parlor for discriminating people," which also happened to carry the finest lines of imported and domestic wines and liquors. One interesting fact was that he offered automobile delivery to any part of the city.

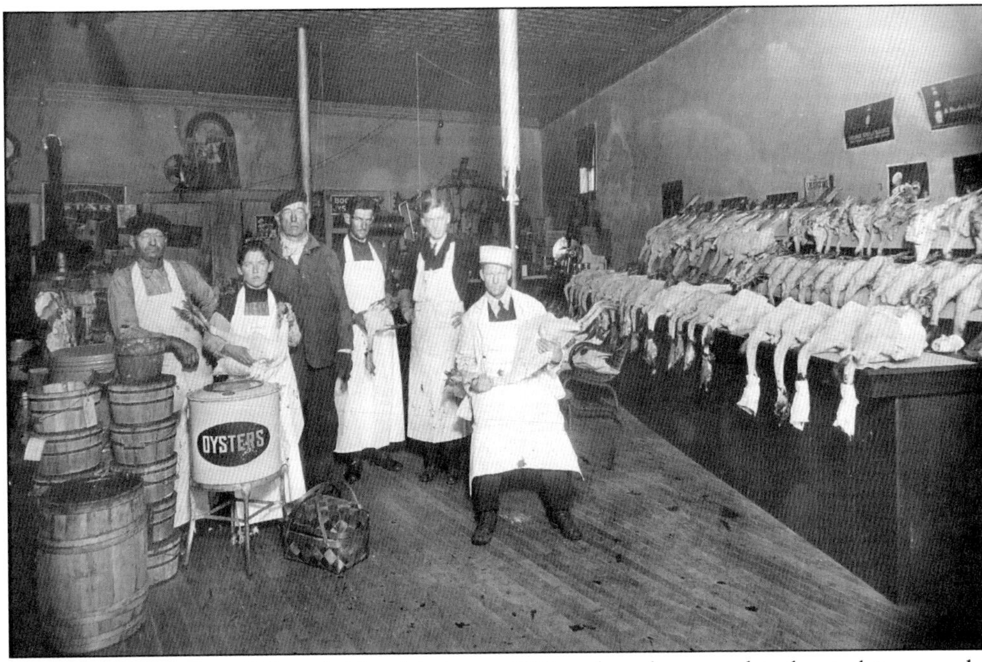

Ed Hagen first operated Hagen's Meat Market in 1912 under sole ownership, but in later years he partnered with Dennis Hagen. They were located on Washington Avenue and Main Street. In 1933, they moved to the north side in a building formerly occupied by Bilstad Hardware Company and later by Swanson's second ax-handle store.

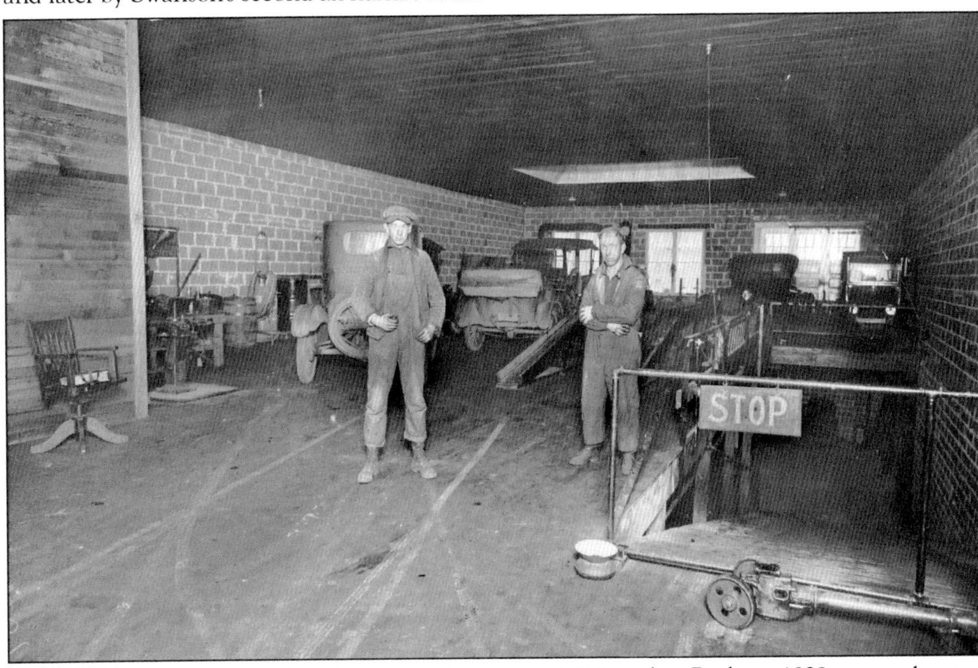

Peoples Garage was owned and operated by George W. Peoples. Built in 1922, it was located opposite of the courthouse with its entrance facing south, directly toward the north entrance of the courthouse. The garage was one-story in height and built of local hollow cement blocks and cement brick. Peoples mainly worked on Dodge automobiles.

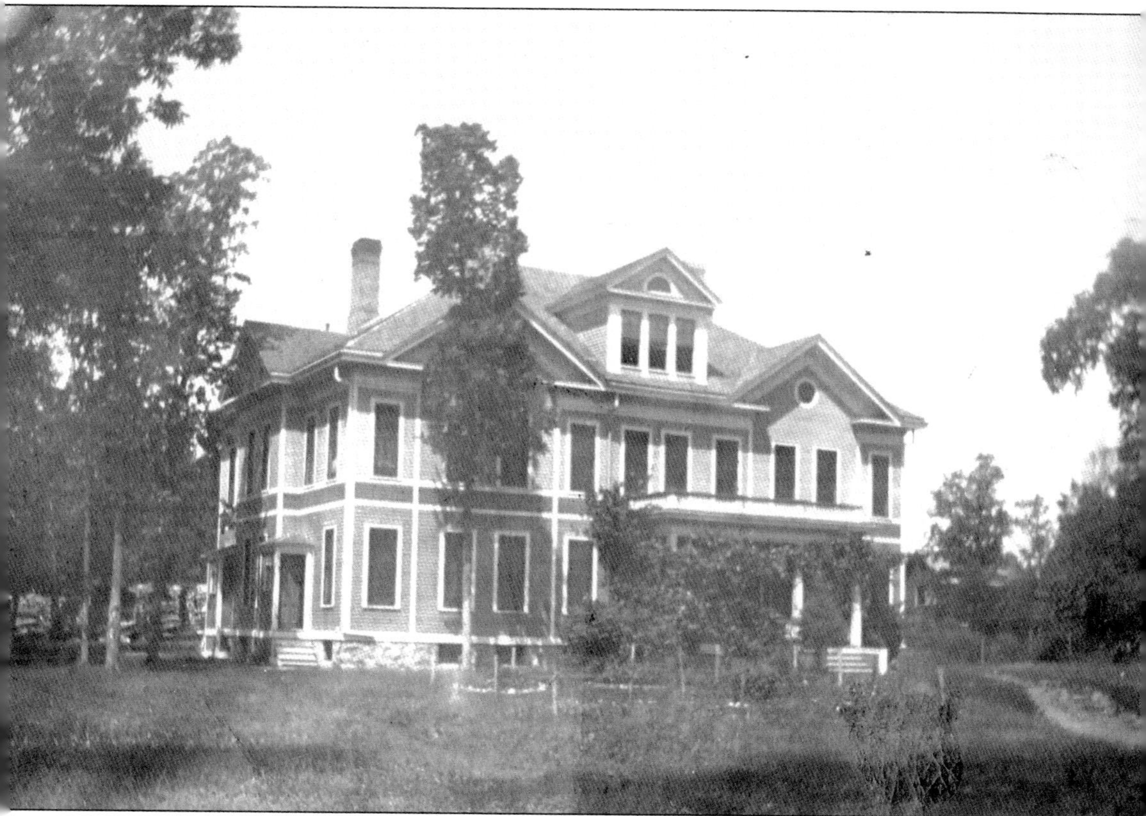

Infirmaries were a common presence in towns at the turn of the 20th century. Originally set up as hospitals to treat the low-income sick, these buildings later became poorhouses for the destitute, much like state hospitals for the mentally ill. Residents were referred to as "inmates," and staff were called "overseers." The environment at times was more like that of a prison than a social service. However, they did provide a necessary service to the community. The original Becker County Infirmary building burned on March 13, 1900. At that time, the building was situated near the Eininger Camp cabins. John Dexter, the overseer, quickly removed the 15 inmates to the barn that was located nearby. Dexter, unable to get the phone to work, mounted his horse and rode into town to sound the fire alarm. A new building was constructed at the fairgrounds, which was considered a good and convenient site on account of its tillable ground, used for growing vegetables to feed the inmates. The infirmary, constructed in 1900 by Brainerd Manufacturing Company for $2,500, was situated on a beautiful wooded ridge facing Detroit Lake. The property consisted of a brick basement and two stories of convenient apartments for male and female occupants. In 1936, it was leased to a private operation before closing in 1940. In later years, it was used as a 4-H clubhouse.

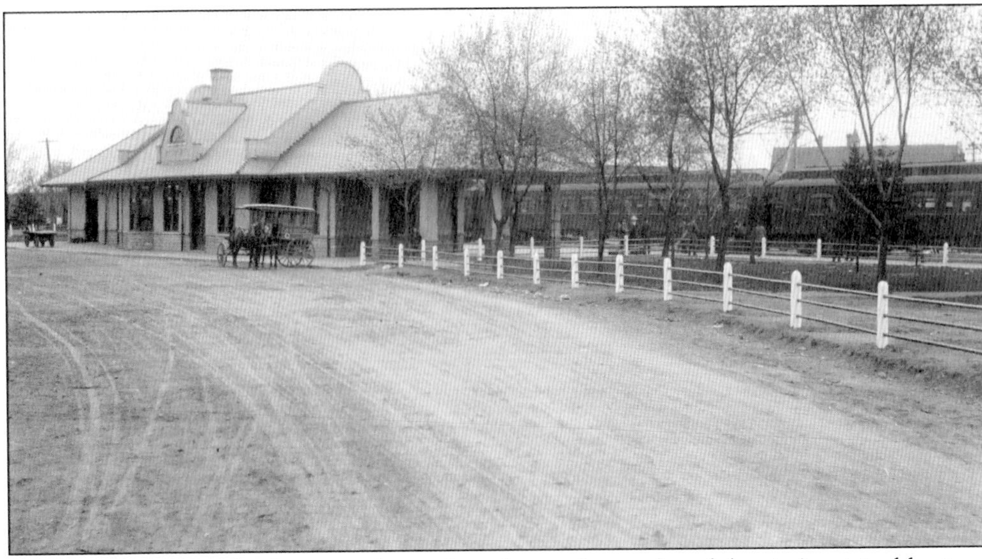

Completed in 1908, the depot was located on the northern edge of the city's original business district. The depot measured 110 by 36 feet and, as originally constructed, had a 36-by-36-foot waiting room with an 18-foot ceiling, a ladies waiting room, a men's smoking room, a ticket office, a baggage room, and bathrooms. The building was visually prominent and serves as one of the best-preserved examples of railroad architecture in northwestern Minnesota today.

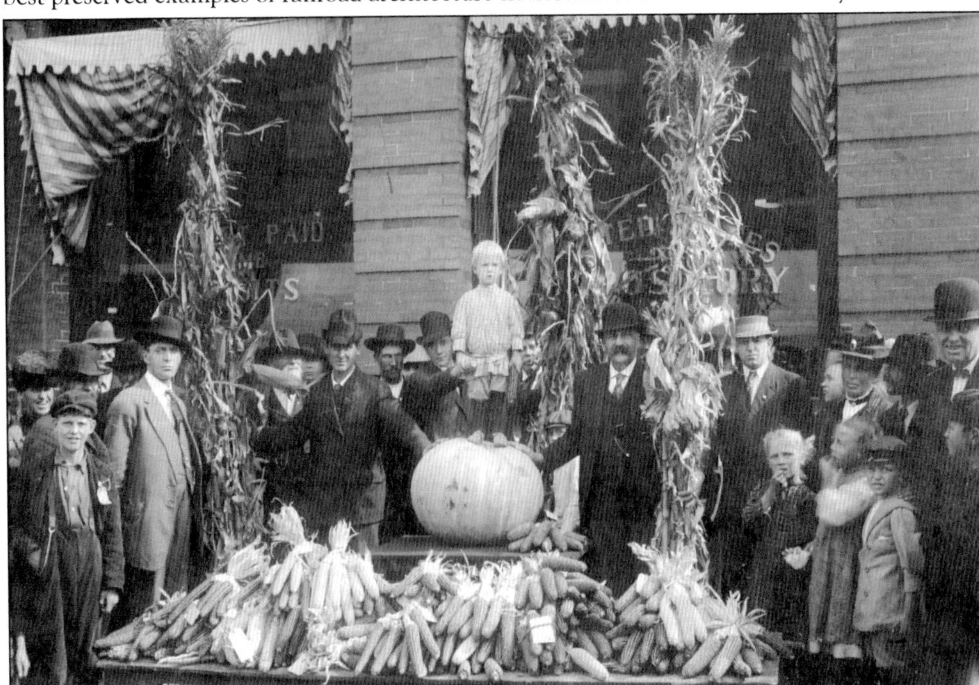

In this 1909 photograph of the first Becker County Corn Exhibit, the corn stalks on the sidewalk were freestanding at 14 feet high. An enrolled member of the White Earth Band of Ojibwe on the White Earth Reservation raised the squash, which weighed 115 pounds and was six feet in circumference. This photograph was taken in front of the First National Bank in Detroit. All vegetables were raised in 1909 in Becker County, Minnesota.

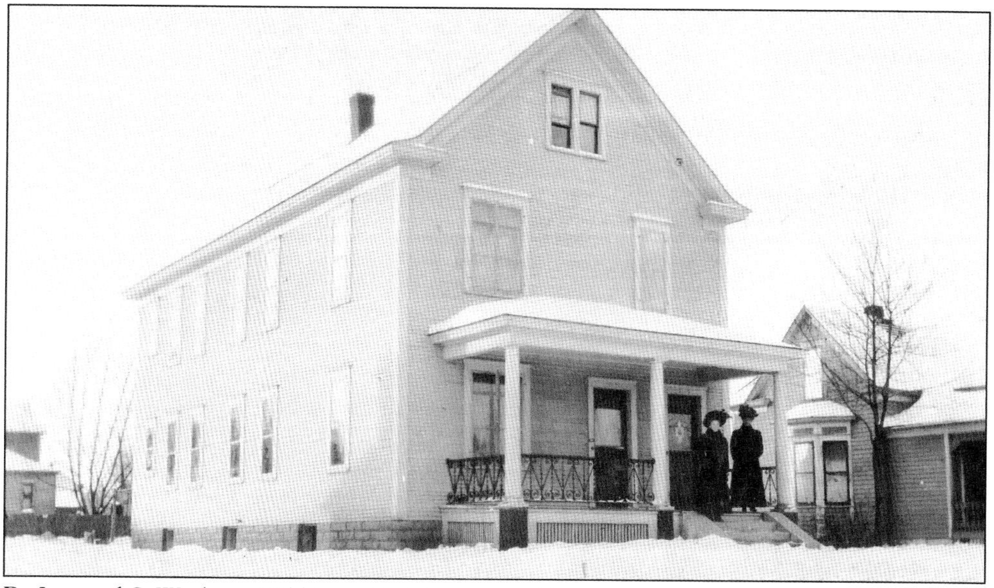

Dr. Leonard C. Weeks, or "Old Doc Weeks," was one of Detroit's pioneer physicians. He took care of his patients in the upstairs room of his home, pictured above, located south of the Congregational Church from 1896 to 1905. He built and equipped a hospital at what is now 207 East Frazee Street (pictured below) before closing it in 1909. The county infirmary served as a hospital until Weeks reopened his community hospital in 1919. In 1928, the American Legion post tried unsuccessfully to get voters to approve a Becker County hospital. However, they did secure stock subscriptions and completed the new hospital in 1929 with the help of the Businessmen's Club. In 1939, the Sisters of St. Benedict at Crookston assumed the bonded debt and converted the hospital into what is now known as Essentia Health St. Mary's.

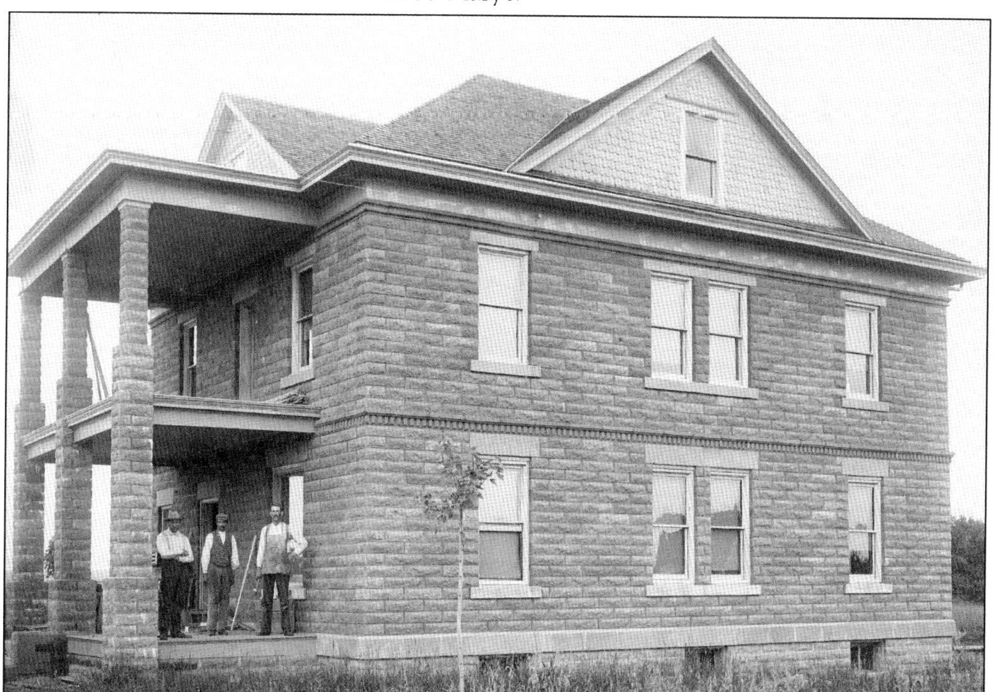

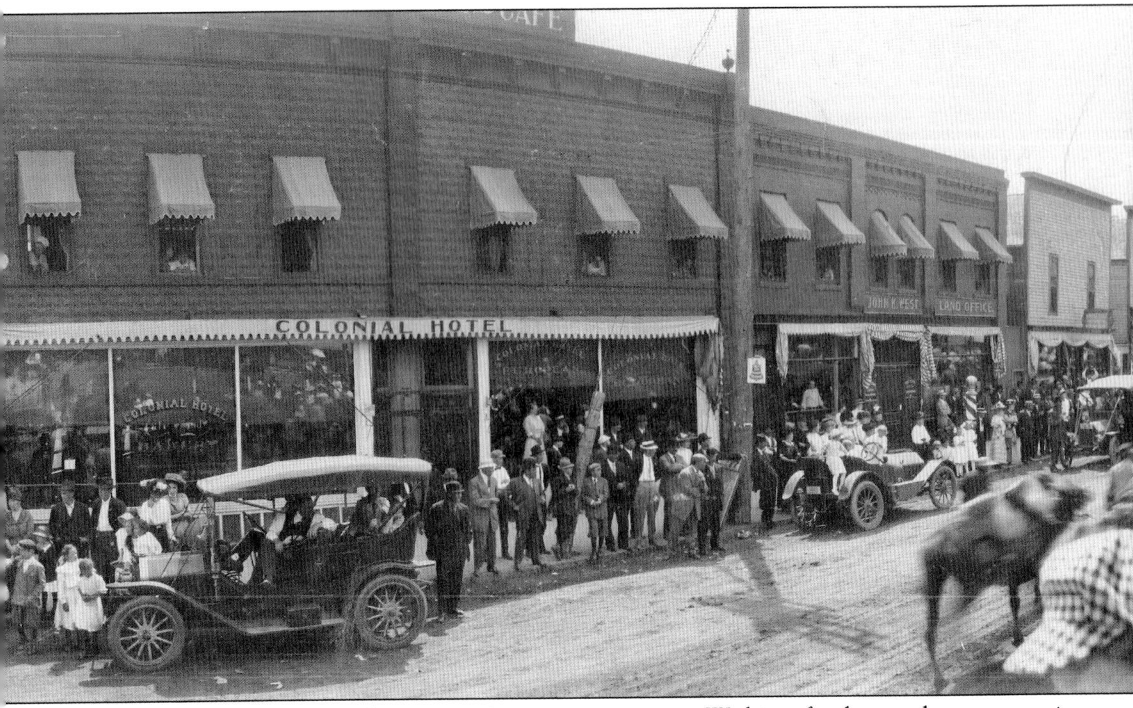

On June 24, 1912, the Gollmar Bros. Circus came to town. Within a few hours, they were setting up. Visitors were given the run of the grounds as they watched all the employees erect the tents and feed the animals. The grounds were probably visited by a few hundred people, many of them coming from surrounding villages. At 10 o'clock, the parade started, and every man, woman,

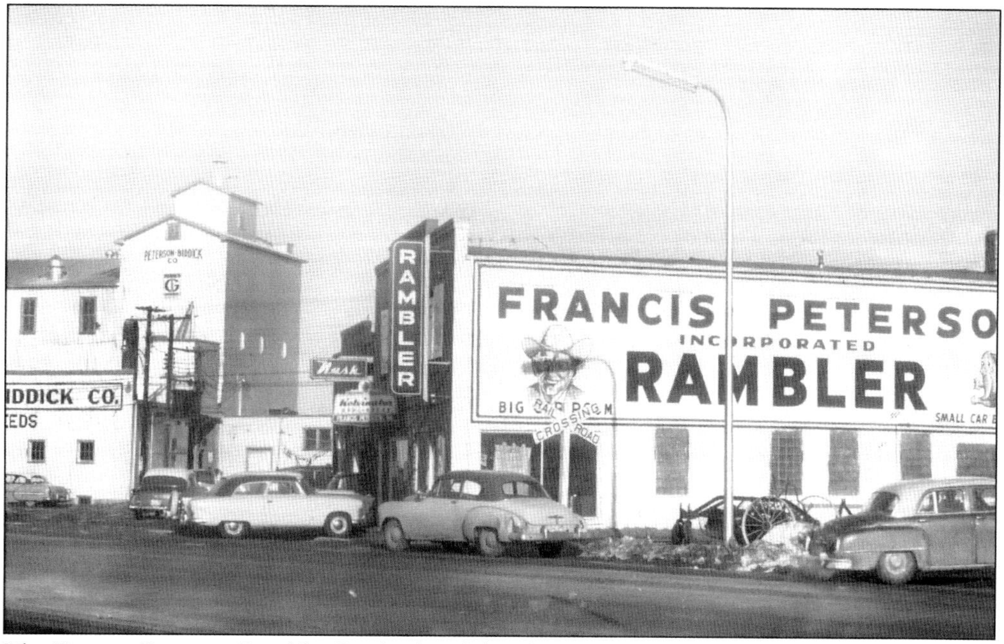

The Francis Peterson Rambler Dealership (above) was located at 819 Lincoln Avenue. They advertised the "smartest cars for town and travel," including the Rambler, Ambassador, and Metropolitan. Owned and operated by Alton Peterson, they remained in business until 1962. Morse Motors (below) was located at 714 Lake Avenue and erected by Charles E. Morse in 1917. In 1926, it was taken over by S.C. "Duke" Halvorson, who changed its name to the Detroit Lakes Motor Company. Beginning in 1931, the business was originally at two different locations on Washington Avenue before purchasing the former Morse Motors building in 1945, renaming it Kandt Motors. Milford Kandt owned the business for 42 years, starting as a part-time salesman in 1934 and working for his father. They began as a Chrysler-Plymouth dealership, but when they moved to Lake Avenue, they became associated with General Motors and began to sell Pontiacs.

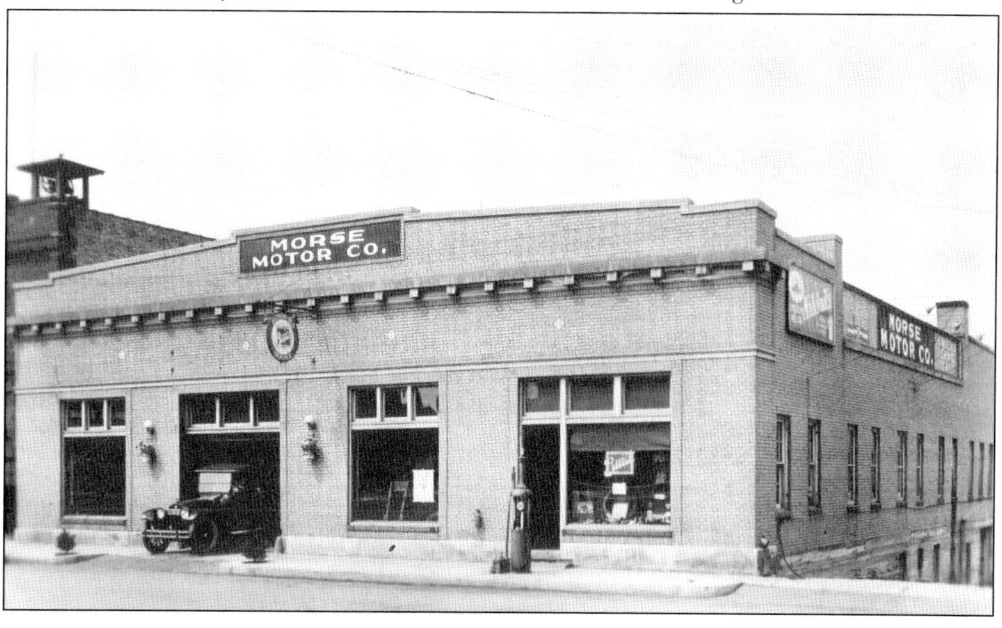

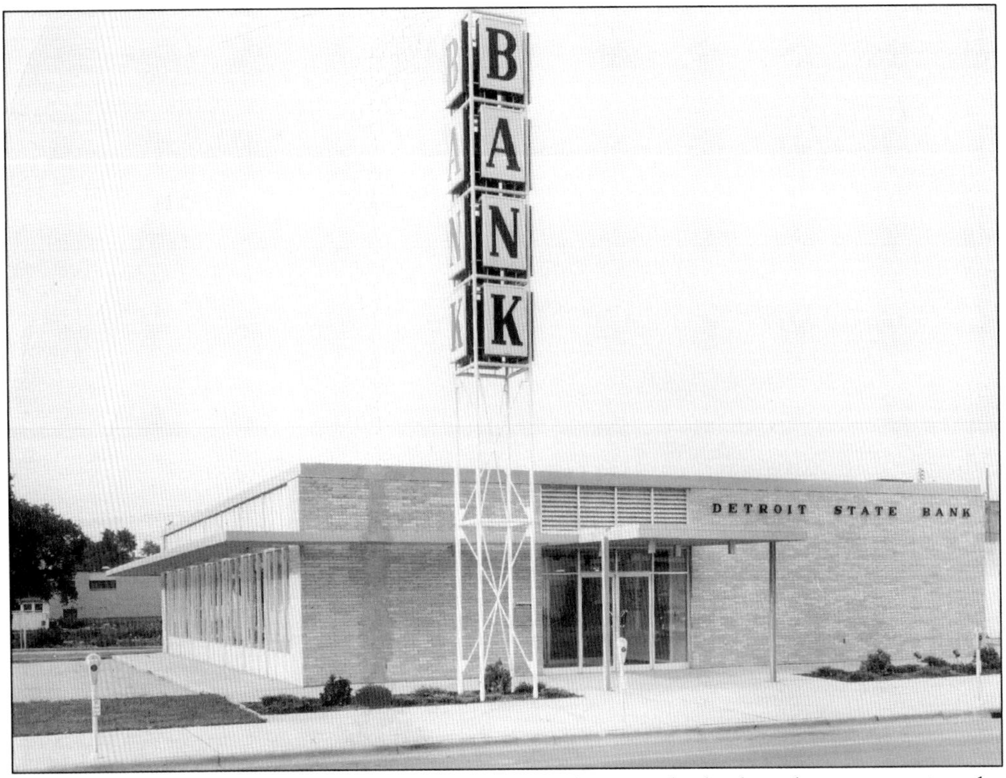

Many of the financial institutions in the Detroit Lakes area had a long history, serving the community for over 50 years. Detroit State Bank opened in 1919 on the corner of Washington and Pioneer Street, with an initial deposit of $62,040.53. During the Great Depression, it was at one time the only financial institution open for withdrawals. By 1960, the bank had constructed a new building at 115 Holmes Street, pictured above. The First National Bank remodeled their building at 717 Washington Avenue in 1961 with new exterior facing, brick on the first floor, and porcelain on the second floor. Floor space more than doubled from 2,200 to 5,400 square feet. In spring 1966, the bank purchased the buildings to the north and added a drive-up teller window, causing the Detroit Lakes Police Department, Ray Hale's Jewelry, and Mattson's Barber Shop to relocate. In 1994, First National Bank became Norwest Bank, and in 2000 they became Wells Fargo Bank.

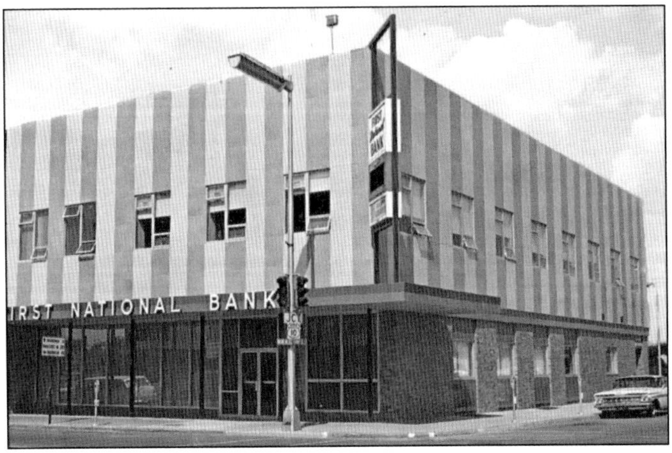

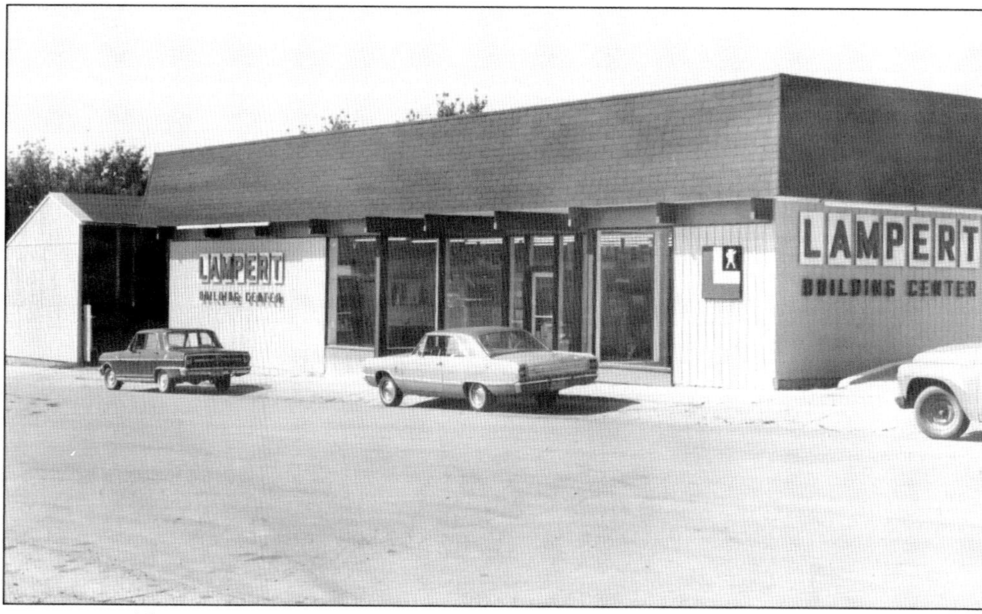

Lampert Building Center was located north of the Northern Pacific tracks at 114 Grant Street, now Mark's Electric. It was known as the Hanson-Hage Lumber Yard until 1943, when it was purchased by the Lampert's chain. The Lampert Lumber Company began when two brothers started a retail lumberyard at Wadena in the 1880s. In 1968, the building in Detroit Lakes was completely remodeled to include 2,500 square feet of sales rooms and offices. At this time, there were more than 60 branches of Lampert's in Minnesota, North Dakota, South Dakota, and Nebraska.

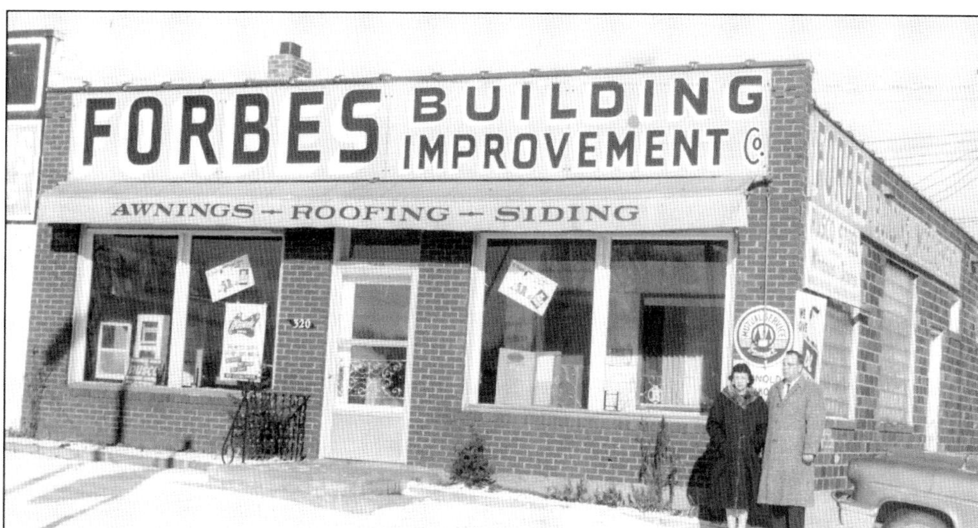

Forbes Building Improvements was owned by Sheldon and Dorothy Forbes and moved numerous times over its tenure in Detroit Lakes. In 1957, Forbes was located at 620 Davis Avenue, and by 1960 the business had moved to 320 Frazee Street. They moved again in 1973 to 714 Randolph Road, which was the last location for Forbes.

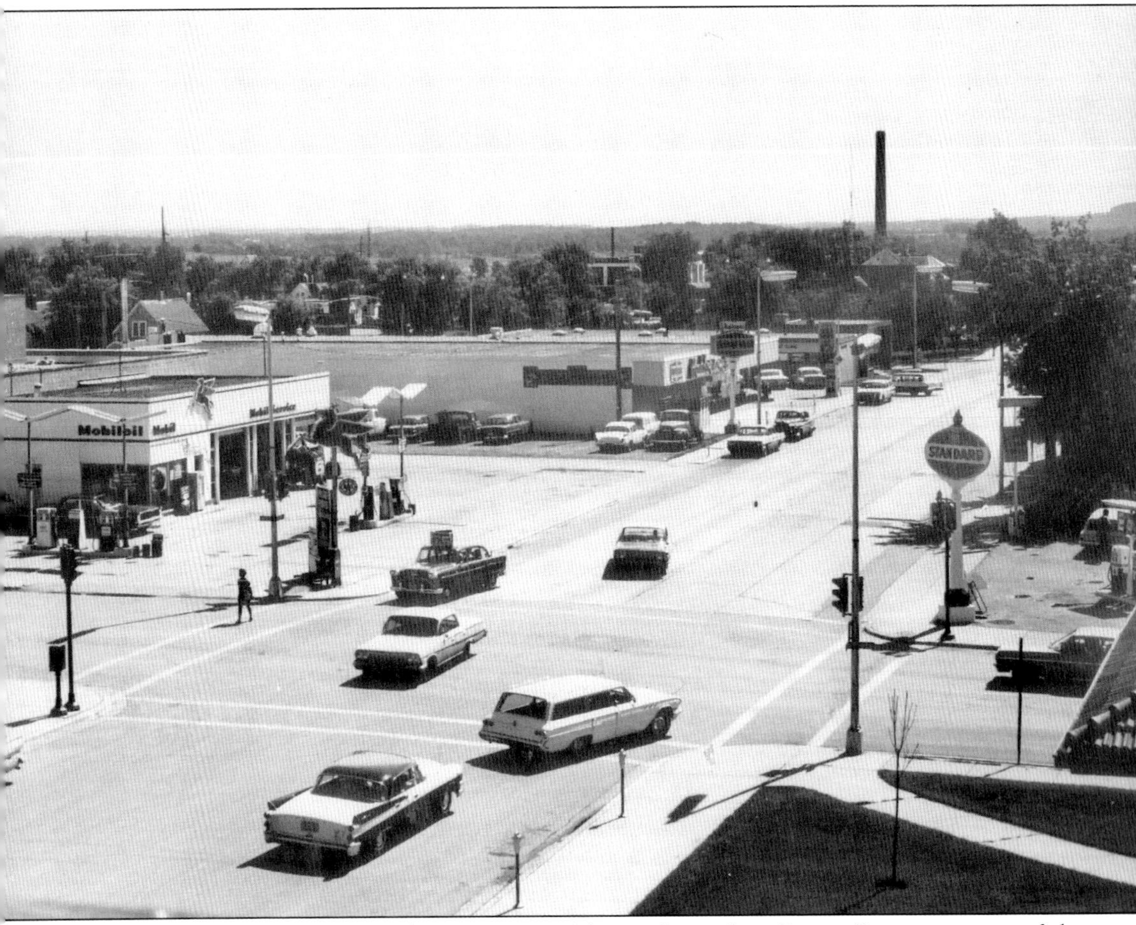

Opened in March 1960, Haldorson's Super Valu was located on Frazee Street, just east of the public library. Seen here in 1968 from the belfry of the Baptist Church, along with the Fingalson's Mobil and the Standard station, the store employed 15 people. Said to contain all the "modern facilities" available, Haldorson's featured in-store music, automatic checkouts, a complete housewares department, air-conditioning, a reach-in dairy case that "eliminated bending and squinting," refrigerated fruit and vegetable cases, and a large self-service meat department. James (Jim) Haldorson was the owner and had been in the meat and grocery business in Detroit Lakes since 1938, with the exception of three years when he served with the US Navy during World War II. The Super Valu retail chain had over 600 locations in 1960, serving over a million customers in eight Midwest states.

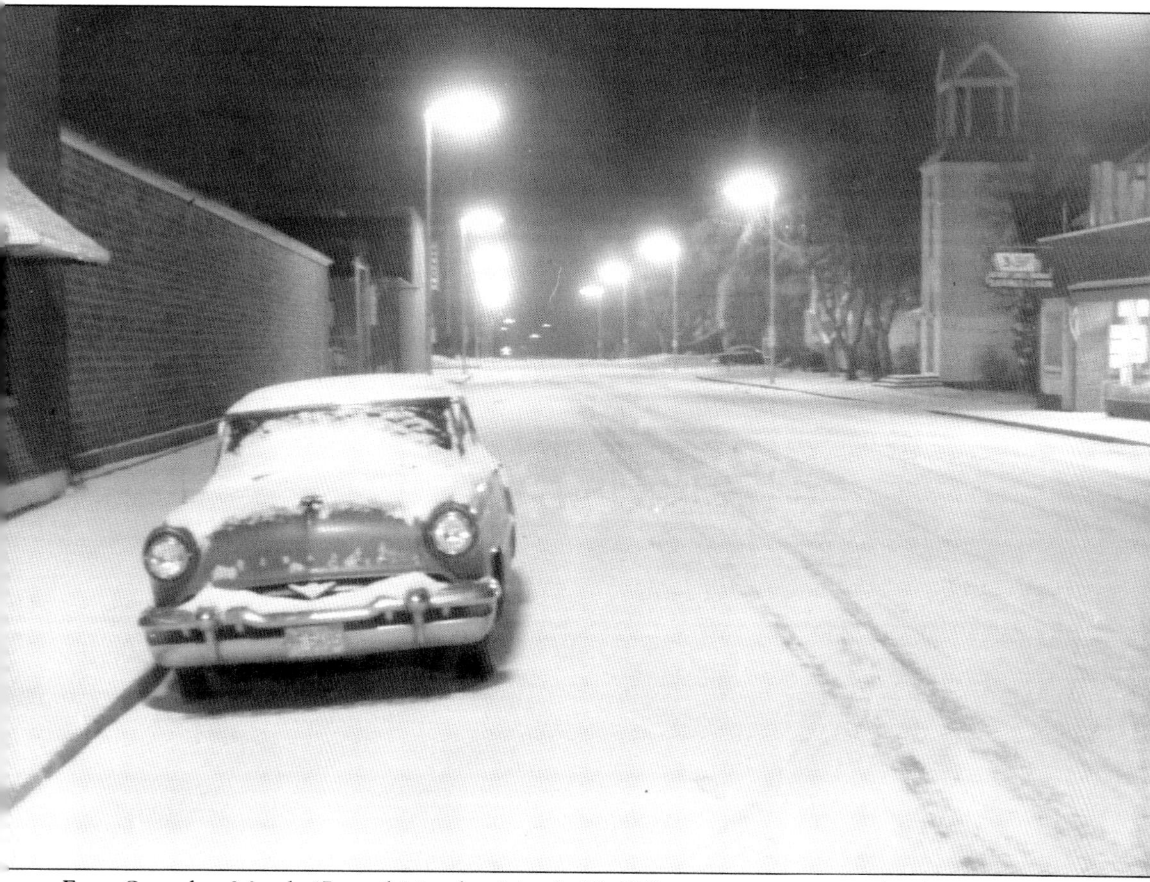

From Saturday, March 17 until Monday, March 19, 1951, a winter storm said to be the worst since the blizzard of 1941 came through Detroit Lakes. More than 500 travelers were stranded in town when 14 inches of snow fell over three days. Hundreds of these folks were on the road returning from the Minnesota State High School Basketball Tournament, including the teams from Felton, Ada, Bismark, Mahnomen, Warren, Fisher, and Oslo. People opened their homes to these stranded motorists after a call was sent out on WDAY from the Graystone Hotel, which was overtaken by requests for sleeping space. Winds up to 35 miles per hour, and temperatures ranging from one degree below zero to nearly 30 below, created havoc on the roads. The highways did not reopen until Tuesday, and the total snow for the winter of 1950 and 1951 was 87 inches, a new record for the Detroit Lakes area.

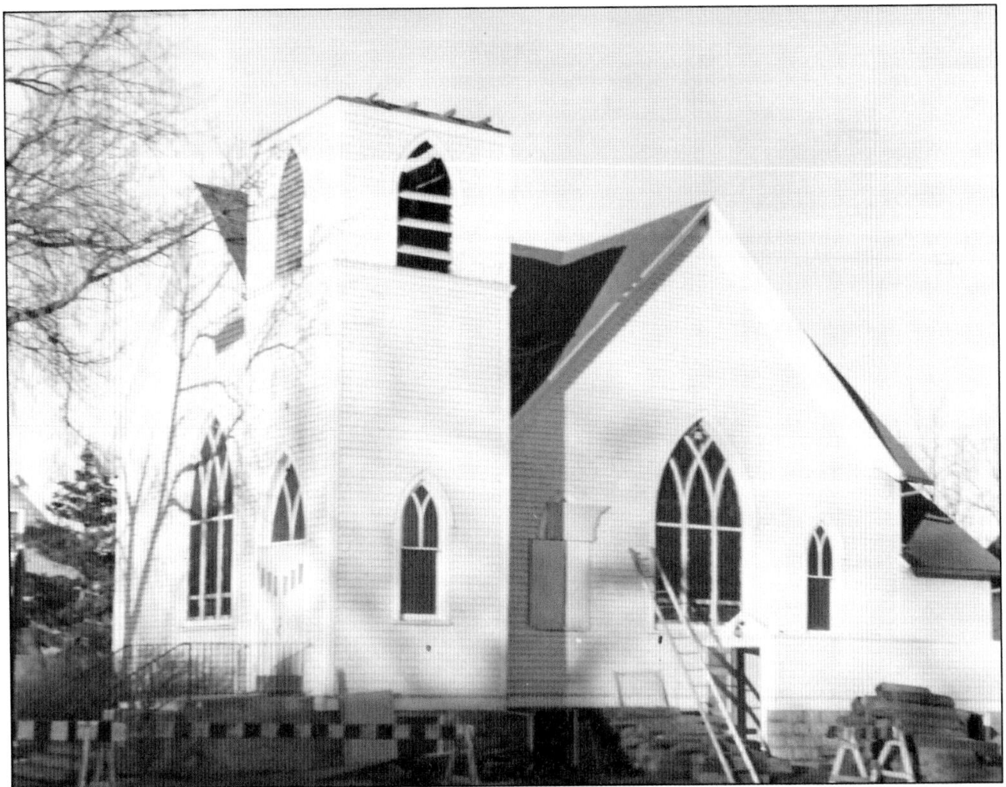

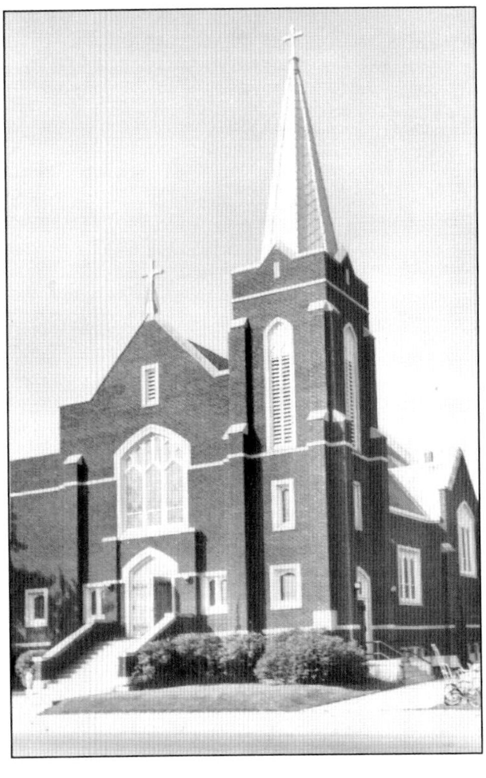

The congregation of Trinity Lutheran Church formed in 1871 as Upsala Lutheran Church, just north of Detroit. By 1897, Upsala, Lund Lutheran, and Swedlanda (Augustana) were sharing ministers. In that year, a centrally located unified parish in Detroit Lakes called Trinity Lutheran formed with members from each of the original congregations. Originally located at the corner of Washington Avenue and Grant Street in a building vacated by the Baptist congregation, Trinity moved in 1961 to its present location at 1401 Madison Avenue.

First Lutheran Church was formed by the merging of three churches in 1917 and became known as the Norwegian Lutheran Church of Detroit. In 1927, the name was changed to First Lutheran Church. In 1961, with the merger of three synods, it became part of the American Lutheran Church. The property at 912 Lake Avenue was purchased as a site for the new church in February 1921. In 1923, the new building was dedicated to seat 500 people. The Parish Education Building was added in 1954, and an extensive remodeling project improved the space in 1978.

Holy Rosary Catholic Church underwent a renovation in 1966, with ground breaking at the new site on August 15. Portions of the old structure, pictured on the right, were reused as a community hall for the Holy Rosary parish. In April 1967, the altar site and cornerstone of the new building were blessed, and in December of the same year, Bishop Lawrence Glenn of Crookston came to bless the three bells to be used in the church, including the original bell from the old tower. The bells, named Ana (dedicated in 1903 in memory of Anna Smith), Joseph, and Mary (donated by Nick and Myrtle Kappel in memory of Mary Coyle) were used to call people to worship. The new building had a capacity of 1,000 parishioners and a reconfigured main entrance to the church from Washington Avenue to Lake Avenue. The blessing and dedication were held May 19, 1968.

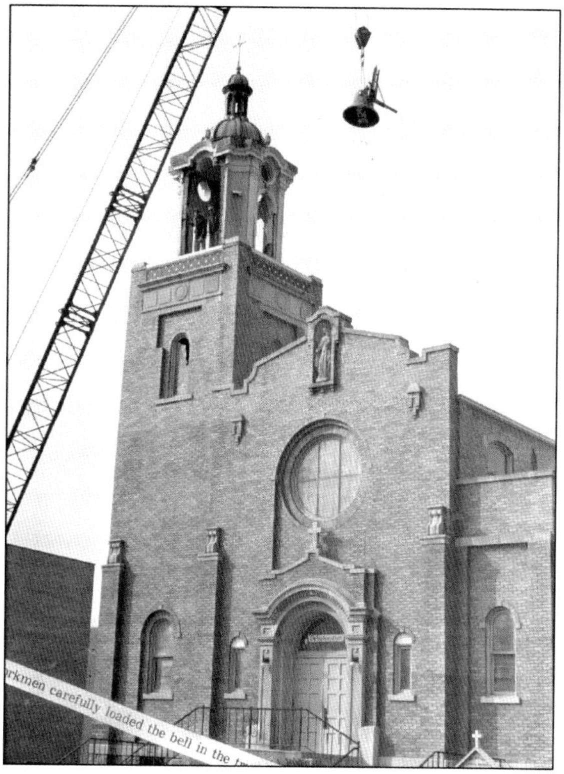

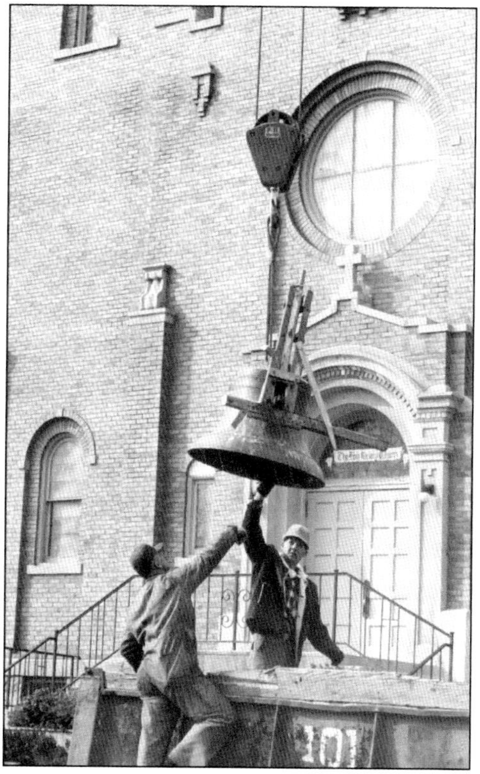

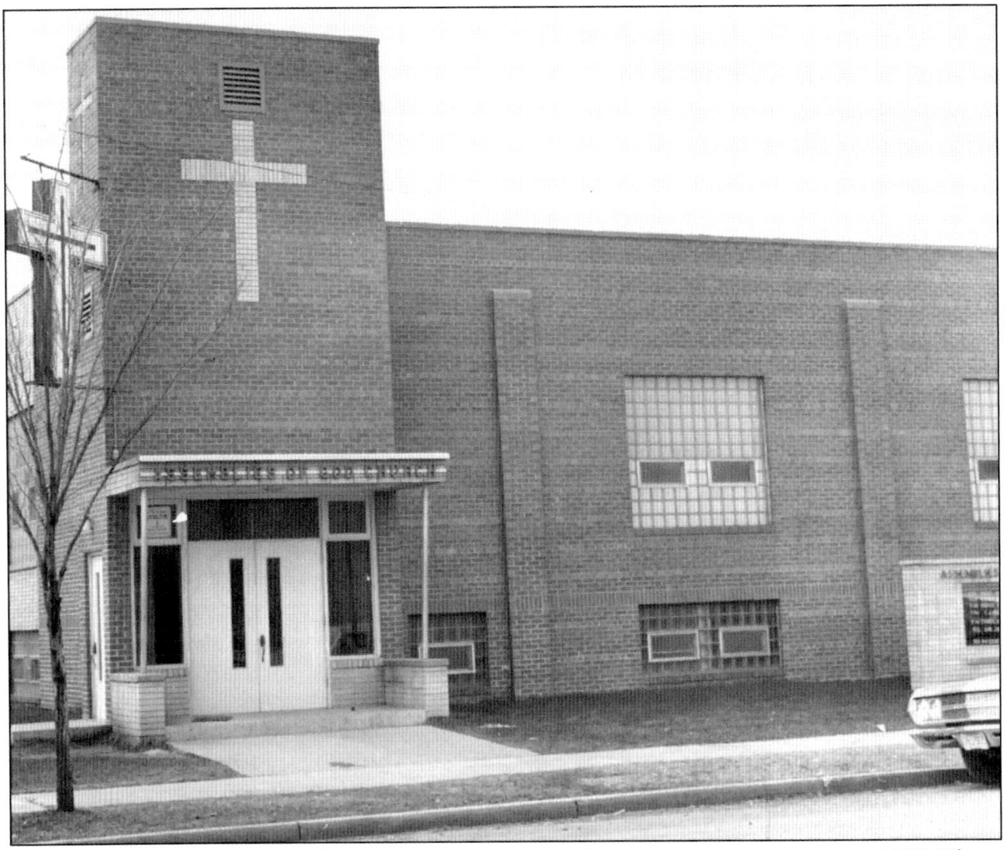

The Assemblies of God Church was started as a series of cottage prayer meetings in 1918. These home-based gatherings were moved to a permanent building in 1928 on north Rossman Avenue, now the Mount Olive Lutheran Church. In 1948, the congregation outgrew their building and purchased the lot at the corner of Summit Avenue and Front Street, with the cornerstone for the new structure being laid on November 25, 1948. On December 12, 1956, a furnace explosion in minus-five-degree weather caused the total loss of the building and contents of the Assemblies of God Church. Church services were temporarily held in the Lincoln School basement and later in the Nazarene Church basement while construction of a new church was underway. A larger building was erected on the same site and the cornerstone was laid in 1958.

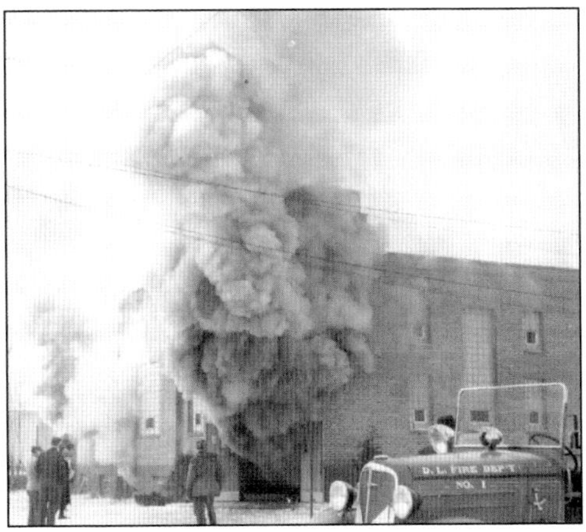

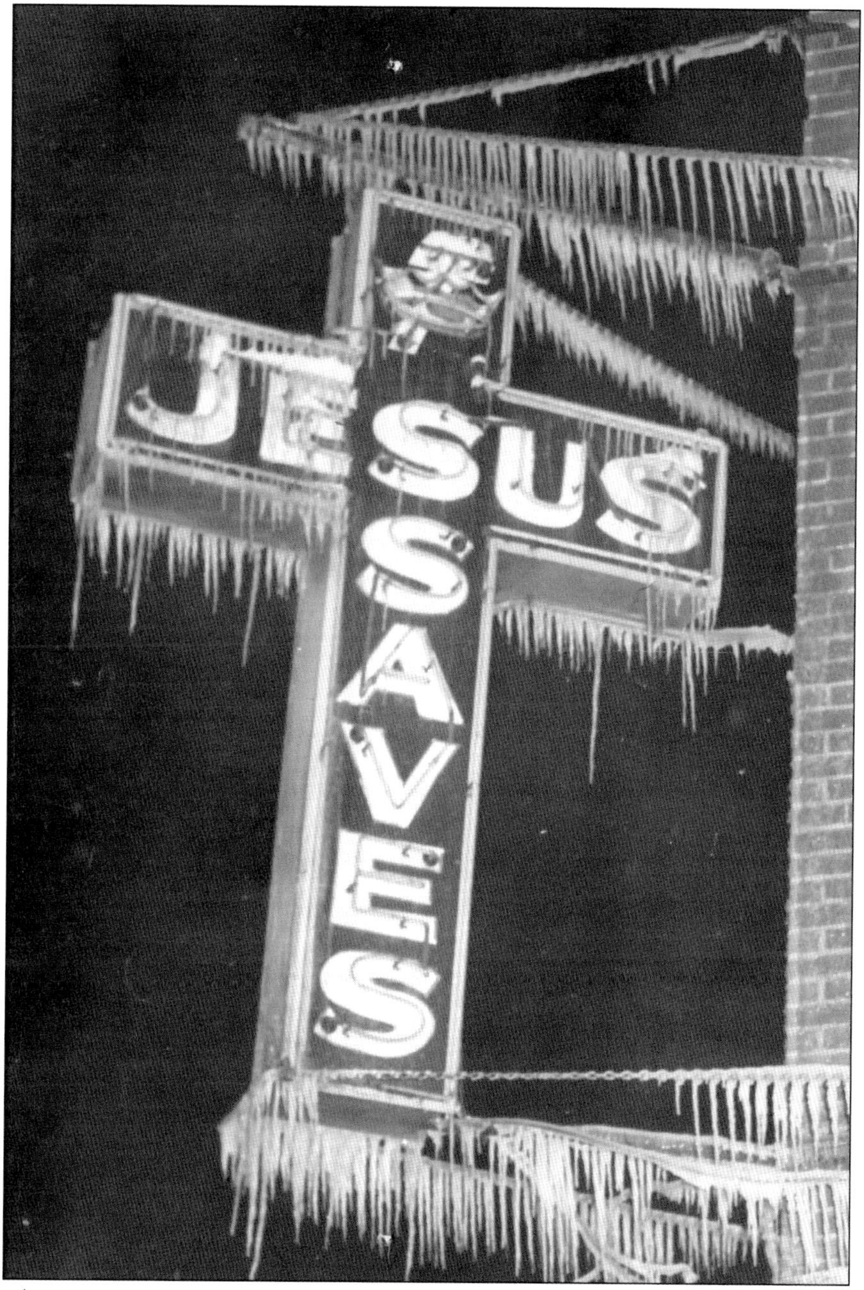

The Becker County Historical Society purchased the Assemblies of God Church building in 1988 and, with slight modification, moved it from its original site in the basement of the Becker County Courthouse to this new museum site. The focus on making the collection and archives more accessible to the public was accomplished in this building by creating a research library, writing grants to get copies of newspapers on microfilm beginning in 1872, building exhibits that showcased artifacts from all parts of the county, and welcoming new types of educational programming. This building, still in use today, has served both its congregation and its museum patrons well and continues to grow and evolve along with the history of Becker County and the city of Detroit Lakes.

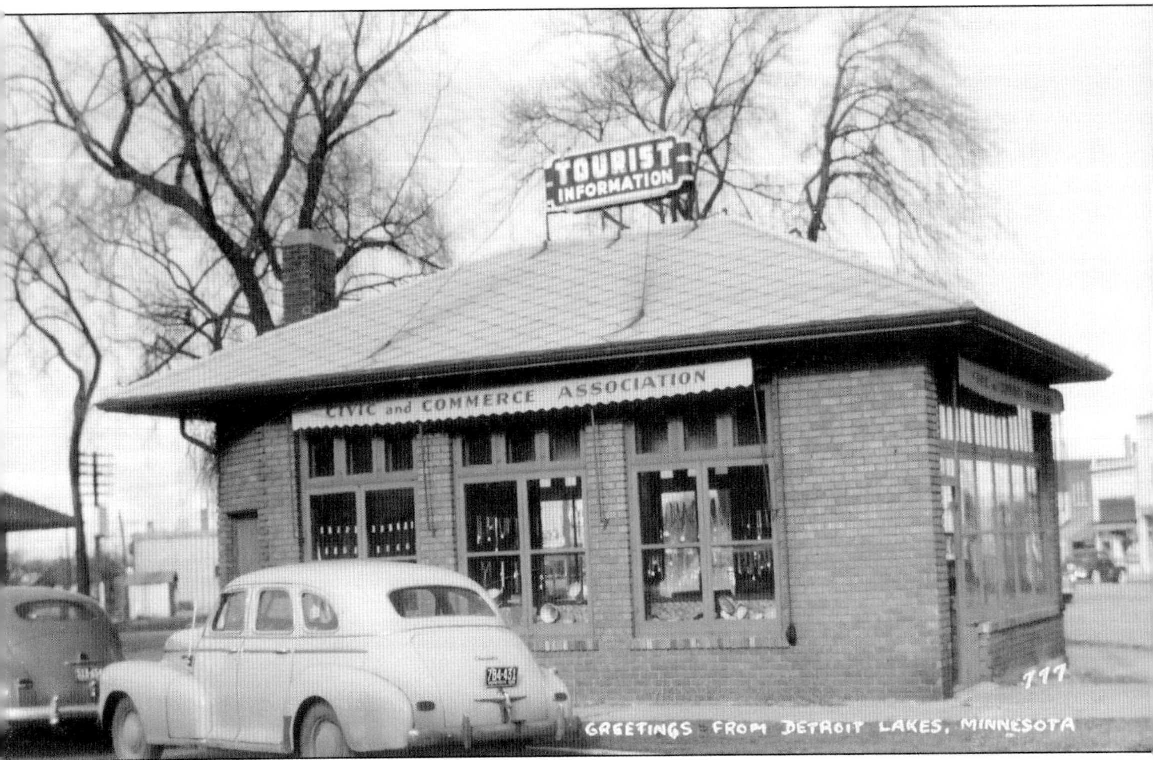

Formed as the Commercial Club in 1921 and renamed the Businessmen's Club and the Detroit Lakes Civic and Commerce Association, the Detroit Lakes Regional Chamber of Commerce has a long history of promoting local business and tourism in the region. Meeting in a variety of locations for some time, the chamber moved to 700 Washington Avenue in November 1936 after a visit to the office of Dan Nelson, secretary, on Pioneer Street, which was a triangular space three by four by five feet, with one chair and a table only about 8 by 18 inches. The new building, formerly the Detroit Floral Company, served the chamber until October 2005, when construction began at the current location at 700 Summit Avenue. Like the businesses it supports, the chamber of commerce has gone through many changes. One suggested plan in 1955 was to construct a new building, built to resemble a giant northern pike that would be 200 by 36 feet. The proposed structure, designed by Ernest Koncikson of Erskine, would house the chamber offices, a game fish aquarium, a wildlife museum, public restrooms, and a reception room. Since no printed results of this meeting exist and the building was not constructed, it can be assumed that it was not met with approval.

Six

Keeping History Alive
1976–Present

In the 1980s, economic challenges struck Detroit Lakes. Approximately 500 people left the city in search of work, and this left local businesses struggling to survive. Many well-established retailers, such as the Blanding Department Store, closed during this time. The Washington Square Mall, situated on the west side of the 700 block of Washington Avenue, changed the style of downtown commerce. Coast-to-Coast Hardware, now Beug's Ace Hardware, moved across the street so that the buildings attached to the mall could be opened from both sides. The industrial park off of Randolph Road grew, bringing new economic opportunity to the city, such as Lakeshirts, established in 1984. As a new base of industry grew, so did the population. By 2000, the city boasted 7,348 residents, a 10 percent increase from 10 years prior. Today, Detroit Lakes sits at 8,569 people.

In 2008, the focus of the city shifted when Minnesota Highway 10, which had formerly gone through the downtown corridor of Washington Avenue, was rerouted to bypass the city. This led to the loss of the earliest street, Pioneer, which had been the hub of the city for more than 100 years. As the citizens adjusted to this new layout, business developments moved west to the outskirts of the city to make space for large chain retailers. City officials have recently responded by working on the development of the central corridor, with improvements being made to Washington Avenue to make it more pedestrian friendly and improve the curb appeal. A new development along Highway 10 is underway that will provide opportunity for more downtown business. The Pavilion has been remodeled and is once again a center point for community activity. The Becker County Fair continues to endure, having just celebrated its 120th year. Tourism thrives. WE Fest, a country music festival established on the east side of Minnesota State Highway 59, is booming, bringing in approximately 10,000 to 15,000 visitors each summer.

As it moves into a new decade, Detroit Lakes and its citizens are optimistic for the future. Its history is alive and its future is limitless. The small settlement once called "Swamp Town" has become a vibrant, bustling city that its pioneers would be proud to call home.

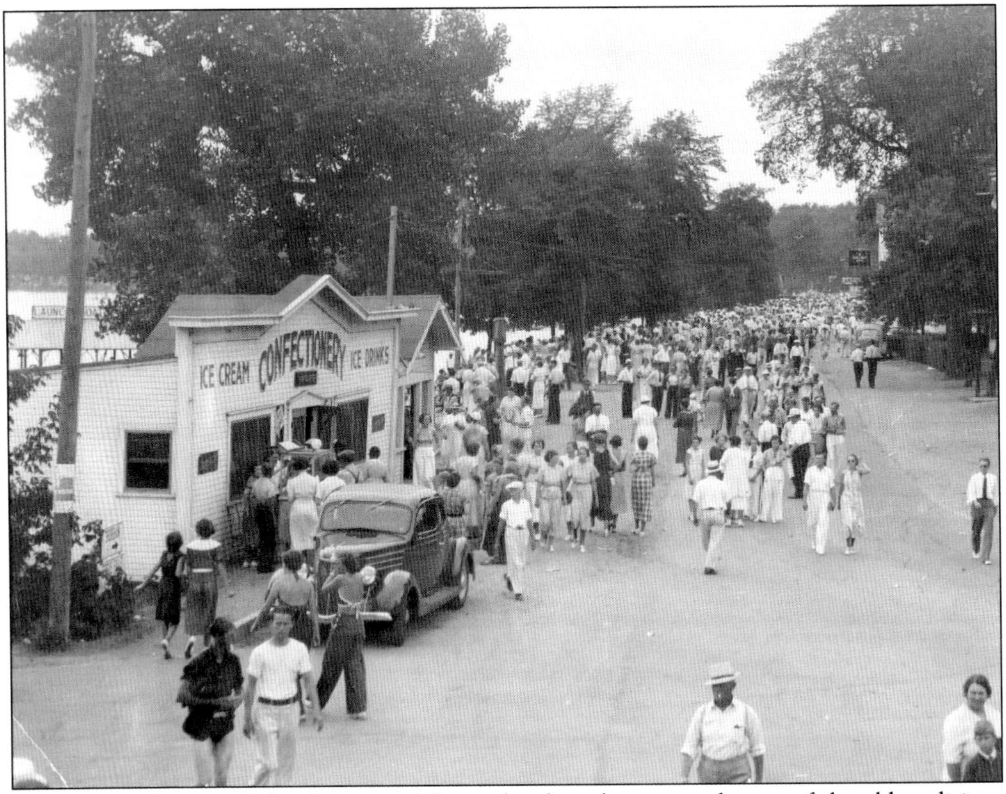

As the city of Detroit Lakes has moved forward, it has also retained some of the old traditions and celebrations. Seen here in 1936, the south end of Washington Avenue is still the hotspot for lake activities. The folks in the photograph above are celebrating the Northwest Water Carnival, which in 2011 marked its 76th year. The confectionery building has since been razed, and J&K Marine stands in its place (below). Today, kayaks, canoes, paddleboats, wave runners, and boats can be rented from J&K and provide a chance for visitors to get out and onto the water. The public swimming beach sits adjacent to the dock and has provided hours of entertainment for the public for generations.

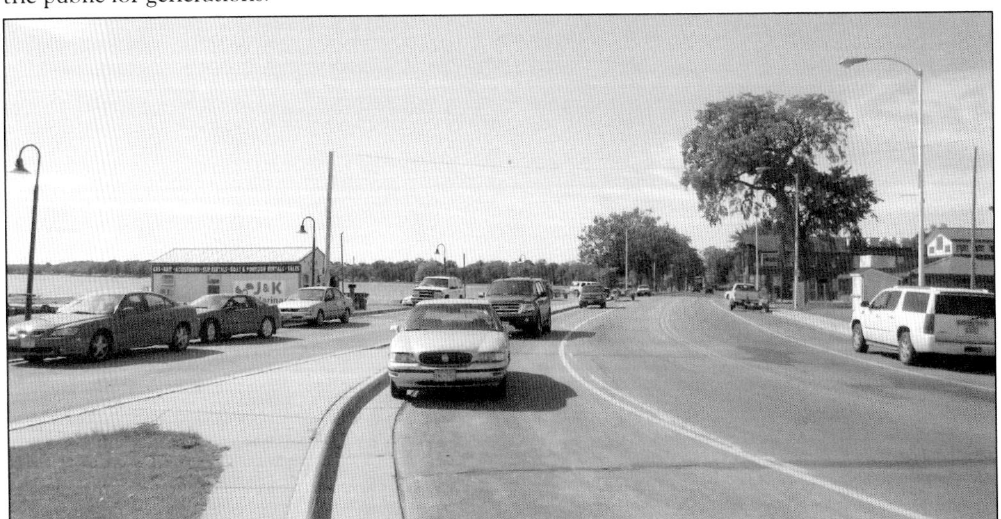

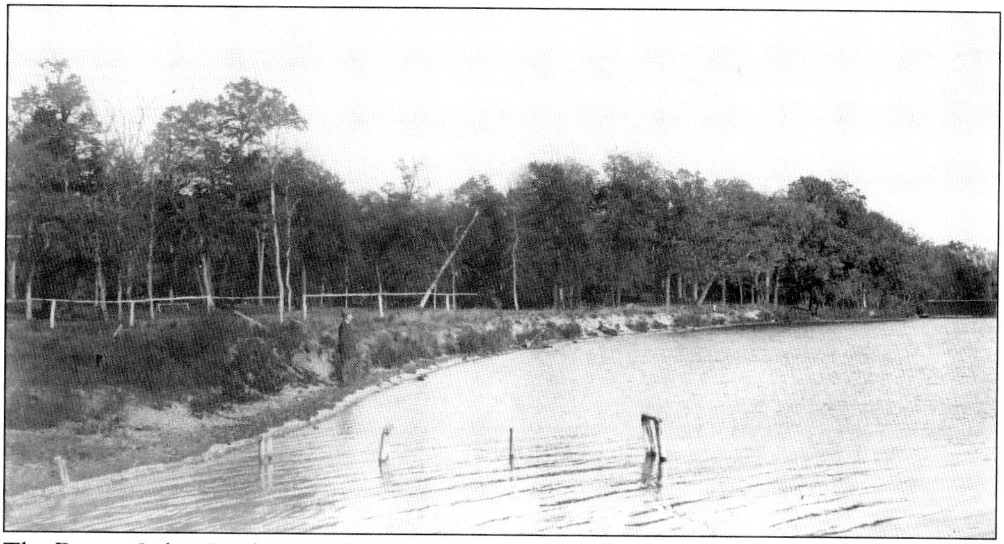

The Detroit Lakes Pavilion, built in 1915, has long served as a gathering space for the city of Detroit Lakes. Music and dances were the most popular activities at the building, but the original lease signed by a group of six young men (H.A. Baker, R.B. Rathbun, C.A. Baker, J.L. Pryor, A.A. Baker, and Fred Sanders) required that the building also provide park concessions, refreshment stands, and amusement attractions, but not ballgames. The renters, who paid $500 per year, were required to enclose the pavilion verandas with glass windows and provide space for public meetings, which were free except on the Fourth of July. They also were required to give one week free during the month of September, used for the Becker County Agricultural Society. Today, the Pavilion, which has been recently remodeled by the Detroit Lakes Area Builders Association, is still a busy space for weddings, the Water Carnival, and Park Fest.

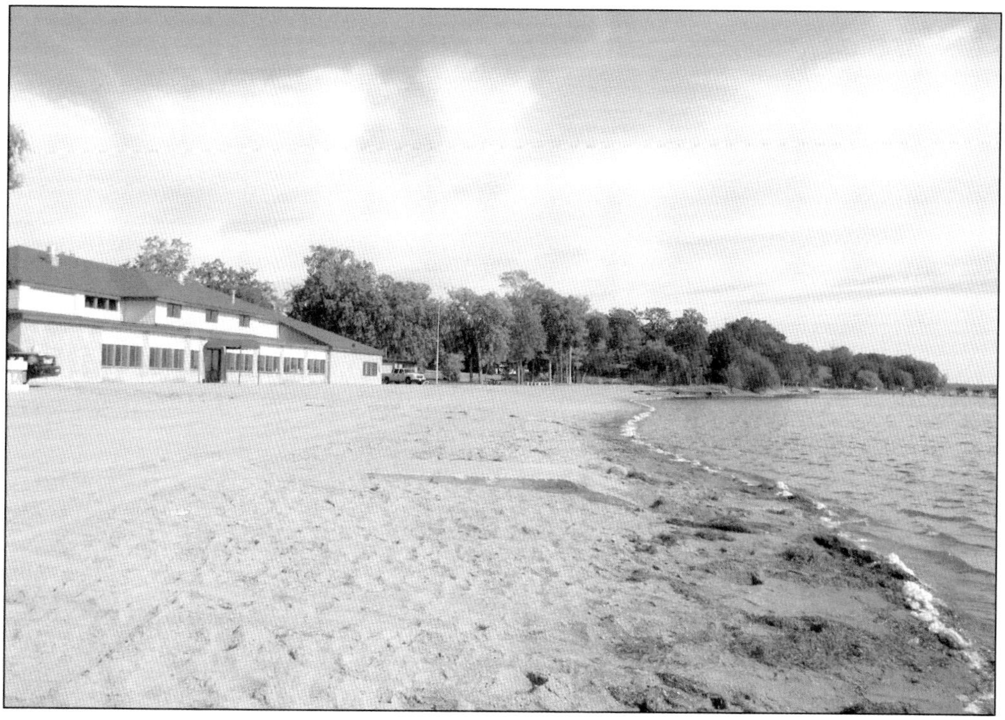

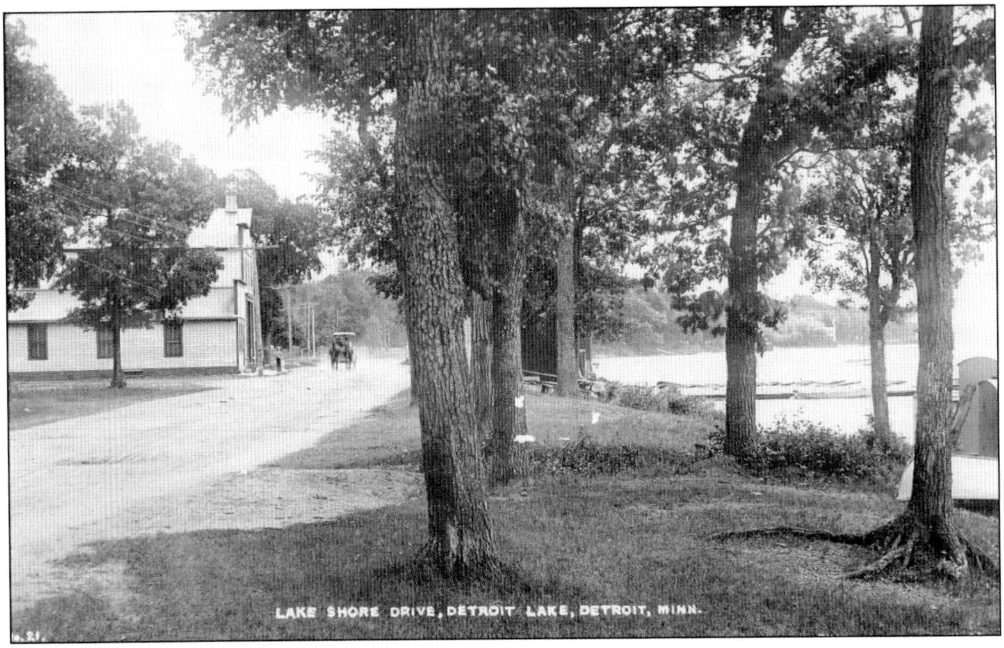

Lake Shore Drive developed from a small, rutted wagon trail to a well-maintained street by the 1920s. Early in its history, this street served the fur traders and American Indian residents that came to the lakeshore for fishing and water. As time went on, Washington and Summit Avenues were extended to the lakeshore and the city began to expand its residential neighborhoods from Frazee Street south. Lakeside Tavern, the white building seen in the early photograph above, is the oldest continuously operating business in Detroit Lakes, established in 1891 and still going strong today. Lake Shore Drive bustles today with both homes and businesses, providing a scenic drive for visitors and a gathering area for residents during events, such as the Fourth of July fireworks over the lake and the Polar Plunge during Polar Fest.

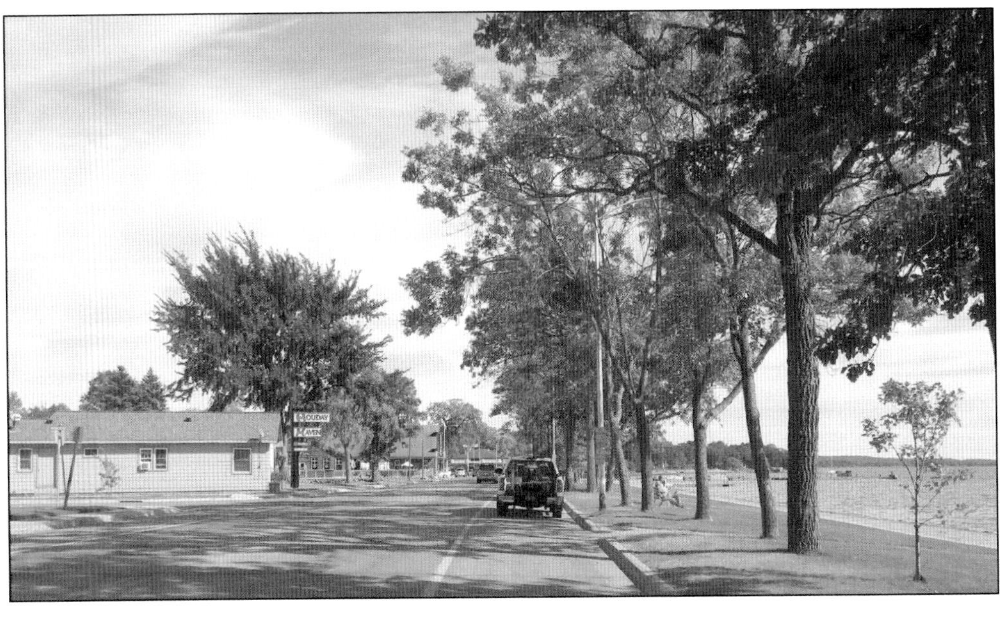

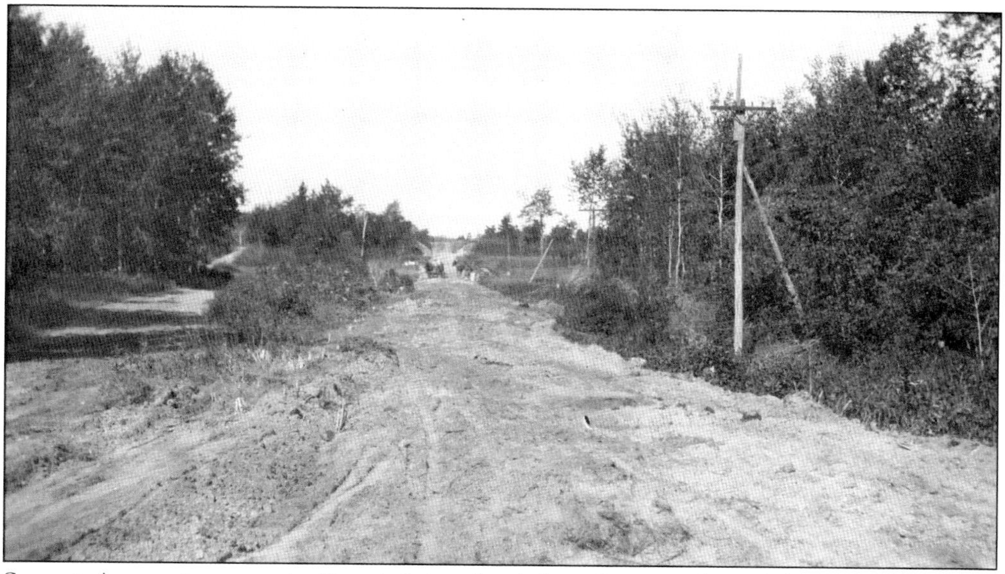

Summit Avenue is a street in Detroit Lakes that is literally a trip through history. Some of the oldest homes in the city sit on this stretch of road, which extends from the lakeshore to the new Minnesota State Highway 10 bypass. Originally created (above, under construction) for access to the lake and as a site for the Chautauqua educational gatherings, Summit remains the center of culture today. On the north end are the Detroit Lakes Cultural and Community Center, home to the Historic Holmes Theater and situated in a building that was the Holmes School, built in 1895. Its neighbor is the Becker County Museum, home to the Becker County Historical Society and Heart O'Lakes Genealogical Society. On the south end, seen below, one finds the cultural icon of Zorbaz, a pizzeria that developed during the 1960s and has now grown to include live music and more than 10 locations nationwide.

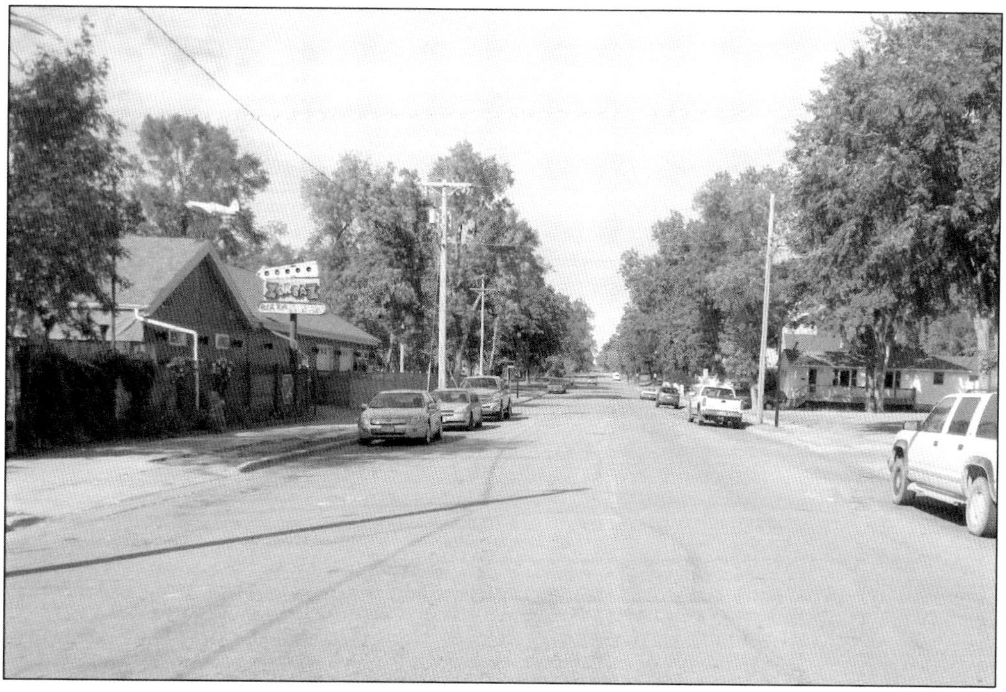

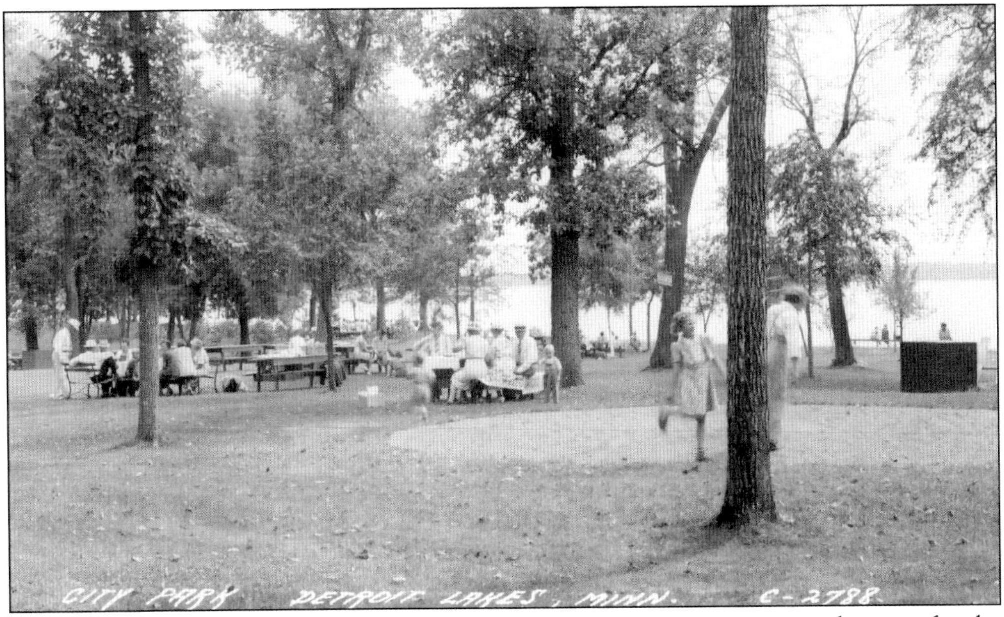

The Detroit Lakes City Park developed in the early 20th century as a natural retreat for the residents of the area. Purchased piece by piece and developed along with the Pavilion, the city park was host to a variety of activities. A band shell was built along with picnic shelters and charcoal grills. Music and festivals filled the space over the summer months. As time went by, the band shell was torn down and the park became instead a hangout spot for the children of the city, with a waterslide and log ride next to the swimming beach. When the Pavilion was recently remodeled, the band shell was also rebuilt, and Tuesdays in the Park brought live outdoor music back to the public. Vendor events, such as Art in the Park and the Detroit Lakes Area Farmers Market, take place in the Detroit Lakes City Park and Peoples Park down the street. The Water Carnival, Fourth of July, and Park Fest also fill the grounds with people and activities.

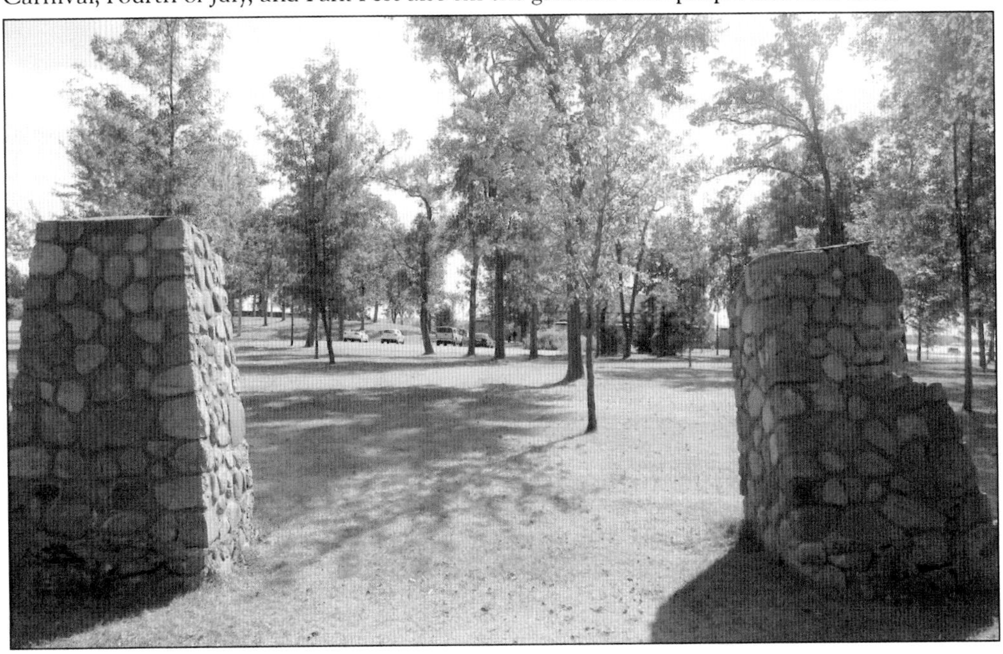

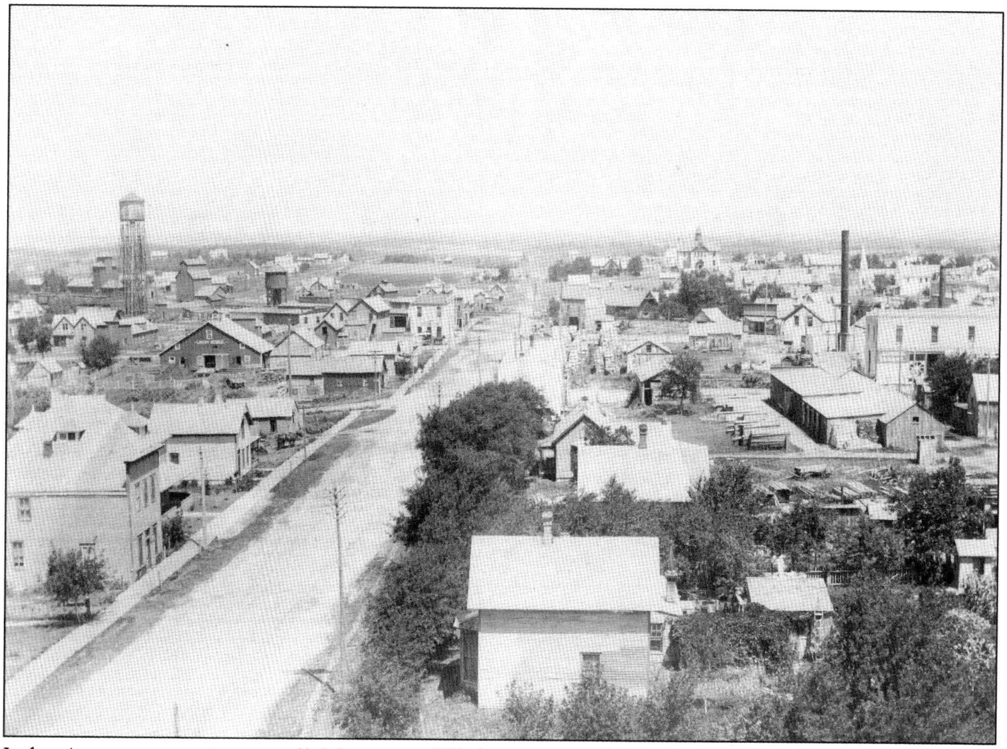

Lake Avenue, running parallel between Washington and Summit Avenues, has served as the civic center of Detroit Lakes since 1884. Seen in the above photograph from the tower of the original courthouse in 1903, the street was originally home to the city hall, fire department, courthouse, and county jail. The courthouse, first opened in 1885, was the tallest building in the city and provided an excellent bird's-eye view. In 1942, a new courthouse was constructed in the Art Deco style. In 1945, the old building was condemned and torn down. Within the last five years, Becker County has remodeled the courthouse and added offices and courtrooms. The Department of Motor Vehicles moved to this location, and the Becker County Museum moved out of the basement and into a building on Summit Avenue.

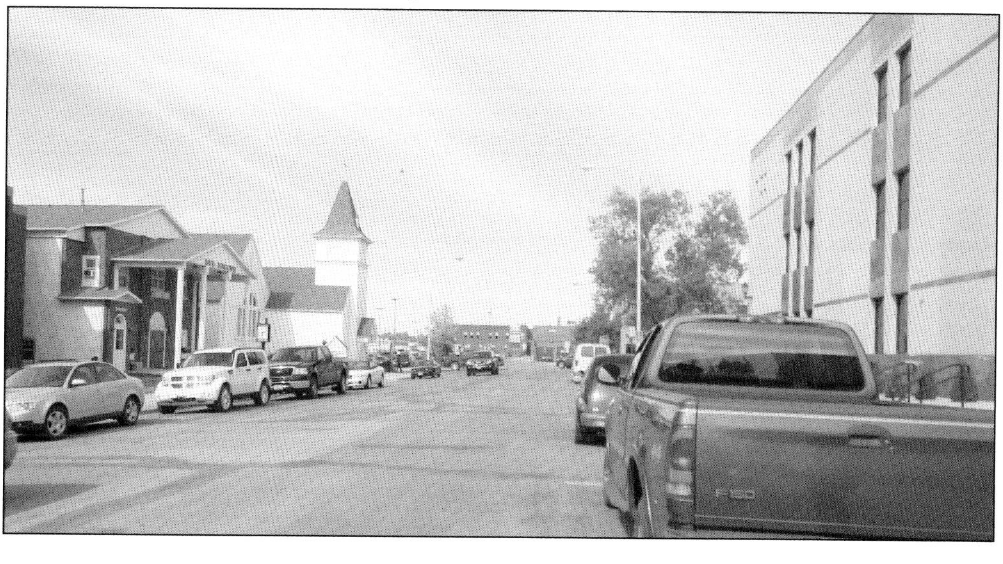

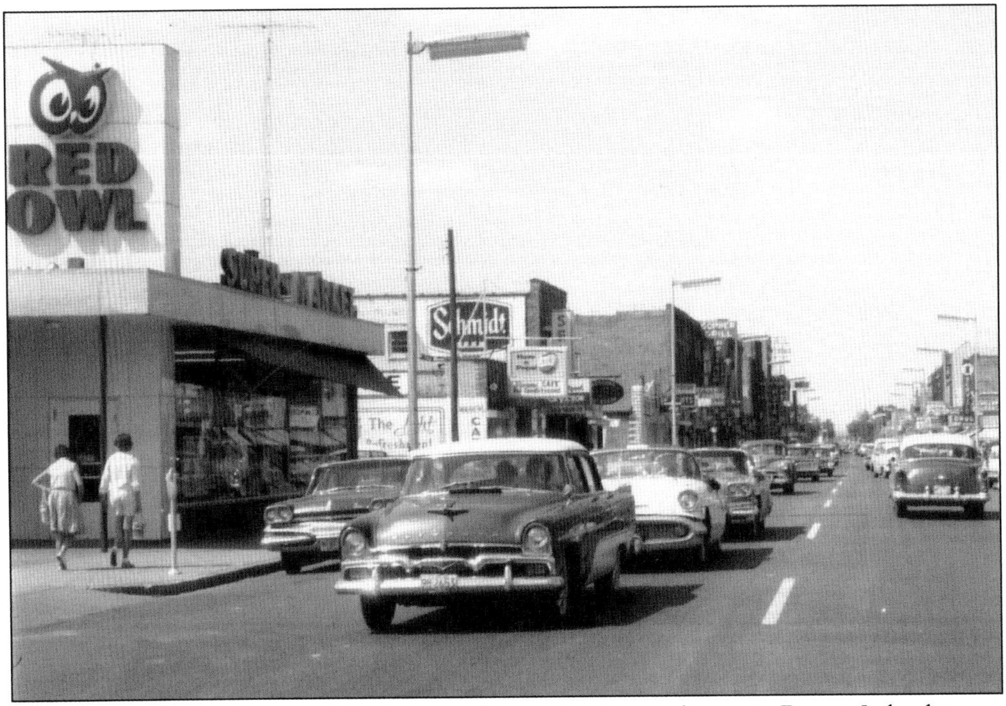

The corner of Frazee Street and Washington Avenue has been a fixture in Detroit Lakes history. In the early years, it stood at the edge of town with the "wilds of Detroit" still existing to the south. In the 1880s, the Hotel Minnesota, a grand two story wooden structure with more than 100 rooms, became a landmark of the city. In 1915, this structure burned to the ground and the Graystone Hotel, on Washington and Pioneer Street, grew up to replace it. Various businesses later sat in this spot including the Red Owl, which opened in its new location here in 1937. Today, Lakes Sport Shop fills the space and provides service to the region for all its outdoor and active lifestyle needs.

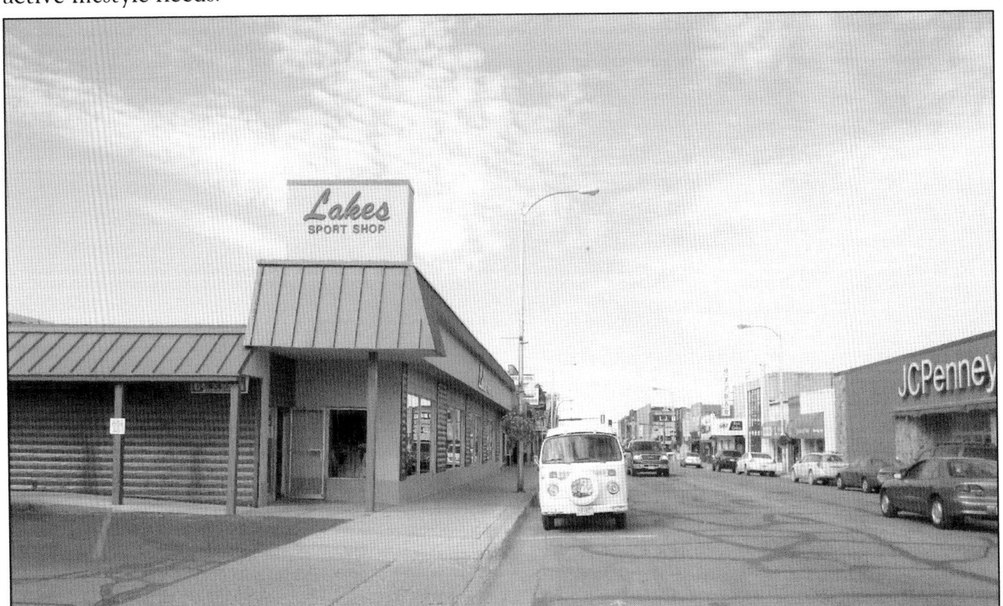

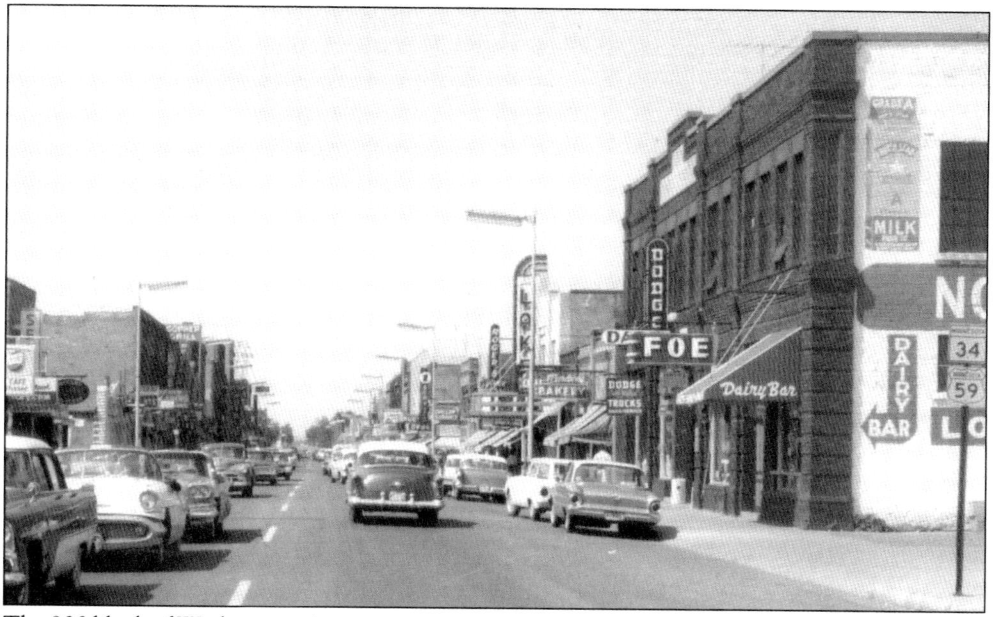

The 900 block of Washington Avenue remains a central business district today. In the photographs seen here, you can see changes that have occurred over the years, with the FOE (Eagles Club) now replaced by J.C. Penney, which originally sat at the north end of the 800 block. The Lakes Theater building, now vacant, was most recently the 917 Club. The Gopher Grill now serves the public as the Main Street Café, one of the few buildings to maintain its original neon sign. Washington Avenue used to serve as Highway 59, 34, and 10, all of which are now diverted around the core of city business. This created an interesting dynamic with one road serving as a county, city, and state entity.

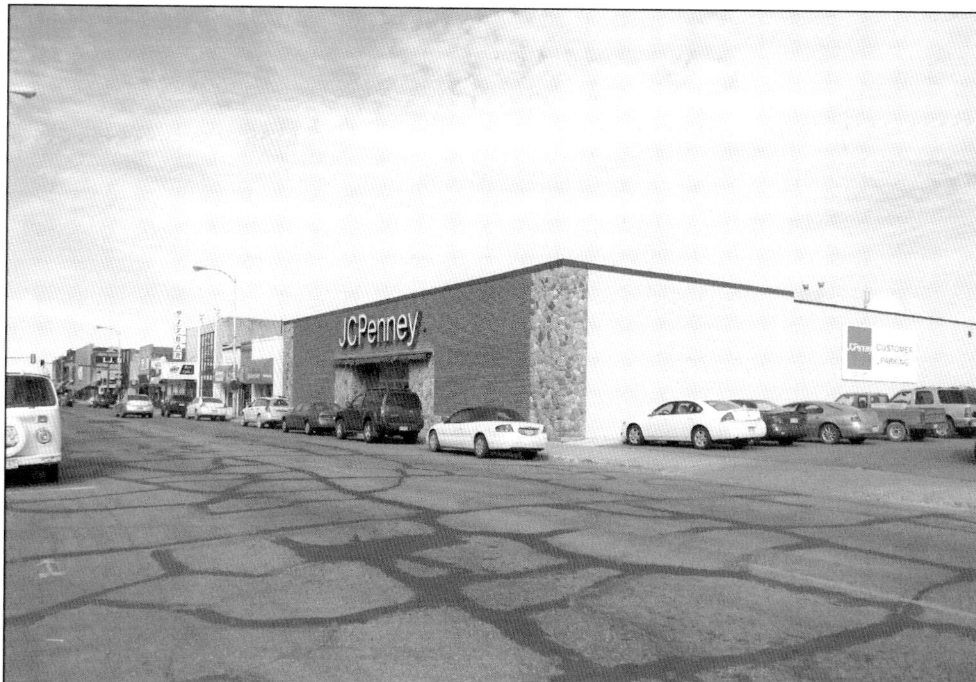

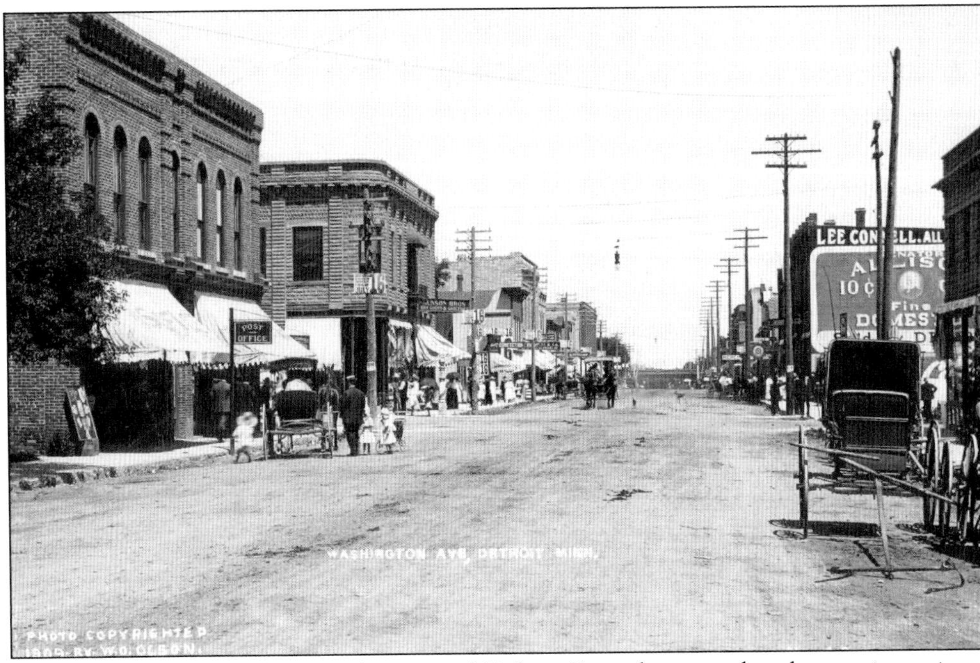

The intersection of Washington Avenue and Holmes Street has served as the crossing point of commerce and civic units in Detroit Lakes for more than 100 years. Seen above, the building that now houses the Main Street Café was once the city and county office building that also included the post office. Civic offices later moved to Lake Avenue, which was the site of the courthouse, town hall, fire department, and post office, pictured here in its fifth location. The Irish Block, named for Jeff Irish, an attorney in the city, featured a curved-corner brick building that later became Schaffer's Ready-to-Wear. This building burned and was replaced by the Washington Square Mall.

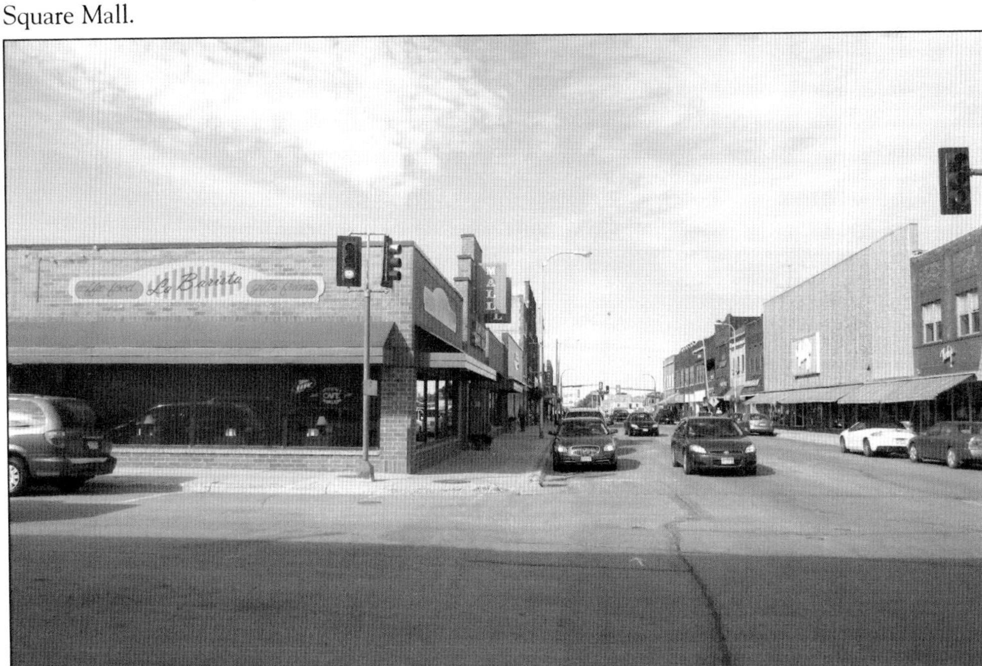

The 800 block of Washington Avenue has, without question, been the heart of the downtown business district throughout the history of Detroit Lakes. Businesses like Schaffer's Ready-to-Wear have become part of the Washington Square Mall. Today, La Barista, a coffee shop owned and operated by Brooke and Courtney Wenzel, occupies this corner. Other former businesses on this block included Diamonds, the McCarthy Hotel, and Mayerson's Clothing. On the east side of the block, the L.J. Norby Company remains, expanding several times over its 105-year history. Originally located in the Teague Block as a Blanding-Norby partnership, the company moved to its present location in 1906 and continues there today.

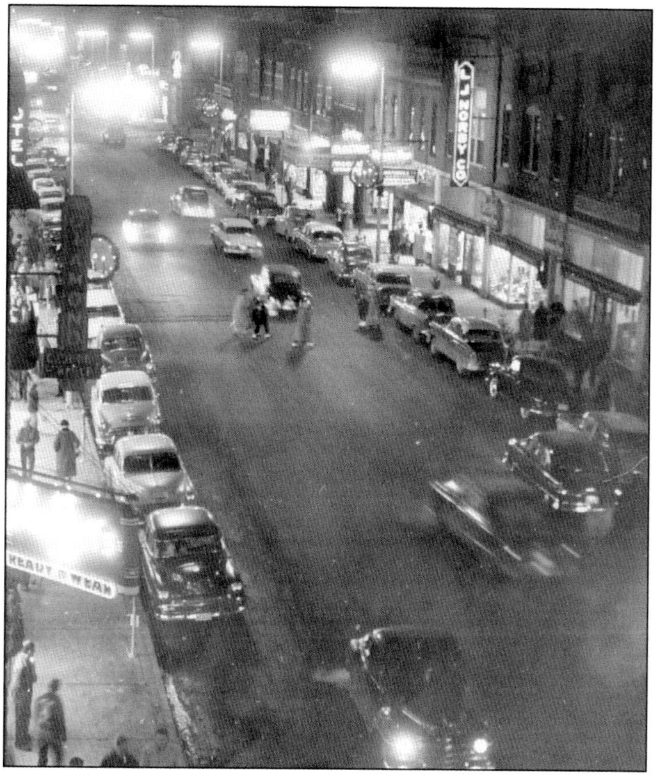

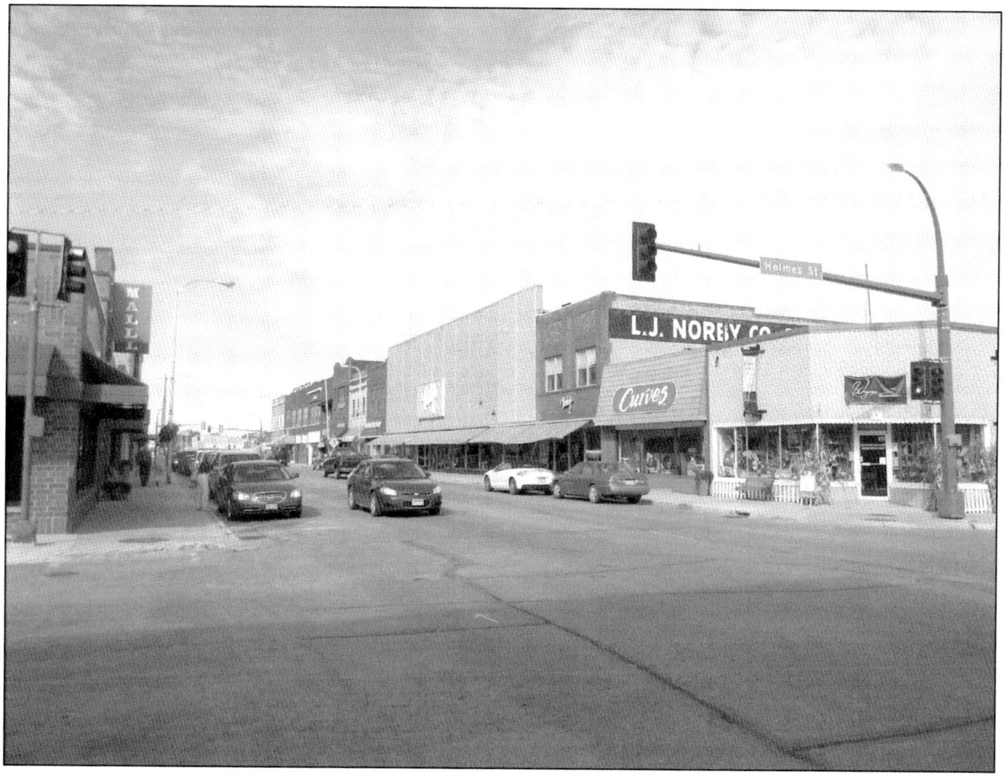

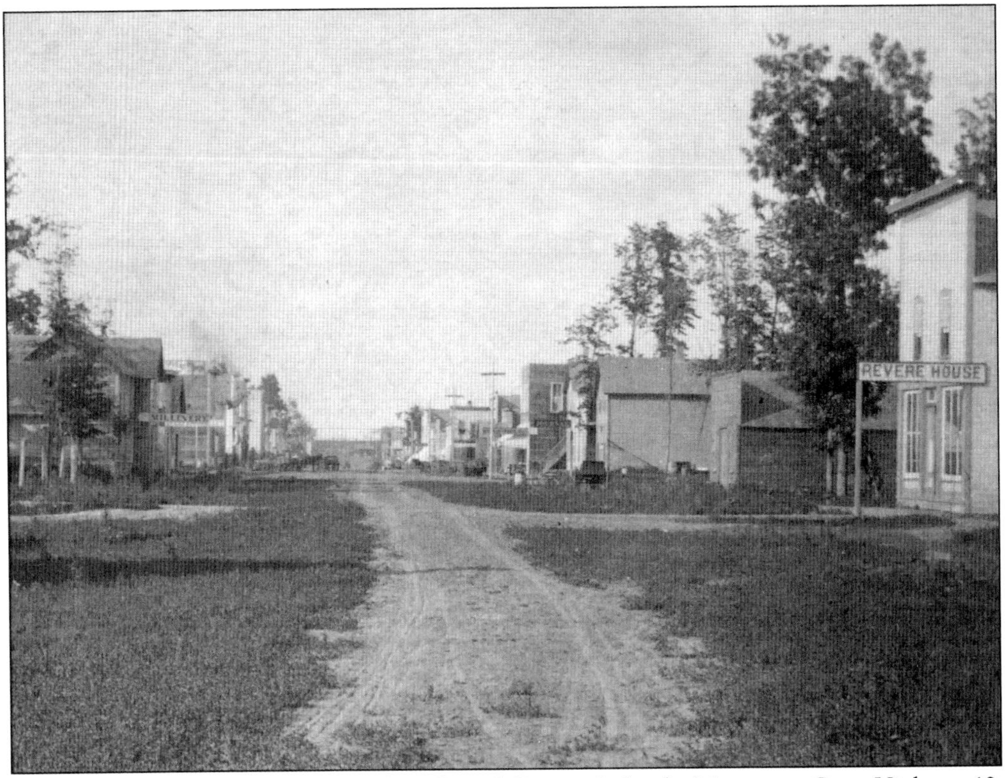

Main Street, now split between north and south Detroit Lakes by Minnesota State Highway 10, was once a bustling commerce district in the city's history. Stores, blacksmith shops, and hotels, like the Revere House seen here, were located within a few blocks of the Soo Line Railroad tracks. As industry shifted, Main Street changed as well. Residential homes sprouted where businesses had stood. Warehouses remained along the tracks, offering storage for freight. In the 1960s, Minnesota State Highway 59 was rerouted to the west of Detroit Lakes and crossed Main Street, allowing it to serve as an access point to the highway and the new business development that started there, including L&M Fleet Supply and Noah's Furniture.

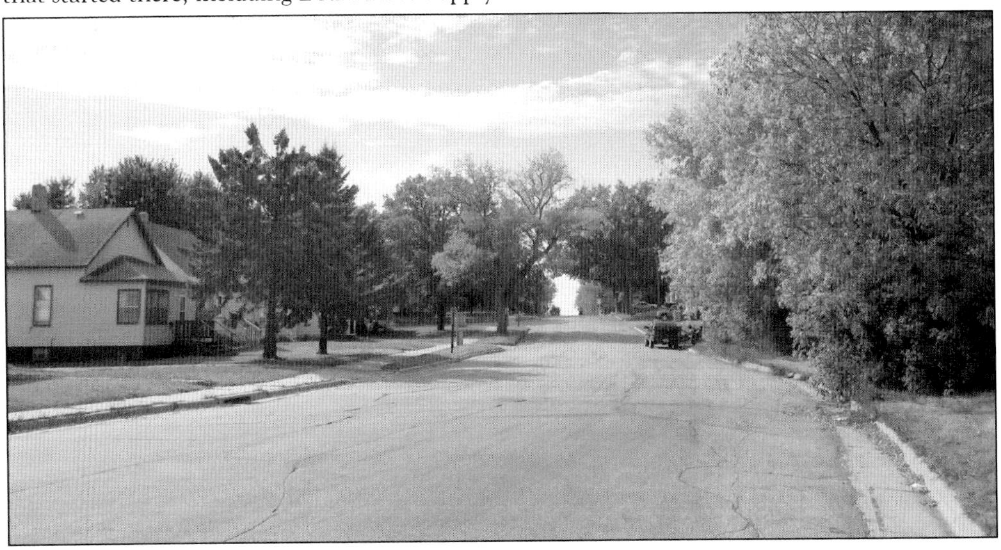

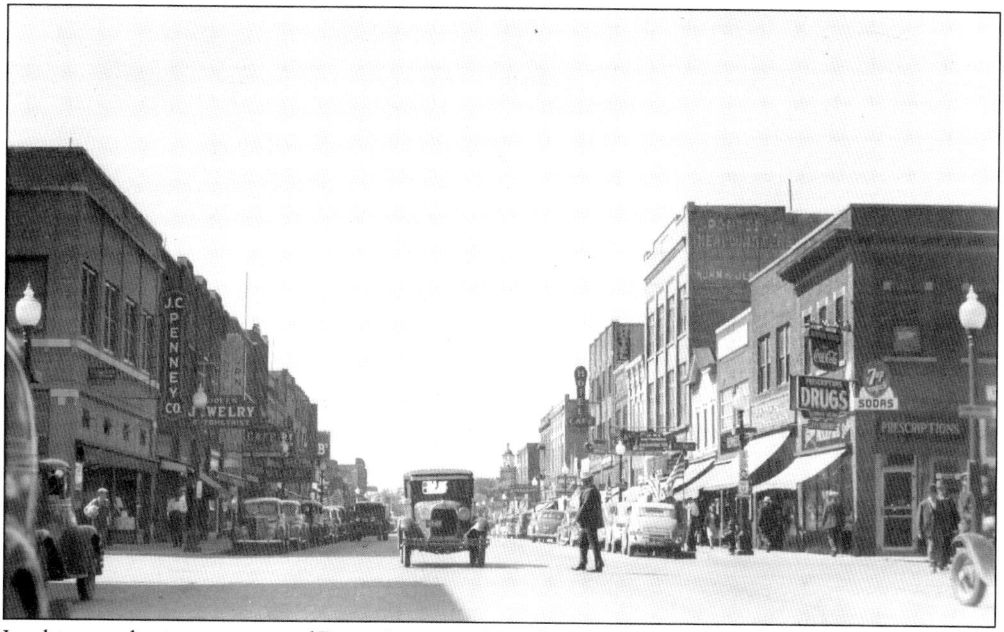

Looking at the intersection of Front Street and Washington Avenue today situates the viewer at the northernmost point of original buildings that still exist before the Northern Pacific Railroad crossing on the east side of the street. This corner, now Beug's Ace Hardware and Vanity, was formerly occupied by J.C. Penney and Nelson Drug. New development brought the destruction of the First Security Bank (Mac's Hardware) building that had stood just to the north, when the Minnesota Highway 10 bypass came through. Today, the area to the east of these buildings is being redeveloped to include Veterans Memorial Park and a strip mall.

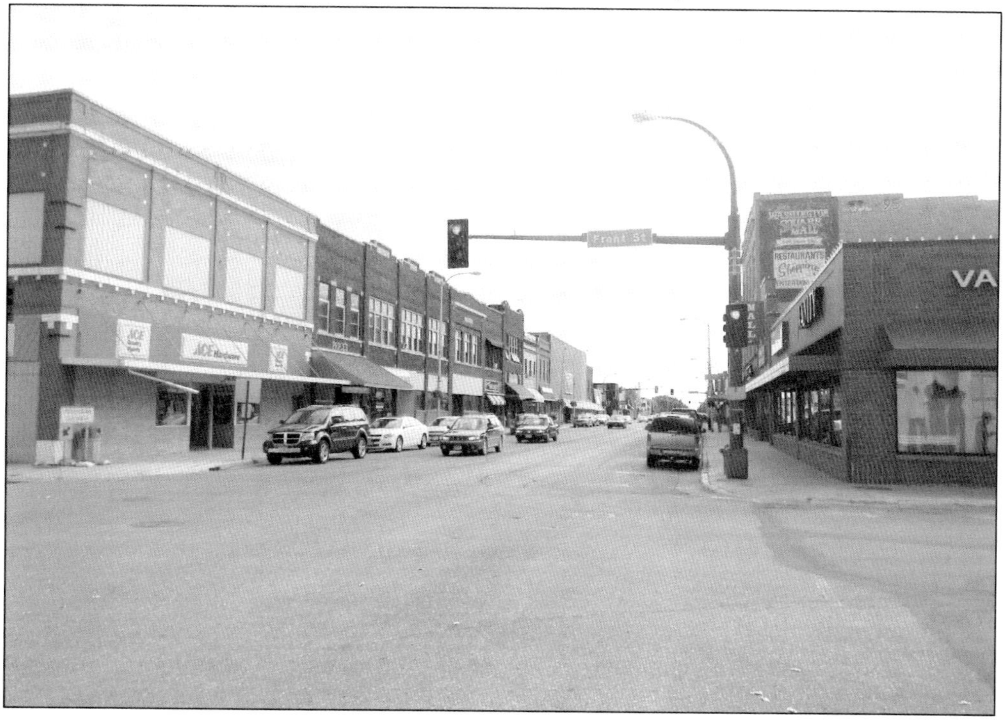

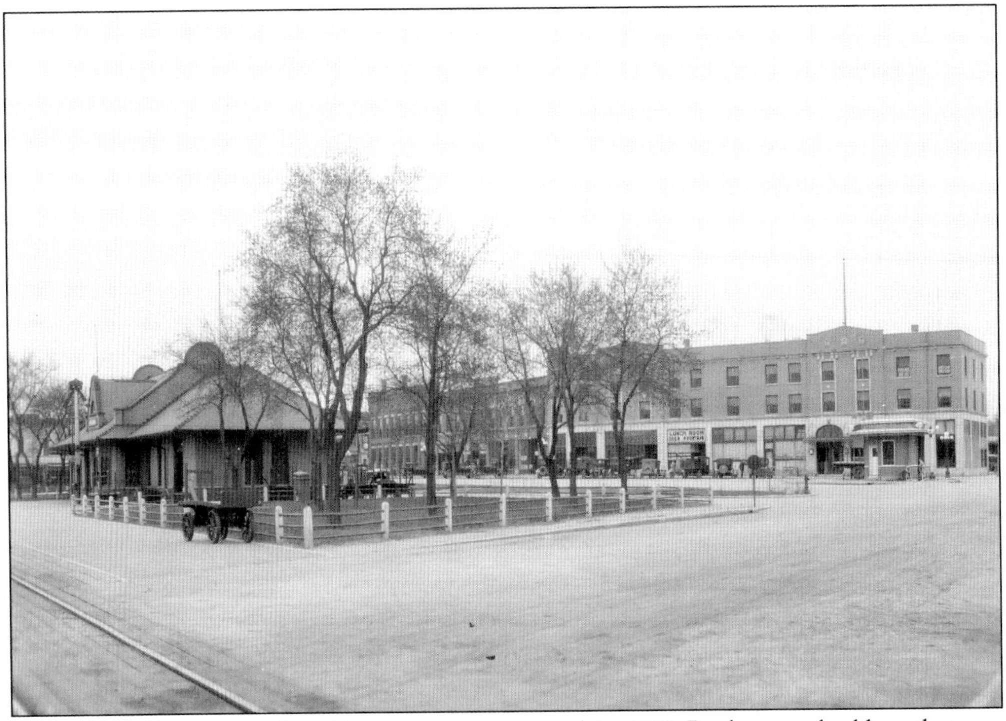

The Northern Pacific Railroad Depot was constructed in 1908. Replacing a building that was originally located north of the tracks, this brick structure offered a tiled waiting area, offices for railroad officials, and indoor washrooms. In 2009 and 2010, the depot was renovated by the White Earth Band of Ojibwe and now serves as a coffee shop and meeting area. It also provides one of only three Amtrak passenger stops in greater Minnesota. Just to the south, the Graystone Hotel building was constructed in 1915 and 1916. It was later attached to the Graystone Annex and then the Holmes and Teague Block to create the angled building we recognize today. Situated on the west end of the Graystone Building, the Saurer Brothers Gas Station, also known as the "World's Smallest," provided quick access to gasoline and basic service for visitors driving through the city. A replica of this station now sits in the Becker County Museum.

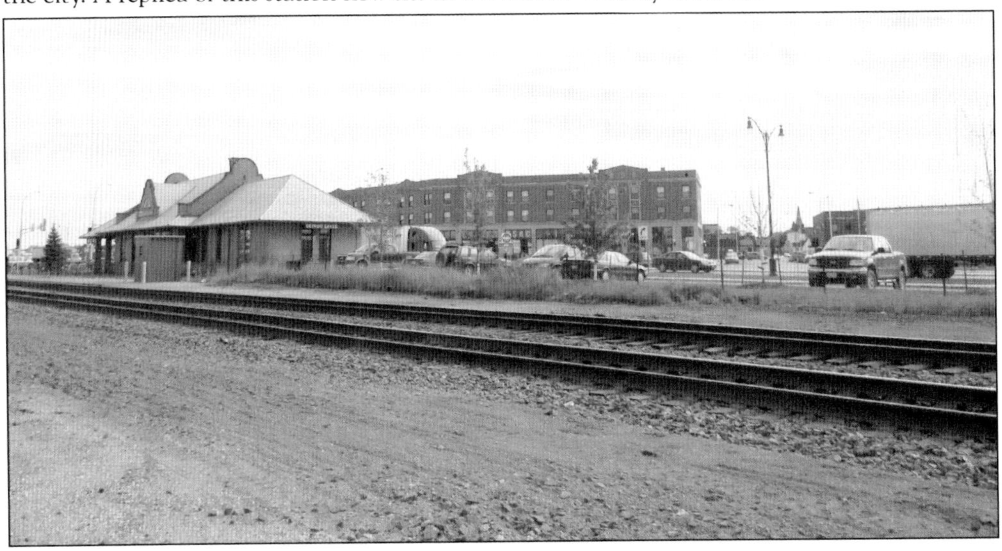

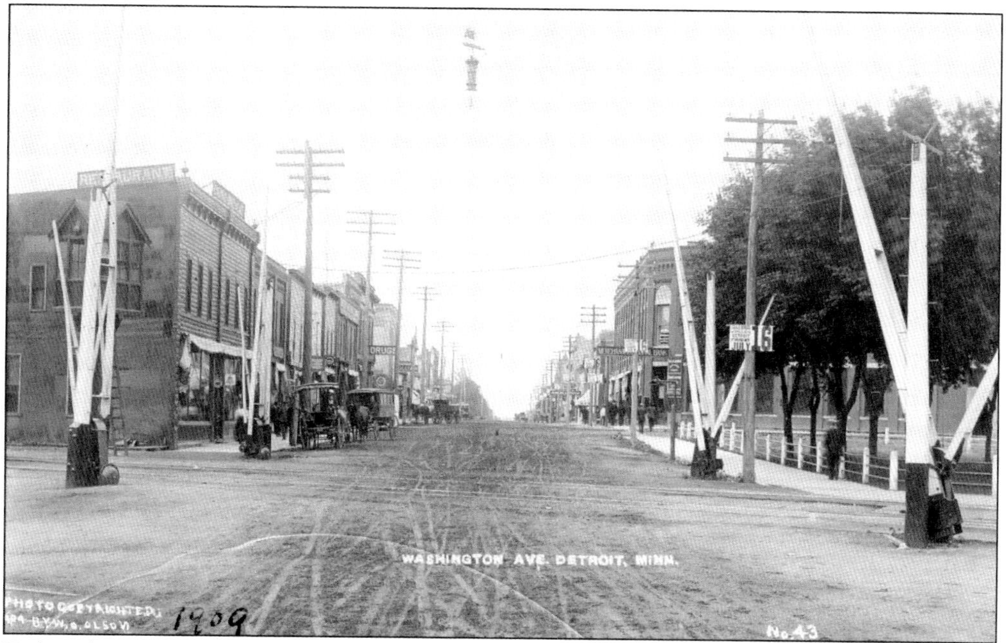

Today, the north side of the Northern Pacific Railroad tracks is a neighborhood in transition. Pioneer Street, which dead-ended just south of the tracks, housed businesses such as the Colonial Hotel and Alvin Wilcox's Land Office. Circuses and parades came down this block, and it was the first that most visitors by train would see of the city. Today, the railroad remains a vital part of the city, going through with deliveries and passengers. Businesses such as TiresPlus and Sinclair's Dinomart keep the neighborhood going. Within the last five years, new brick crosswalks and pedestrian bump-outs have been added, making this busy street easier to cross.

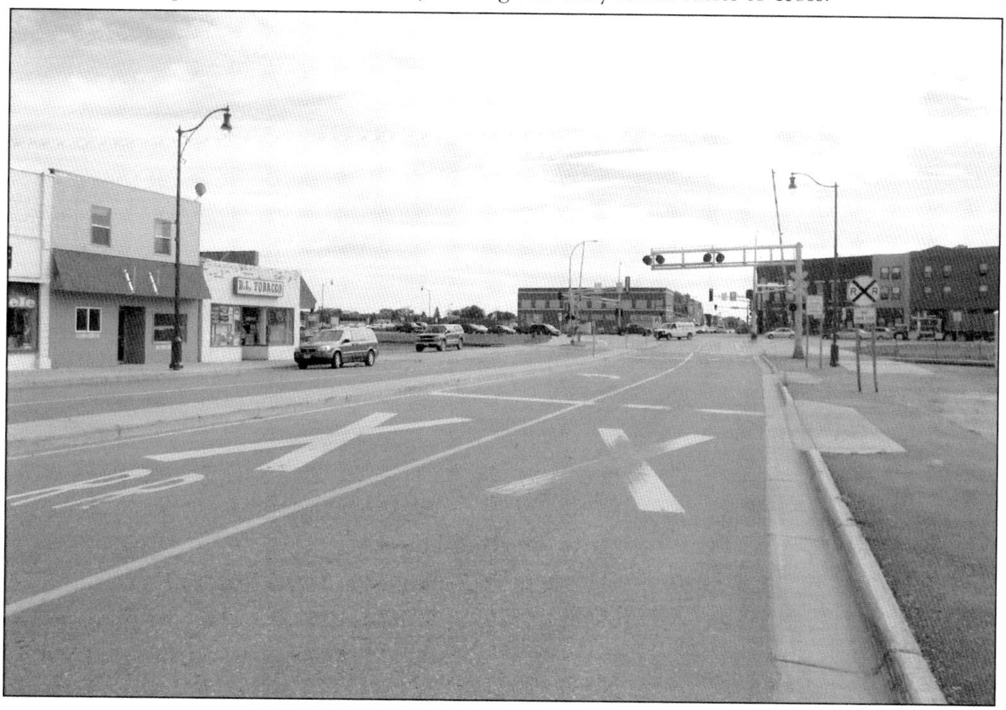

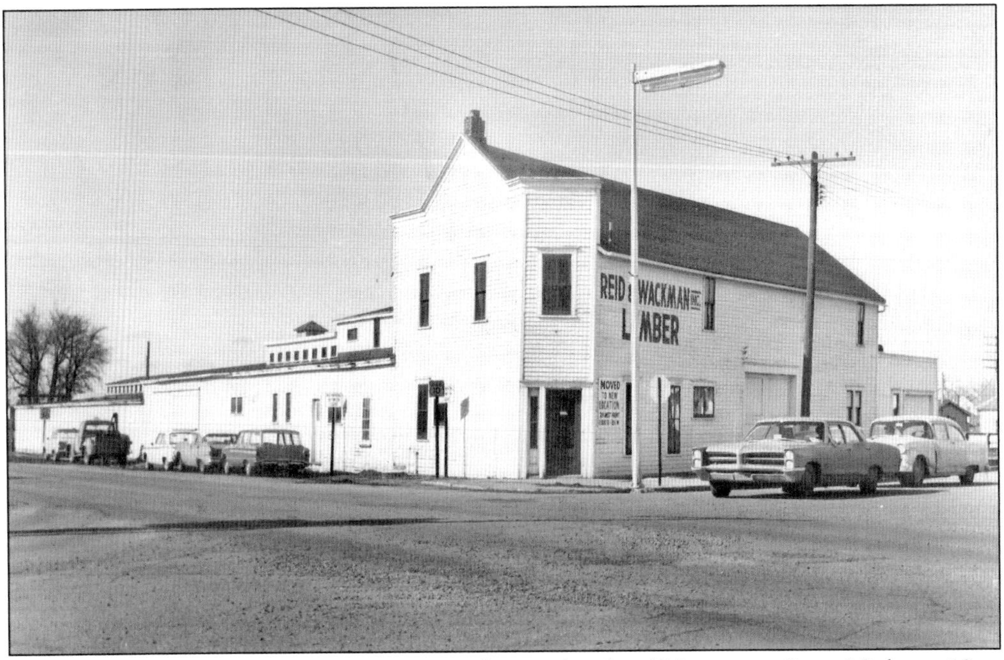

Main Street and Lake Avenue intersect on the north side of Minnesota State Highway 10 at the former site of Reid & Wackman Lumber. A useful site in its day, located directly next to the Northern Pacific Railroad Tracks, this location had many uses before becoming a lumber company. Reid & Wackman was a long presence here, opening in 1886 and closing at this location in 1966. Many other service industries also occupied this neighborhood, including beer warehouses, Hartman Hide and Fur, and numerous freight buildings. Today, the westbound lanes of Highway 10 and parking lot for the depot occupy this spot.

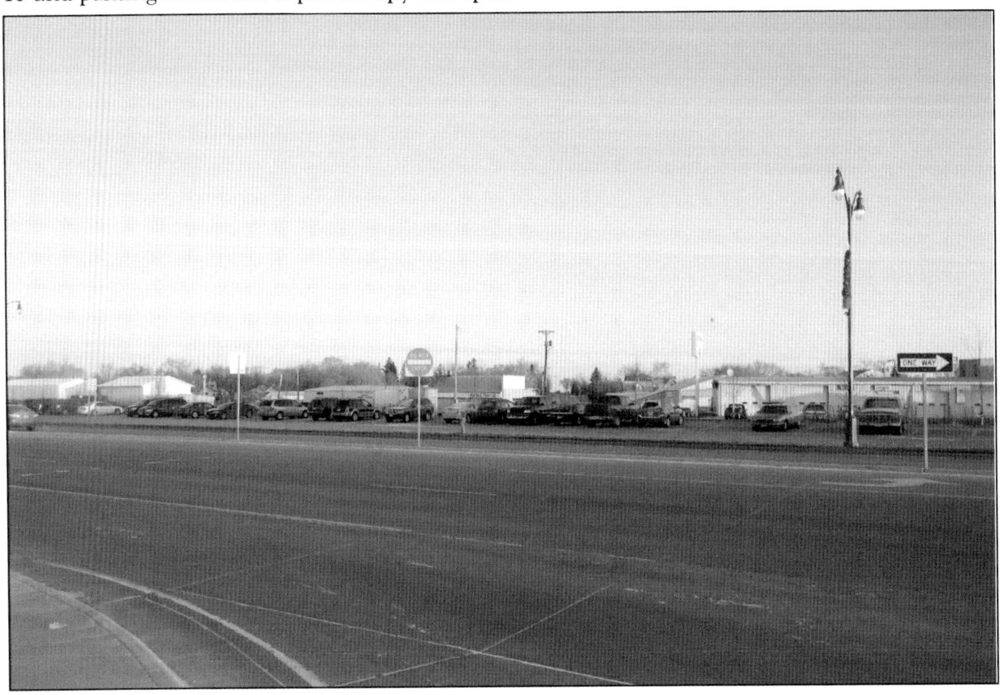

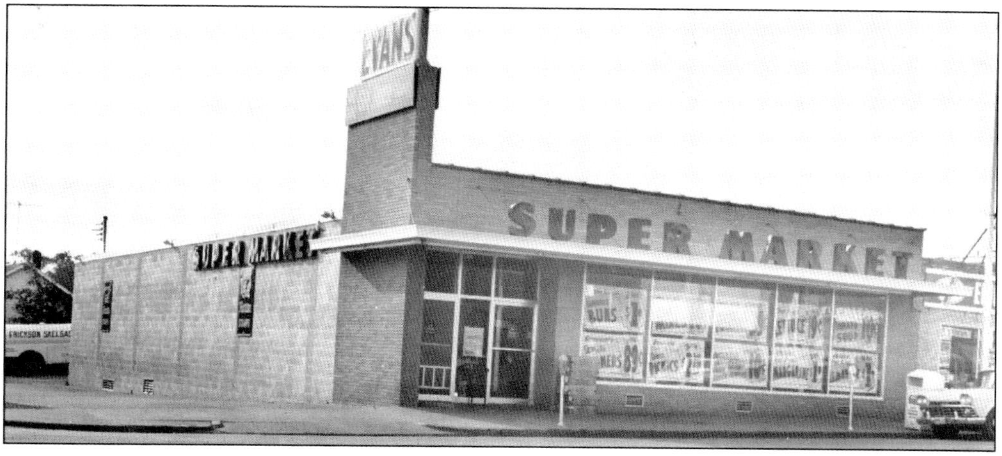

The corner of Washington Avenue and Grant Street is now being revitalized. The Baptist Church, later the first site of Trinity Lutheran, sat in the parking lot of what is now Michael's Furniture and the Social Cup Coffee Shop. The offices of Detroit Lakes Newspapers occupies the building that once housed Evans Super Market, pictured above. The VFW sits on the east side of the intersection, offering a gathering place for veterans. The northern part of the city is now also home to M-State (Minnesota State Technical and Community College), which is part of a five-campus system that brings an influx of students to the community each year. As with any city, Detroit Lakes has gone through many periods of change, emerging as a community with a rich history and bright future.

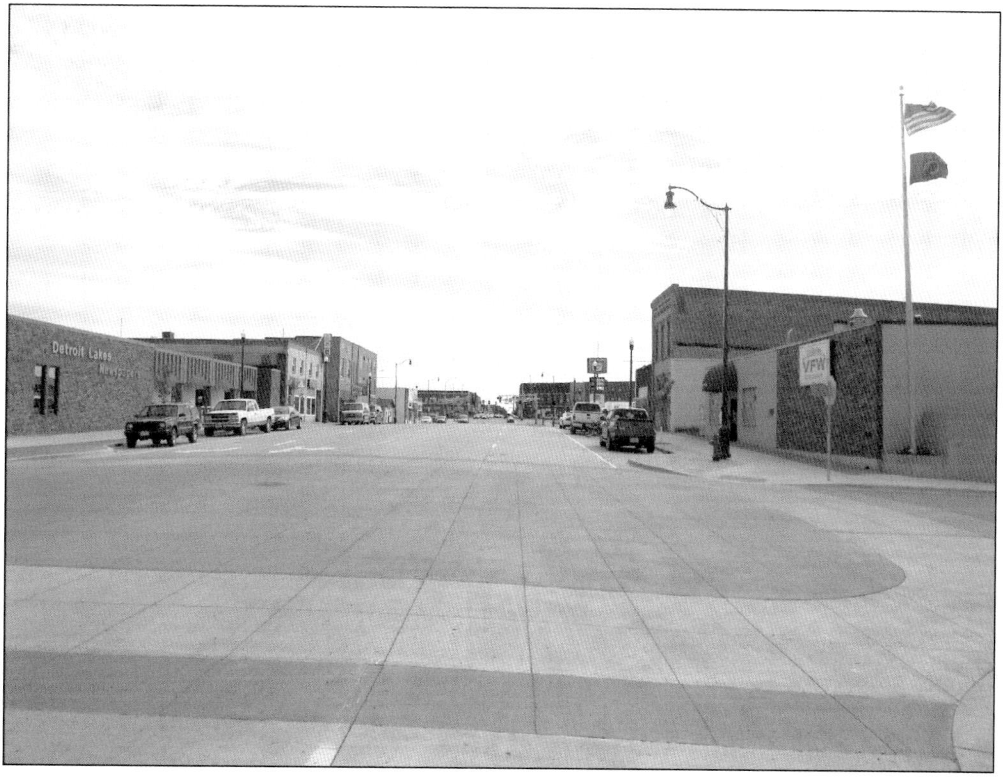

Bibliography

Becker County Historical Society. *The Soldiers of Becker County*. Detroit Lakes, MN, 2011.

City of Detroit Lakes. *100 Years of Progress: Sod to Shoreline*. Detroit Lakes, MN, 1971.

Detroit Lakes Middle School. *Historians 1998*. Independent School District 22: Detroit Lakes, MN, 1998

Lake Park Historical Society. *People's History of Becker County*. Dallas, TX: Taylor Publishing, 1976.

Mayfield, Pippi. *150 Years of Becker County*. Detroit Lakes, MN: Detroit Lakes Newspapers, 2009.

Prentice, Ken and Guy E. Teague. *Horse and Buggy Days at Detroit Lakes*. Detroit Lakes, MN: Lakes Publishing, 1971.

Wilcox, Alvin H. A *Pioneer History of Becker County Minnesota*. St. Paul, MN: Pioneer Press, 1907.

The Becker County Historical Society

The Becker County Historical Society, established in 1882 as the Pioneer Settlers Union, resides in Detroit Lakes, Minnesota, which is the county seat of Becker County. Offering a museum with exhibits, collections totaling more than 10,000 artifacts, a research library with more than 5,000 archival documents, newspapers on microfilm beginning in 1872 to present day, tax records, township records, and countless books, the history of Becker County can be discovered there. The Becker County Historical Society also houses over 18,000 photographs, which help the staff tell the visual history of the county, as they have done in this book. Donations of artifacts, photos, and documents are continuously taken, so please consider preserving a piece of your family's history in our collections. An institution that is dependent on many forms of support for its operations and programming, the Becker County Historical Society appreciates your investment in history by purchasing this book, and hope that you may be inspired to join our society and keep history alive in your county. Information about donations, membership, and volunteer service can be found on our website, www.beckercountyhistory.org, or by visiting the Becker County Museum at 714 Summit Avenue, Detroit Lakes, Minnesota 56502, or call 218-847-2938. For further research and reading, please visit the Becker County Historical Society Research Library at 714 Summit Avenue, Detroit Lakes, Minnesota 56502, or call 218-847-2938.